The Civil War in the South
Carolina Lowcountry

The Civil War in the South Carolina Lowcountry

How a Confederate Artillery Battery and a Black Union Regiment Defined the War

Ron Roth

McFarland & Company, Inc., Publishers
Jefferson, North Carolina

ISBN (print) 978-1-4766-7710-1
ISBN (ebook) 978-1-4766-3836-2

Library of Congress and British Library
cataloguing data are available

Library of Congress Control Number 2019055171

© 2020 Ron Roth. All rights reserved

No part of this book may be reproduced or transmitted in any form or by any means, electronic or mechanical, including photocopying or recording, or by any information storage and retrieval system, without permission in writing from the publisher.

On the cover: *top* a rare photograph of a Confederate artillery battery (Library of Congress); *bottom* the only known photograph of the 1st South Carolina Regiment (Library of Congress)

Printed in the United States of America

*McFarland & Company, Inc., Publishers
Box 611, Jefferson, North Carolina 28640
www.mcfarlandpub.com*

In memory of David Shannon McGrael

While it is impossible for us to foresee our national future, we can yet see enough to warrant us in believing that if the alternative placed before us be the abandonment of the institution of slavery or the dissolution of the Union ... the dissolution of the Union is the next step in the path of our glory.

—William Henry Trescot, Fourth of July address to the Beaufort Volunteer Artillery, 1850

If we hadn't become soldiers, all might have gone back as it was before; our freedom might have slipped through di two houses of Congress and President Lincoln's four years might have passed by and nothin' been done for us. But now things can never go back, because we have showed our energy and our courage and our natural manhood.... Another thing is, suppose you had kept your freedom widout enlisting in de army; your chilen might have grown up free, and been well cultivated so as to be equal to any business, but it would have been always flung in dere face—"Your fader never fought for he own freedom"—and what could they answer? Neber can say that to di African race any more. Thanks to dis regiment, never can say dat anymore, because we first showed 'em we could fight by dere side.

—Corporal Thomas Long of Company C, First South Carolina Regiment, Sabbath message to the First South Carolina Regiment, March 27, 1864

Table of Contents

Acknowledgments ix
Preface 1
Prologue: "It was a jolly time and we were young" 3

One. "The finest product of Southern civilization" 13
Two. "What do I think ob slavery? Murdering of de people" 19
Three. "He die but he die for doin' de right" 32
Four. "We can make one long, last, desperate struggle, for our rights and honor" 39
Five. "The dissolution of the Union is the next step in the path of our glory" 48
Six. "A grand show of war" 53
Seven. "The Mosby of the Islands" 63
Eight. "The bullets were like hail" 72
Nine. "Ours is the gentlemanly company" 87
Ten. A Glimpse of Total War: The Burning of Bluffton 97
Eleven. "Freedom is sweeter than life" 102
Twelve. "Never have I seen such terrible havoc" 123
Thirteen. "It is now a question of very few days" 133

Epilogue: "Everything was going to confusion and ruin" 147

Appendix I: Rosters 159

Appendix II: Two Addresses 171

Chapter Notes 177

Bibliography 181

Index 185

Acknowledgments

It is a pleasure to acknowledge here, however inadequately, the help and encouragement I have received in bringing this book to completion.

I am especially indebted to Dr. Stephen Wise for his encouragement and review of my manuscript. Steve is coauthor of the definitive history of Beaufort County, an indispensable volume for my research.

At the top of every historian's list of those who deserve thanks are librarians and archivists, dozens who through the years patiently and professionally assisted me in finding resources critical to my research. One of them is the peerless Grace Cordial, Senior Librarian of the Beaufort District Collection of the Beaufort County Library. Grace and the Beaufort District Collection are both treasures.

Another South Carolina research treasure is the South Caroliniana Library Collection of the University of South Carolina, the archive that houses the correspondence of Stephen Elliott, Jr., and where I spent many hours making many requests of its staff.

Many thanks to my editor at McFarland, Natalie Foreman, who was helpful in every way.

Graphic artist Hal Jespersen's maps fulfilled my goal of providing battle maps of precision and clarity for the readers of this book.

My dear friend Dave McGrael provided insightful observations and suggestions, and it is to him that this book is dedicated.

And who knew that my sister Nancy Bursey was an ace proofreader? Any suggestion of grammatical expertise demonstrated in this book is the result of her careful review of the text.

Last but hardly least is my wife Pat's daily encouragement and her unflinching belief in this project and my ability to complete it.

Preface

The purpose of this book is to provide a portrait of the Civil War as it unfolded in the South Carolina Sea Islands, specifically that region known as the St. Helena Parish that encompassed the areas surrounding the towns of Beaufort and Bluffton. The two subjects of the book—the Confederate Beaufort Volunteer Artillery battery and the United States 1st South Carolina Regiment—are portrayed not just in full battle array, but within a narrative that encompasses the social, political and racial factors that informed their experiences both before and during the war. For African Americans, that history is extremely painful and keyed by their experiences of slavery. For the Southerners, it was the harsh reality that their way of life, built on slavery, was coming to an end. Understanding these parallel narratives in my view requires an understanding of events that led up to the conflict itself, and for that reason I have spent greater time on that part of the narrative than is typical of the standard military history.

The Civil War is rife with paradoxes, and some of the most dramatic of them played out in the coastal Lowcountry of South Carolina south of Charleston. Few Civil War locales could claim to have as radically opposed narratives existing side by side. Here was a region where just miles from each other radically disparate events took place. On one hand we hear fire-eater Robert Barnwell Rhett's inflammatory 1844 secessionist speech delivered under the canopy of an ancient oak tree in Bluffton; then two decades later, just 30 miles away at a spot south of Beaufort, we see the creation and recruitment of the first black Union regiment to fight in the Civil War.

Despite the small size of the region, an examination of its Civil War history takes its place in dispelling some of the core myths of the Civil War.

Among these is the enduring "lost cause" myth claiming that that the Confederacy was overwhelmed by a massive Union advantage in men and materials. Subsequent scholarship has demonstrated that the Confederate army "suffered no crippling deficiency in weapons or supplies." Similarly, in the South Carolina Lowcountry, my research makes clear the Beaufort Volunteer Artillery (BVA) was not at any time lacking in men or material. Indeed, at the time of its surrender in 1865, its roster was substantially larger than that at the time of its mustering in 1862. And its proximity to the Charleston Armory, a Confederate production center of cannons and ammunition, could certainly have been an advantage in maintaining adequate supply of ammunition.

Another topic this book explores is the value and impact of black Union troops to the success of the Union war effort. Soon after the U.S. naval flotilla attack on Port Royal Sound on November 1861 and the occupation of Beaufort, African American soldiers could be seen drilling on the streets of Beaufort. Mansions on elegant Bay Street were converted to army hospitals and black children and adults were being taught to read and write. Practically overnight the South Carolina Lowcountry had become a laboratory for the new frontier of race relations that was emerging with emancipation of the enslaved. Thus, the salient irony of the region of St. Helena Parish was that what was once the heart and soul of Southern secession would be the headquarters of the United States' first two black regiments, units whose men were inspired by the Emancipation Proclamation as they undertook their first steps toward freedom. Like other newly formed black regiments, the 1st and 2nd South Carolina evolved steadily from non-combatant roles to experienced, hard-fighting units. While the engagements in which they fought were minor, they were epochal in overturning the widely held belief by white soldiers and the Northern public in general that blacks would not make good soldiers.

The crucible of the unique character of the war in the South Carolina Lowcountry resulted in a different kind of warfare, a guerrilla style of fighting in which the BVA artillerist would excel. It also forged a new type of soldier, a former slave that would fight with a fierce moral conviction and tenacity driven by his thirst for freedom.

Prologue

"It was a jolly time and we were young"

It was a wedding of South Carolina's Lowcountry royalty—the marriage of the season. Stephen Elliott, Jr., future captain of the Beaufort Volunteer Artillery, was taking the hand of Charlotte Stuart at her father's plantation at Page Point, two miles upriver from the Elliott plantation. In the cold December air young friends of the Elliotts and Stuarts from nearby plantations on St. Helena Island were being rowed across the Broad River by their slaves on a twelve-oared boat to join the wedding party. One of them, Elliott's friend and future cannoneer for the Beaufort Volunteer Artillery, James Reeves Stuart, described the scene:

> The girls were in their ball dresses, but we had the awning up and the mattress spread on the platform, which was wide enough for them to sit flat down with their backs against the sides and their feet towards the middle. The boat hands sang all the way about.
>
> It was a jolly time and we were young. Relatives from Charleston were there and from the plantations miles around. (All the planters, relatives, Elliotts, Pinckneys, Heywards were there, a swarm of carriages. We did not leave for home until long past midnight.)
>
> The return home in the morning was quite as jolly. Uncle Henry [Elliott's father-in-law] had some old madeira that he had been keeping for such an occasion for thirty years. But I will say positively we were merry perhaps, but not one of our party was *tipsy*. The negroes had had their share of the good things and were all also in a good humor.[1]

Because of the many islands and waterways between plantations, boats were necessary transportation. Landing the boat was a precarious task in waters that rose and fell with the tides six to eight feet twice a day. Women and children were carried off in a chair held between two of the slave oarsmen. Slave women on board would be carried off unceremoniously by the oarsmen, their arms wrapped around their necks. When the war came, these boats would be used by Elliott and Reeves for guerrilla attacks on Union forces.

The islands were a natural paradise for the plantation owners, and Stuart nostalgically described them in his memoirs:

> A small creek of salt water wound close up under the shore, in which the tide constantly rose and fell. And some large live oak trees hung over the water, their long limbs extending over to the salt marsh grass beyond, the lower ones sometimes dipping under the water at high tide and the moss trailing in festoons into the flood.... There were other sights too, and sounds. The shriek of the fish hawk, the squawk of the great blue heron and the cackling cry of the marsh hens.
>
> While on the beach were many tracks of the raccoon, among the countless holes of the little fiddler crabs, his prey. And under the great massive gnarled roots, the home of the mink and the otter.[2]

Centrally located to these islands, the village of Beaufort rested on the banks of the Beaufort River. It was referred to by some as the "Newport of the South," and visitors waxed effusively on its beauty. In 1845, a Scottish geologist, Charles Lyell, toured Beaufort marveling at the unique Lowcountry views of salt marshes and sea grasses and the picturesque vistas of the planters' villas, their long verandahs shaded by towering live oak trees.

Beaufort, South Carolina, was referred to as the "Newport of the South." Its elegant mansions along Bay Street were home to some of the wealthiest families in the country (Beaufort, 1861, Timothy O'Sullivan, photographer, Library of Congress).

Even one of the officers of the occupying Union troops in 1863 succumbed to its aura, describing it in the purplest of prose: "Words are feeble to describe this isle of the bay, this fairyland of the South with a gem of a town in it.... The stranger is surprised and bewildered at the number of fine structures all along the bay, so large, modern and costly. These mansions and their surroundings were all that wealth, taste and art could suggest. The air is freighted with aroma of flowers, the oleander, magnolia, fig tree, lemon and orange, as well as the live oak."[3]

BVA cannoneer James Reeves Stuart remembered fondly the view from a window at his family's plantation: "I do remember the old live oaks with their drapery of grey moss and the pine trees, the yellow pine with their foliage of long pine needles, and how I used to lie on the clean pine straw covering the ground below and gaze up at the blue sky through the branches and the white clouds drifting by and listen to the sea breeze as it swept through them uttering strange cries and calls and distant almost human shrieks. No other tree is such an aeolian harp as the long-leaved southern pine."[4] Planter families enjoyed privileged lives, and during the hot summer months made excursions to the shore described by Stuart in his memoirs:

> Sometimes our families would go down to Bay Point for two or three weeks, where there were a number of Pest Houses, very plainly built of wood. No sashes, but shutters in case of a storm. Here we went bathing in the surf. It was at the mouth of the harbor looking right out to sea. The lightship on Port Royal entrance faintly visible at night [*sic*].
>
> We caught turtles on the beach and terrapins and found their nests in the sand with from 70 to 100 eggs in them. We had a royal time and went back to school well-tanned and our faces and arms peeling. We boys generally slept in a tent. The mornings and forenoons were very hot and glaring. But at noon every day the sea breeze began to blow and continued to blow until about 9 PM. This salt breeze was very bracing and invigorating.[5]

Like many planters, Stuart and Elliott were avid hunters and fishermen. In April during the cotton planting season the planters would call a halt to work, have their slaves slip their boats into the water and head toward Port Royal Sound where the drum fish were spawning. The drum fish were large, edible fish weighing between thirty and forty pounds. East of St. Helena Island, Hunting Island was a favored destination for hunting.

These pastimes were supplemented by exceptional educational and cultural resources. One of Beaufort's leading citizens, Robert Woodward Barnwell, extolled Beaufort's literary and intellectual achievements in poetry with a decidedly patrician tone:

> Books and the boats I sing:
> And this old town of note.
> Where each had a library
> And every man a boat.
>
> Leisure and Island homes!
> For them old Homer wrote,
> And oft they went to Odysseus
> To learn about a boat.
>
> They'd sit upon a balcony
> With Gibbon, Hume and Grote,
> And the they'd take some exercise
> With six oars and a boat.
>
> Plantations all had muscled crews
> A landing and a boat.
> Each lad was taught to sail and row,
> But also how to quote.
>
> On summer morns they loved to read,
> On summer eves to float,
> Woe to the man who had no books
> Or chanced to have no boat!
>
> For Beaufort was a strange old town
> In those old days remote!
> One had to have a library;
> One loved to have a boat.[6]

Beaufort's libraries were well stocked. Established in 1807, the Beaufort Library Society held more than 3,000 books on its shelves on topics of history, science, religion and politics. Numerous books, magazines and newspapers were found in most Beaufort households, and the Beaufort Post Office reported that in one year 33,120 newspapers and 3,406 periodicals were delivered to Beaufort residents, a total seldom exceeded by other American towns.[7]

Prominent Southern literary lights had associations with Beaufort. The Confederacy's unofficial poet laureate, Henry Timrod, made frequent visits to Beaufort. South Carolina's most celebrated poet, William Gilmore Simms, expressed admiration for Beaufort College. The leading zoologist of the antebellum era, Dr. John E. Holbrook, was born in Beaufort.

During the summers, families escaped the heat of their plantations living in second homes in Beaufort. As their wealth accumulated in the 1840s and '50s, they could afford to travel to resorts in Flat Rock, North Carolina, Saratoga and Newport.

Antebellum Beaufort was aptly described as the "wealthiest, most aristocratic and cultivated town of its size in America, a town which, though small in number of inhabitants, produced statesmen, scholars, sailors, and divines whose name and fame are known throughout the country." The St. Helena Island and Beaufort planters who comprised the BVA were uniquely blessed with the near exclusive production of one of the most valuable commodities in the world: long staple cotton. Long staple cotton differed from the more common short staple variety in the length of its long, silky fibers. Its fiber measures between one and a half to two inches long, compared with the ⅝-inch short staple variety typical of the rest of the South. Since the quality of cotton is judged by the number of "hanks" that can be spun from a pound of cotton, the Sea Island variety could spin about twice as much as that of the short staple.

In 1850, the average worth of the St. Helena Parish planters' rice and cotton crops totaled $2,170,264. The following decade leading up to the Civil War the planters expanded their tillable acreage, and many of them found themselves among the wealthiest of Americans in the country.[8]

The soaring economy during the 1850s drove construction and real estate booms. St. Helena Parish planters flaunted their wealth, building impressive plantation homes on Port Royal and St. Helena Islands and luxurious summer residences along Beaufort's elegant Bay Street overlooking the Broad River. In 1853, the newly formed Port Royal Road Company built a sea shell-lined road connecting the important Port Royal Ferry and Beaufort, an internal improvement that would stimulate commerce. Relatives of the BVA men profited from the construction boom including carpenter John Zealy, builder Frank Tailbird and shipbuilders Saxby Chaplin and John J. Rhodes.[9]

An elite group of 48 families owned the 141 plantations in the St. Helena Parish. Among this privileged cream of Beaufort society were names on the BVA's roster: Elliott, Stuart, Fuller, Rhett, Stoney, Fripp, Barnwell and Jenkins.

Stephen Elliott, granduncle of future BVA Captain and Brigadier General Stephen Elliott, Jr., was one of the most influential men of letters in of pre–Civil War Beaufort. Born in Beaufort in 1771 and raised by his brother William Elliott II—scion of one of Beaufort's most affluent families—he graduated Phi Beta Kappa from Yale in 1791, then returned to Beaufort to run his family's plantation. More than any other person, he was individually responsible for improving the educational and cultural life of the town, organizing the Beaufort Library Society in 1807, and serving on the first Board of Trustees of Beaufort College. As a state senator he established a reputation as one of South Carolina's preeminent educators and founder of the public school system, a reputation enlarged in 1824 as one of the key organizers of the Medical College of South Carolina.

His work as an amateur botanist attracted national and international attention, culminating in the publication of his *Botany of South Carolina and Georgia* which became the definitive work on this subject and cemented his reputation as one of the most important scholars in antebellum South Carolina. His scholarly credentials notwithstanding, his reputation as a Southern gentleman was unimpeachable, combining "the manners of a refined gentleman with the most exact and comprehensive acquirements of natural philosophy." He died in 1830, leaving in his estate a private library of approximately 2,500 volumes.

His grandnephew would later exhibit a similar intellectual curiosity and interest in libraries. In a letter written to his wife, Charlotte, while on temporary leave recovering from an injury during the siege of Petersburg, Virginia, he describes a discovery in the house where he was recovering.

> An old gentleman paid me a visit and sent me the key of his library which is a very valuable one, and I have been having a fine time there. The only trouble is that all this comfort has made me so well that I must file off and leave it. I have had much occasion to think of you more than usual since I have been staying here where the comforts remind me much of home.
>
> Looking over the books I have come across Samuel Pepys diary and the constant way in which he carried his wife all about with him to see plays and all such sights—made me think more than all of you. However, poor fellow, if he did not take her he sometimes "had but an ill time" when she found out that he had been to the theater without her ... on which occasions she used much foul language and there was no contentment until morning when affairs were happily adjusted, he promising that he would not take pleasure by himself again. He took good care of her wardrobe and bought many petticoats "fine and gay with silver and gold lace." The picture of domestic life so artlessly and quaintly told was too much for me and I became afraid that a longer stay among the civilized haunts of men would make me homesick. I have only one ambition now, and that is to be at home in peace with you and my boys.[10]

Perhaps the most famous member of Beaufort's antebellum elite with familial connections to the BVA was Robert W. Barnwell. Two of his sons would serve in the BVA: 5th Corporal Robert Hayne Barnwell and Private Stephen Elliott Barnwell.

Barnwell's Old South, aristocratic bearing was best described by historian Clement Eaton: "With beautiful manners, a modest and unassuming personality he possessed the poise and graces of an aristocrat of an old family." His pedigree was impeccable: son of a Revolutionary War hero and descended from "Tuscarora Jack," the legendary founder of Beaufort.

He would serve two terms in the United States Congress, and in 1835 was appointed president of the South Carolina College in Columbia (1835–41). After a successful tenure as president and professor of political and moral philosophy, he returned to Beaufort where he led the Beaufort College Board of Trustees as its president and held court over Beaufort's social and intellectual affairs. Nothing got done in Beaufort without consulting "Cousin Robert."

He was a forceful and vocal apologist for the South's planter class, particularly those planters in the St. Helena Parish claiming that he "found nothing in the Word of God condemning the institution [slavery] and they now felt they could hold slaves in good conscience."

The men of the Beaufort Volunteer Artillery (BVA) played central roles in the social and educational life of antebellum Beaufort, holding public musters, organizing parades and hosting the annual Fourth of July banquet at "the Arsenal," a Gothic Revival style mock fortress housing the BVA's cannons and ammunition. At one of these banquets host Major John G. Barnwell, captain of the BVA, called it to order to the beat of a huge brass drum that sat next to him. Not all the pursuits of the BVA volunteers were so high toned. One of its men, F. F. Sams, founded the Beaufort Billiard Club, and the planters had a reputation for hard drinking, gambling and cock fighting.

In 1852, future BVA volunteers including Lewis Reeves Sams, Henry Fuller, Henry Middleton Stuart, and Stephen Elliott were among the trustees of the newly chartered Beaufort Female Seminary.[11] For a town of its size, Beaufort had an unusually large number of schools, both public and private, including Beaufort College, a grammar school, three private schools for women and an academy for women. It had a weekly newspaper, *The Palmetto Post*, and ten churches including white and African American. Beaufort's close connection to the sea resulted in an unusually cosmopolitan and diverse population for a South Carolina town. In July 1850, one could find French, Scots, Germans, Irish and even a Dane walking the streets. At Susan Morcock's boarding house one found a dentist, three teachers from New York, students and an itinerant Alabama artist.

In 1860, the fruit of Beaufort's wealth was produced on the backbreaking labor of St. Helena Island's 7,644 slaves. According to Stuart, the lives of the plantation slaves were idyllic: "It was a wonderfully secure life, that old Plantation life in the days of slavery. They were 'the negroes' or 'our people.' They were a part of us. They themselves used the expression habitually *our* plantation, *our* cattle, *our* horses, *our* family, or *our* white folks. We went to bed at night with a feeling of perfect security and yet our house was never locked up." While Stuart's description of the slaves suggests his family's plantation practices with their slaves were relatively benign, its tone and condescension reveal a typical attitude of the planter class. More to the point was the widespread belief that the enslaved were of an inferior race, "a vast burden," but one that generated immense wealth.[12]

Stuart's rosy characterization of his feeling of security was not shared by all. Some planters lived in fear of slave conspiracies and revolts. They remembered a slave conspiracy in 1804 in St. Peter's parish north of Beaufort that resulted in the hanging and beheading of approximately a dozen slaves. The memory of Denmark Vesey's conspiracy in Charleston in 1822 was well known to the planters. This widespread plot to revolt involved hundreds of blacks, thirty-five of whom were executed by hanging.

The BVA participated in slave patrols. Militias like the BVA were often the point of the spear, enforcing oppressive measures to control the slave population. Organized by plantation owners, the patrols policed slaves, monitoring their activities and watching for runaways. Slave patrols could whip any slave—on the spot—if they found him or her outside their master's property. They could search slave cabins with impunity for arms, ammunition or runaways. They broke up meetings or assemblies of slaves suspected of providing reading instruction, or church services if they were held outside of certain, prescribed hours. More often they degenerated into excuses for drinking and carousing.

Compared with other slave holding regions in the south, the plantations of Beaufort and the St. Helena Parish islands of Port Royal, Lady's and Parris Islands were relatively free from slave conspiracy activities. No slave plots were discovered, nor were there slave uprisings. Only once was a black person charged with killing a white, though there were several reports of isolated killings of whites.

Nonetheless, the St. Helena Parish planters like plantation owners throughout the South were profoundly shaken by news of John Brown's Harpers Ferry raid in October 1859. Brown, driven by a fanatical hatred of slavery—a fugitive from justice with a price on his head for killing slavery sympathizers in Kansas—entered the small Virginia village of Harpers Ferry with eighteen men determined to capture the United States Arsenal there, distribute its weapons to Virginia slaves and ignite a slave uprising.

Brown's Harpers Ferry attack failed militarily. Brown and his exhausted men were captured, and ten of their own, five innocent bystanders, and one Marine were killed in the process.

But if the military goal of his attack failed, the impact of his mission was spectacularly successful. He became a household name generating adulation in the North and infamy in the South. The impact of the raid on the plantation owners of the St. Helena Parish was electrifying. Historian Steven Channing aptly described the mixture of fear and defiance that overtook plantation owners: "The spasm of fear which swept across South Carolina in the days and weeks after Harpers Ferry was not willfully created by extremists. With unconscious insight John Brown had struck at the deepest and most intimate anxieties of the white South. The fear and rage he had aroused were at the heart of the secession movement."[13]

Particularly alarming were Brown's personal maps including one of South Carolina with mysterious markings of crosses in areas thought to be targeted for slave insurrection. The mistress of the family plantation "Badwell" in Abbeville voiced the fear of many, noting that Abbeville was one of the towns marked on Brown's map. "God have mercy on us," she wrote to her husband. "Such revelations make one wonder how insecure is our situation and fear for the Future [sic]."

Rumors abounded in South Carolina newspapers that lieutenants of Brown were roaming through the state looking to foment chaos. A series of destructive fires in Talbot County, Georgia, were attributed to Brown's agents by the *Savannah Republican*, noting that the county was one of those with an "X" on Brown's map of Georgia. With the constant drumbeat of alarms in the newspapers in the months after the raid, slave patrol and vigilance committee activities ramped up to a fever pitch. Not far from Beaufort, in the town of Gillisonville, the parish seat, a public meeting was held on the court house steps including plantation owners, merchants, farmers and others to listen to outraged citizens rail against John Brown who had targeted their town on his maps. Five new vigilante committees were formed to clamp down on the slave population. Unlike previous slave patrols, whites suspected of being sympathetic to abolition were targets of the vigilante committees. In the new paranoia, teachers, ministers, and salesmen and others thought to be closet abolitionists were called out. An Irish stonecutter in Columbia was singled out for using "seditious language," jailed, whipped and put on a ship bound for New York.[14]

A victim of the post-raid hysteria was the widely held belief of the basic loyalty of slaves to their masters. A Beaufort District resident writing to the *Charleston Mercury* under the pen name of "Vigilance" feared the imagined John Brown agitators roaming the Carolina countryside were fomenting unrest and encouraging slaves to cut their masters' throats. Vigilance further maintained that the slaves in Beaufort had been corrupted by abolitionists. He worried that Northerners traveling across Beaufort were arming the slaves, plying them with false hopes. His own slaves had been told by a black freedman that the Aurora Borealis was an omen that civil war was imminent.

Brown's raid stoked the tensions between planters and slaves in Beaufort and the St. Helena Parish. A perfect storm was brewing that would forever change the fortunes of the planters and the slaves whose interests were inalterably opposed to each other.

One

"The finest product of Southern civilization"

The Sea Island cotton boom between 1790 and 1825 introduced the privileged families of the Beaufort Volunteer Artillery to a level of wealth unheard of in other parts of the country. New fortunes were made, and as South Carolina became America's largest cotton-producing state, the sleepy village of Beaufort was transformed into a social and cultural mecca crossroads, one of the wealthiest towns in America. On nearby St. Helena Island, the land adjoining a circular, fifteen-mile road was among the greatest pieces of wealth producing real estate in the United States.

In 1850, two of the largest cotton plantations in St. Helena Parish were owned by men with numerous family members that would serve in the BVA. Benjamin Chaplin Sr. owned the largest number of slaves in the Lowcountry, 272, working 1,373 acres. Thomas A. Coffin owned several plantations on totaling 2,911 acres and 301 slaves.[1]

The planters' place on the spectrum of gentility was weighted far toward the higher end. Educated at the elite universities of the northeast, those on the highest social level, the self-styled "eminent class," had the wealth to maintain part-time residences at their plantation home during the cooler months of the year, then retreat during the hottest summer months to their residences in one of the summer resort towns such as Bluffton, McPhersonville, or even resorts in North Carolina.

Their showcase mansions in Beaufort were decorated to impress. On their walls hung paintings by French and Italian artists, perhaps their own portraits painted by a leading American artist like Thomas Sully. Floors were covered by Turkish carpets, and personal libraries replete with expensive, tooled leather bindings attesting to their intellectual attainments.

Such was Beaufort's renown that in 1825, the Marquis de Lafayette—beloved friend of George Washington and hero of the American Revolution—included Beaufort as one of the stops in his triumphal tour of the United States. Lafayette arrived in Beaufort on the plush new steamboat SS *Henry Schultz*. Among the highlights planned for his visit the Beaufort Volunteer Artillery attired in their dress uniforms would honor him with a parade review and a gala ball in the evening at the Elliott house.[2]

One typically entered a plantation on a long avenue lined with stately live oak trees, their limbs overhanging the road draped with luxurious sprays of Spanish moss. The road ended at the entrance of the *big house*, the term for the plantation house used by the slaves. Various outbuildings were spread over the property near the big house: storage barns for cotton and corn, cabins for the house servants. Groves of peaches, oranges or figs might be planted nearby. A few hundred yards to the rear of the house might be found the slave cabins.

One of the northern missionaries living on St. Helena Island after the Federal occupation in 1862 described some of the plantation houses as "being all built of hard pine, which is handsome on the floors, but the rest of the woodwork is painted ... an ugly green which is not cheerful.... The place is very attractive looking, grapevines and honeysuckles and pine woods nearby."

"The big house," describes historian Theodore Rosengarten, "was the center of a dense social life. Friends, relatives and slaves, all with strangers in tow, invaded the house by night and day, making privacy impossible. One lived in public and earned a good name by knowing how to get along with people of different social standings.... Status among whites was measured in capital goods—in the numbers of acres and slaves he owned."

The burden of managing the big house fell on the plantation mistress who faced an endless round of tasks crowding her typical day.

> Almost every half hour during the day she would be called to administer to some want or to grant or refuse some request of her many dependents. At nine the plantation nurse arrived with a list or "tally" of the sick. The serious cases had to be visited first, and, if necessary, a physician summoned; for the others, medicine to be prescribed, weighed and measured.
>
> At eleven the wagon from the quarters came, with the whole carcass of a beef or sheep, and she was required to direct the cutting of the joints reserved for the table and kitchen. The cook must have a personal interview and minute directions. The same was demanded by the fisherman, who wishes to show his catch and receive orders regarding the opening of oysters, clams or the boiling of crabs or prawns.
>
> At twelve the three seamstresses, whose perpetual work was the fashion of plantation garments, arrived with their baskets of completed coats, pants or shirts. These must be "checked up" against the cloth, buttons and thread measured and

One. *"The finest product of Southern civilization"* 15

The Tombee plantation "big house" owned by Thomas B. Chaplin. Chaplin struggled to attain the lifestyle expected of a "gentleman" planter (photograph by the author).

> delivered. And by now the butler wishes to know what he had best serve to the gentlemen returning from their hunt.
> At two a tired and weary woman sank into a chair, hoping for a brief rest.³

The short life of the wife of St. Helena Island plantation owner Thomas Chaplin and BVA volunteer attests to the toll plantation life could exact from the mistress, both physically and emotionally. Daughter of a wealthy Charleston merchant, Mary McDowell married the young seventeen-year-old Chaplin in April 1839. During the first years of their marriage, Mary and Thomas enjoyed good times including entertaining, partying in Charleston and Beaufort, and horseback riding.

But in April 1845, Mary's health began a long, painful decline after the birth of one of her children, Edmund. By the end of the final six years of her life she became an invalid, having given birth to seven children. Enduring seemingly unending pregnancies and frequent sickness, she seldom left her room except to take meals with her family.

Mary died on November 2, 1851. While her death could not have come as a shock, Chaplin's grief was real, and for the moment, inconsolable, writing in his journal, "The saddest day of my life. My poor, poor wife breathed her last, and was relieved of all her sufferings (many and great they were) about 12 o'clock today. Scarcely with a struggle, her pure soul departed, to realms of peace and love and joy, above, where will be no more sorrow, and care, and where her troubled soul will be at rest."

Hunting and entertaining were the chief recreations of the Beaufort St. Helena Island planters. The nearby Hunting Island and its 2,000 acres, well stocked with deer, was set aside as their exclusive hunting preserve. An informal clubhouse was maintained for the sportsmen, and each month one of them had the responsibility to provide the food, service, and liquor. Dinners could be quite elaborate, with all the aristocratic trappings of a formal dinner. A description of a hunting club dinner in 1851 at St. Simons Island, Georgia by one of its members provides a picture of the opulence and conviviality that was expected at these feasts.

> The hour is five pm.... The room is warmed and cheered by the glowing coals in a great fire-place; the table with cover laid for fourteen, is clothed in the snowiest of damask and lit by a score of candles made from the wax of the myrtle berry which cover the salt marshes; the brass candlesticks shine like virgin gold.
>
> The two soups, one a clam broth, the other chicken mulligatawny, were brought on first, the fish, shrimp pies, crab roasts, and vegetables were all placed in one service; the dessert was simple, tartlets of orange marmalade, dried fruits and nuts. The dishes disposed of, amid general gossip and talk, and the cloth drawn, the great punch bowl with its mixture of rum, brandy, sugar, lemon juice and peel, was brought in. The wine glasses were pushed aside, and bottle-shaped glass mugs were handed round; and the chairman of the meeting ... rising, announced that the health of the President of the United States would be drunk, standing and with cheers.[4]

The boisterous libations and drunkenness common to these affairs would occasionally lead to quarrels and fistfights. Thomas Chaplin became enraged by a slight from fellow plantation owner Dr. William Jenkins. Chaplin was perpetually short of cash, pestering friends and family for loans. Jenkins pointedly referred to this at one of the banquets, and the insult resulted in an attempt by Chaplin to throw him out a window. For a week after the incident Chaplin remained in his house, brooded over the incident and his wounded pride.

The confrontation might have resulted in a duel. Chaplin recorded in his journal four separate occasions when acquaintances of his delivered challenges which were ritually received and accepted. While the actual consummation of a real duel was always a possibility, the simple completion of the ritual and acknowledgment of the grievance by the challenged to the challenger was normally enough to clear the air, while observing the code of gentlemanly behavior. Chaplin himself was a "second" for his cousin Captain Jenkins, in a challenge issued to John Webb over an affair regarding Webb's intentions toward Jenkin's sister Emma, attentions which apparently were not clear to her and needed to be resolved as a matter of honor. Chaplin was greatly relieved when Emma's honor had been restored, possibly by a promise from Webb to marry her. We will never know for sure the circumstances of the affair, but Webb kept his promise and eventually married Emma.[5]

Sometime in the 1820s the planters' most important social organization was established: the St. Helena Agricultural Society. The association was ostensibly a forum to discuss horticultural practices, planting techniques and swapping cotton seeds. The commodity that enabled planters to build their wealth was the fabulously profitable Sea Island cotton, grown with a seed imported from the Bahama Islands.

The silky luxury of its sleek, long fiber grew and thrived in the light, sandy soil fringing the salt marshes of the coastal islands and the long growing season afforded on the islands. Planters spoiled it with the care of a Thoroughbred horse, fine-tuning its strains to a level of quality that commanded the highest prices. Among those families who would profit most from Sea Island cotton were those of the Chaplins and Fripps, families who would contribute many cannoneers to the Beaufort Volunteer Artillery.

The small yields of the very best cotton seeds forced them to cultivate large areas while exhausting their fields fertility in a few years, moving on to the next available area of virgin soil. Their plantations could be a strange sight. In their haste to plant as much seed as possible as quickly as possible, they girdled the huge oak and palmetto trees to kill them, but left the stumps intact, giving the land the eerie feeling of a cemetery. This method also prevented the use of plows, immeasurably adding to the backbreaking work of the slaves.

Planters discovered that saltmarsh mud was a superior manure, spread about forty cart loads to the acre. Slaves were dispatched to the creeks and marshes in boats, loading them with mud, then returning to unload it into ox carts or baskets and taken to the fields to be spread.[6] Colonel Edward Barnwell of St. Helena was so enamored of the value of manure and his recipe for compost that he put it into his will. He bequeathed to his son one of his slaves who knew the recipe for good compost and how to apply it.

The production of one crop of cotton was a long and laborious process and an uncertain crop to raise. For every year of profitable yields there were as many of poor ones. The vagaries of the weather produced devastating assaults of blight, cut worms and leaf worms (caterpillars), diseases that could spread rapidly and wipe out a whole crop.

Most Beaufort and St. Helena planters employed overseers to manage their plantation's day-to-day operations, with the larger estates having as many as six overseers. The overseers had a difficult job. They were responsible for the success and profitability of the cotton crop and managing relations with the slaves. To help them in their tasks overseers often relied on experienced slaves, "drivers," to "tame" new slaves in the ways of the plantation, and most importantly, to obey orders and stand still when a white man spoke.

When the conch blew in the early morning and slaves were sent to the fields, drivers would walk among them with their "wand of office," a hand club or small whip. More than the overseer or planter, a driver would closely control nearly every detail of the slaves' lives. He distributed rations, made sure the workers had completed their tasks and inflicted punishment when he saw fit. But whether the driver was cruel or fair-minded, the work had to be done and the slave paid the price.

Two

"What do I think ob slavery? Murdering of de people"

Sam Mitchell was a slave on the Woodward plantation not far from Beaufort. At age eighty-seven he was interviewed by a researcher for the Federal Writers' Project collecting first-person accounts of former slaves describing their experience of slavery. His powerful account describes many of the key aspects of the life of a Beaufort District or St. Helena slave. He speaks in Gullah, the language of the Sea Island blacks, a combination of English words and words derived from his West African origins.

Wen war come, I been minding cow for my master. My father been Moses Mitchell and my mother been Tyra Mitchell. We belong to John Chaplin and lib on Woodlawn plantation. Mr. Chaplin had seven plantations. He lib at Brickyaa'd plantation in winter and in Beaufort in summer. He hab many slaves, but I don't know how many. As near as I can remember, dey been fifteen slaves on Woodlawn plantation. De slave lib on de street, each cabin had two room, de Master don't gib you nutting for yo house—you hab to git dat de best way you can.

In our house was bed, table. My father mek dem. My mother had fourteen chillen—us sleep on floor. Eb'ry Tuesday de Master gib each slave a peck ob corn. Wen potato dug, we git potato. Two time in de year we git six yard ob cloth, calico in spring and homespun in de winter. Once a year we git shoe.

De slave had 'bout two task ob land to cultivate for se'f in wat call Nigger field. Could raise one pig. All my mother chillen dead cept me and one sister Rhina, who lib wid me. My father hab a boat and he gone fishing at night and sell fish. Master let him cut post and wood at night and sell, too. He had to do dis work at night 'cause in daytime he have to do his task. He was carpenter, but when dey was no carpentry work to do on de plantation, he plow. Little boy and old man mind cow. My mudder hoe. Little girl ... mind baby.

On Woodlawn dey was no overseer. We had nigger driver. Maussa didnt 'low much whipping, but slave had to do task. If did't, den he git whipping. Driver do whipping, but if he whip too severely, Maussa would sometime tek field hand and mek him driver and put driver in field.

If a slave was sick, Maussa would come and see w'at was de matter. Sometimes he would give de slave jollip to mek him womit. If he was sick, the Master would tek him to Beaufort to de doctor. If a wooman slave sick, Big Missis would go and see dem.

Slave had only one holiday in de year. Dat Christmas. Maussa would kill a cow on every plantation on Christmas and gib all de slave some. On Maussa John Chaplin plantation slave have to tell him soon as dey begin to court. If Maussa say No you can't marry dat gal, den dat settle it, you can't marry urn. He dont lak his slave to marry slave on nodder plantation, but if you do den you hab pass to wisit yo wife. W'en slave marry, w'ite preacher marry um in de Maussa house, but Maussa don't gib you anyt'ing.

Slave had dey own chu'ch on plantation wid nigger preacher, but on communion Sunday, you had to go to white folks chu'ch in Beaufort and sit up stair. Wasn't no jailhouse on de plantation, but dey was a barn w'ere sometimes Maussa put slave w'en dey been bad.

Never saw any slaves sold, but I hear tell of de banjo table. W'en slave die, Maussa let me berry um in de daytime. Nigger preacher preach funeral.

Slave on Maussa plantation could come to Beaufort on Sattidy night, but dey have to be back by 9 o'clock or patrol would get um. Maussa had nine chillen, six boy been in Rebel army. Dat Wednesday in November w'en gun fust shoot to Bay Pint [Point] I fought it been t'under rolling, but dey ain't no cloud. My mother say, "son, dat ain't no hunder, dat Yankee come to gib you freedom." I been so glad, I jump up and down.

My father been splitting rail and Maussa come from Beaufort in de carriage.... He told de driver to git his eight-oar boat name Tarrlfy and carry him to Charleston. My father he run to his house and tell my mother w'at Maussa say. My mother say, "You ain't gonna row no boat to Charleston, you go out dat back door and keep a-going." So my father he did.

After freedom come everybody do as he please. De Yankee open school for nigger and teacher lib in Maussa house to Brickyaa'd. My father git job as carpenter wid Yankee and buy ten-acre ob land on Ladies Island.

I been married two time. My last wife, Florence, living right here in Beaufort, but she left me long time ago. I nab two chillen, one daughter live to Philadelphy and de odder lib on Ladies Island. I got four grand-chillen, all ob dem grown.

Did I ebber hear ob Abraham Lincoln? Right here in my house. I got his history. He was de president of de United States that freed four million slave. What do I think ob slavery? Murdering of de people. I t'ink freedom been a great gift. Lak my Maussa and I guess he was as good to his slave as he could be, but I ruther be free.[1]

At several points in his narrative Sam mentions the importance of completing his "task." This refers to the task system of plantation management, a system that became the primary form of labor management in the St. Helena Parish plantations. The system had advantages for both planters and slaves. Unlike the traditional system of unrelenting, sunup to sundown work schedule that physically punished slaves and diminished their productivity, under the task system a slave's daily responsibility was to complete a specific, well defined, individual job: split one hundred rails, gin thirty pounds of cotton or gather three carts of marsh mud for fertilizer.

The system was refined to take into account an individual slave's physical capacity. The slaves were assessed annually and classified as to their ability to perform either full, half, or quarter tasks. This enabled the overseer or driver to make daily assignments based on the rigor of the task and the capability of the individual slave. So, for instance, hoeing weeds in the cotton fields was a less strenuous activity, enabling the more physically able slaves to perform several tasks during the day. On the other hand, the rigors of picking cotton were far more physically demanding, resulting in fewer tasks being assigned to the slave.[2]

Sam Polite was a slave born on the St. Helena Island plantation of Marion Fripp. The Fripp family provided many artillerymen for the Beaufort Volunteer Artillery and their slaveholdings in the St. Helena Parish were extensive. In an interview later in life, he described the task system from the slave's point of view: "Every slave have task to do; sometime one task, sometime two task and sometime three. You have for work till task through. When Cotton done make, you have other task. Have to cut cord of marsh grass maybe. Task of marsh been eight feet long and four feet high. Then some you have to roll cord of mud in cowpen. Woman have to rake leaf from wood into cowpen.... When you knock off work you can work on your land."[3] This last point was extremely important to the slaves. When the plantation slaves' task for the day was completed, what time remained would be used to work their own gardens (if they were permitted to have them) tend their pigs and chickens, and fish. Sam Polite greatly valued this time: "Maybe you might have two or three tasks of land round your cabin what master give you for plant. You can have chicken, maybe hog. You can sell egg and chicken to store and marster will buy your hog. In that way slave can save money for buy thing like fish and whatever he want ... sometimes you can throw out net and catch shrimp. You can also catch possum and raccoon with your dog.[4]"

Some masters encouraged their slaves to earn their own money, and purchased produce, chicken, eggs and fish from them. Slaves might be permitted to build boats and canoes for fishing, and crafted intricate, beautiful baskets. Indeed, Sam Mitchell makes note that when his father's task was completed, he went fishing at night then sold the fish later.

Some masters would pay their slaves for extra work. One planter provided a separate field where twenty-five of the men could plant using half of their Saturday workday. At the end of the season the men sold the produce and divided the $1,500 of proceeds between themselves. This practice was permitted not so much for humane purposes, but the planters' experience that slaves permitted to have some personal property were usually more compliant in their attitudes.[5]

Women slaves could use the extra time to learn new household skills. Beaufort slave Rebecca Grant learned to weave and dye cloth and make her own clothes. Adaline Gray, a St. Peters Parish slave, learned how to process indigo to create blue dye and make soap for her mistress and the slave community.[6]

Mitchell makes note of his master John Chaplin's prerogative to approve his courting of a female slave, and the necessity to seek and receive his consent for marriage. This was standard operating procedure on St. Helena Parish plantations.

As a rule, planters encouraged their slaves to marry a woman on their own plantation, reinforcing their control of the couple. This had its advantages to the male slave guaranteeing a wife would prepare meals and look after his meals,[7] and provide the master with another "breeder," to maintain an adequate work force and slaves to sell for profit on the slave market. The Sea Island plantations were major suppliers of slaves for plantations on the interior, an important source of income that could have a profound impact on the plantation's profitability.

Chaplin's requirement that a marriage ceremony for the couple take place in the plantation house was also a standard practice. Most planters in the St. Helena parish required that their male slaves choose one wife for life. To reinforce this practice planters organized marriage ceremonies and required the men to ask permission to marry a specific woman. A ceremony could be very informal, no more than a one sentence pronouncement by the planter that the couple were man and wife.

The significance of the marriage was sometimes reinforced by a plantation-wide celebration featuring a cake, and special foods including beef and rice to make a stew, and molasses and water for drink. Sometimes the mistress would make a white veil made from a discarded window curtain, or if the slave had any money saved from the sale of produce from their gardens it could be used to buy material for a dress.

John Chaplin's cousin, Thomas B. Chaplin, owner of the St. Helena plantation at Coffin's Point, scorned what he saw as the pretense of the slave marriage ceremonies. They somehow offended his "religious sense." He would deliberately absence himself from a wedding of his slaves. He resented the festivities celebrating the marriage writing in his diary, "I did not wish to be here to see the tomfoolery that was going on about it, as if they were ladies of quality." He was angry with his wife for giving them a "grand supper," using "very foolishly, my crockery, tables, chairs, candlesticks, and I suppose everything else they wanted." As late as 1876 he was still greatly annoyed at his wife for using some of his good liquor to make a bowl of punch.[8]

While the firmness of these marriage bonds varied considerably with individual slaves, many husbands and wives formed strong, permanent bonds of love and devotion. On Edisto Island, a slave known as "Old Jeff" remained devoted to his wife Sandy long after her death. Daily he visited her grave, then slept next to it at night. After a time, his friends became concerned by his unusual behavior, but he responded by claiming he intended to dig up Sandy's bones and take them to his house to have with him always.

The system of slavery disrupted black family life in the cruelest of ways. One of Thomas Chaplin's slaves, Charles, made periodic visits to his wife Phoebe, formerly of Coffin's Point plantation, but sold four years earlier to a plantation off the island. After one of those visits Charles informed Chaplin Phoebe's master had moved to Texas and had sold Phoebe to a new owner, who in turn was trying to sell her. This would likely mean she would be sold to a plantation in the interior, separating them permanently. She was on the market for $150. Charles pleaded to Chaplin to purchase her, but he refused. Chaplin, like many of the planter class, looked on his slaves as less than human. As such, he could not believe the permanent separation of a slave wife and husband would be as painful as that between a white couple.

Chaplin's indifference to his slaves' well-being was demonstrated in his attitude toward the slave children on his plantation. One of his slaves, Nelly, had three of her infant children die in three consecutive years prior to 1861. Breeding was one of the most important tasks of the women slaves, and Chaplin looked on Nelly's losses as a failure to fulfill her responsibilities. His journal suggests no compassion for his slaves' personal losses and the overall high mortality rate on his plantation. Indeed, he went so far to accuse them of killing their babies in the ultimate act of defiance.

It did not occur to him there might be medical or health related causes of these fatalities—pneumonia, dysentery, fever—similar to those of white children in his parish. The unhealthy, squalid conditions in the slave cabins and poor nutrition of the slave diet compounded the slaves' susceptibility to disease.[9]

As a rule, Beaufort District and St. Helena Island planters were attentive to their slaves' health—not necessarily for humanitarian reasons, but because it was good business to do so. Healthy slaves meant productive slaves, and many planters made sincere efforts to provide adequate medical treatment.

Plantations sometimes had a building called the "sick house" by the slaves where they would receive medical care. Typically, a sick house would be managed by the mistress or the wife of the overseer, with the day-to-day activities of the facility provided by a woman slave. Often it was the mistress who would stay up all night with a sick child, not the mother. The mistress of one of the plantations observed, "When people talk of my having so many slaves, I always tell them that it is the slaves who own me. Morning, noon, and night, I'm obliged to look after them, to doctor them, and to attend them in every way."[10]

Some planters tried to educate themselves on home medicine, including books on treating minor diseases. One of these books, *The Planters' Guide and Family Book of Medicine*, published in Charleston in 1848, details common slave ailments and diseases with suggestions on how to treat them.

Planters could be especially attentive to the health of their infant

Five generations of Smith Plantation slaves, Beaufort, South Carolina (Timothy Sullivan, photographer, Library of Congress).

slaves and pregnant mothers, providing incentives to mothers to carefully nurture their infant young and attend to their own care during pregnancy. Women on the Middleton plantation near Charleston were not permitted to work during the winter months. The plantation's owner, Henry A. Middleton, would require that they reduce their workload by half during pregnancy. He rewarded mothers with infants one month old with a gift of a dollar and gave the same amount to a mother with a one-year-old. At Christmas in 1859 he distributed dollar awards to twenty-six mothers with month-old infants, and fourteen mothers with one-year-olds.

When the mother returned to the fields, a "granny" would take over the care of the child during working hours. Middleton would reward her as well with seventy-five cents for every infant in her care that survived. Despite these incentives and precautions, infant mortality rates on plantations remained high, both for slaves and the children of their white masters.[11]

Mitchell's slighting reference to "the white folks chu'ch in Beaufort" where they would have to sit "up stair" in the slave gallery refers to the "Brick Church" in the center of St. Helena Island. After the Civil War the church would be taken over entirely by blacks and used to teach hundreds of them to read and write.

The slaves' church on the plantation he refers to was likely a "praise house," often the cabin of one of the community's religious leaders. Several times a week, people would gather there to "sing, pray, and exhort." Edward Pierce, a special agent of the Department of the Treasury that was administering the Island after the Federal occupation described a praise house service he witnessed: "The praise meeting usually opened with a 'sperichil' followed by a hymn which the leader 'deaconed' two lines at a time, reading from a well worn psalm book, if perchance he had learned to read … holding the book nearer the flickering light … all calling out the lines from memory."[12]

At some point during the service the "shout" began. Pushing the church benches to the wall, the worshippers began a distinctive, shuffling dance. Harriet Ware, one of the educators and leaders from the north who would later come to St. Helena Island after the Battle of Port Royal in 1862 described it:

> Old and young, men and women, sprucely-dressed young men, grotesquely half-clad field hands—the women generally with gay handkerchiefs twisted about their heads and with short skirts—boys with tattered shirts and men's trousers, young girls barefooted, all stand up in the middle of the floor, and when the "sperichil" is struck up, begin first walking and by-and-by shuffling around, one after the other in a ring. The foot is hardly taken from the floor, and the progression is mainly due to a jerking, hitching motion, which agitates the entire shouter, and soon brings out streams of perspiration. Sometimes they dance silently, some-

The slaves' churches were typically referred to as "praise houses." Several times a week they would gather there to "sing, pray and exhort." This photograph is of "Colored Folks church, Beaufort, SC," ca. 1863–66 (Hubbard and Mix photographer. Library of Congress).

times as they shuffle they sing the chorus of the spiritual, and sometimes the song itself is also sung by the dancers. But more frequently a band, composed of some of the best singers and tired shouters stand at the side of the room to "base" the others, singing the body of the song and clapping their hands together or on their knees. Song and dance alike are extremely energetic, and often, when the shout lasts into the middle of the night, the monotonous thud, thud of the feet prevents sleep within half a mile of the praise house.[13]

Slave attempts to escape their bondage were not uncommon, but the motivations varied. For some, it was simply the desire to leave temporarily to visit a relative, usually a husband or wife, living at a nearby plantation. There was risk with this, for without a pass, a slave caught by slave patrollers would likely receive a flogging. Some fled fearing punishment for some infraction on their plantation, others because they were fed up, or that they had received especially cruel treatment from their master. Some simply wanted to get away for a while.

Indeed, the likelihood of a South Carolina slave successfully fleeing 2,000 miles to freedom in the North, traveling barefoot with no map, at night, was highly unlikely. At best he or she might stumble onto a "maroon" community of slaves, more common in North Carolina. Maroons were encampments of escaped slaves existing in remote areas far from roads and towns.

Plantation owners sometimes delayed a search for a missing slave. The planter might be aware of a spouse or relative of the slave on a nearby plantation and assume the slave would return in a few days. If after a week or longer the slave had not returned, the master would usually run a classified advertisement like the one following in a Charleston newspaper describing the slave and offering a reward for his capture or information on his whereabouts.

> **Runaway**
> From the subscriber, on the 27th of May, his negro boy Isome. Said boy is about 21 years of age; rather light complexion; very coarse hair; weight about 150 lbs.; height about 5 feet 6 or 7 inches; rather pleasing countenance; quick and easy spoken; rather a downcast look. It is thought that he is trying to make his way to Franklin county, N.C., where he was hired in Jan. last, of Thomas J. Blackwell. A liberal reward will be given for his confinement in any Jail in North or South Carolina, or to anyone who will give information where he can be found.
> W. H. Privett, Canwayboro, S. C.

On the morning of July 14, 1856, one of Thomas Chaplin's slaves, his man Jim, pretended to go to a well for water but did not return. Jim's disappearance was particularly galling to Chaplin. Jim was Chaplin's "man," had worked side by side with him for thirteen years and had received more privileges than most of the other slaves. He thought he could be trusted. He had been sent overnight to Beaufort numerous times and returned, carried messages and mail to his mother—a three-day trip—and always returned. He could only remember having flogged him once and worked beside him on special jobs. There was no hint of dissatisfaction. What could have been the motivation? A missing hen.

Each night one of Chaplin's male slaves was assigned the task of guarding the plantation's livestock. Although the night of the disappearance of the hen was not Jim's night to watch, Chaplin concluded that Jim was responsible for the hen's disappearance. Furious, he stormed into Jim's wife's cabin on an adjoining plantation and took his clothes, a rebuke of Jim's negligence and a warning that he was in jeopardy of losing all the "privileges" he had earned. Over the next two weeks Chaplin received no word of Jim's whereabouts; but just as he was about to organize a hunt for his slave, Jim returned.[14]

By Chaplin's standards, Jim's punishment was modest. He wrote, "Gave

Jim a very moderate punishment, say about 60 paddles, put on his bare hide, with my own hands." Not long after, Jim's privileges were restored.

Treatment of the slaves by their masters in the Beaufort District and St. Helena Island varied with the master. Some St. Helena slaves described their masters as "good Massa," while other planters were "Debil heself." Edgar Fripp was singled out as one who "would whip any Negro who upon meeting him did not remove his hat." After the occupation of Beaufort by Union forces in 1862, the newly freed slaves showed their scars from whippings to the northern missionaries, one woman claiming she lost four babies during her pregnancy due to whippings. One of the missionaries, Laura Towne, found a whipping post in the dining room in one of the plantations.[15]

On the other hand, Captain John Fripp's slaves spoke well of him. His was one of the few plantation homes not plundered by slaves after the Federal occupation. Justice for slaves in the St. Helena parish was controlled entirely by their masters. A disturbing event occurred in February 1849, and Thomas Chaplin was called to serve on a jury of inquest—a panel made up entirely of island plantation owners. The death of a slave had been reported on James Sandiford's plantation, and the circumstances of the death were serious enough to merit investigation.

During the proceedings Chaplin reveals an uncharacteristic streak of compassion for the slave, Roger, as well as disgust at the venomous cruelty that led to his death. He vigorously dissented from the verdict of the inquest that the death was accidental and required no trial of Sandiford for murder. His description of Roger's ordeal remains one of the most powerful surviving accounts of the unspeakably inhumane treatment of a slave and merits extended citation.

> Monday I received a summons while at breakfast, to go over to J. H. Sandiford's at 10 o'clock a.m. this day and sit on a jury of inquest investigating the death of Roger, a Negro man belonging to Sandiford. Accordingly I went. About 12 m. there were 12 of us together (the number required to form a jury, viz.—Dr. Scott, foreman, J. J. Pope, J. E. I. Fripp).
>
> W.O.P Fripp, Dr. M. M. Sams, Henry Fripp, Dr. Jenkins, Jr. McTureous, Henry McTureous, P. W. Perry, W. Perry and myself.
>
> We were sworn by J. D. Pope, magistrate, and proceeded to examine the body. We found it in an outhouse used as a corn house, and meat house. Such a shocking sight never before met my eyes. There was the poor negro who all his life had been a complete cripple, being hardly able to walk and used his knees more than his feet, in the most shocking situation, but *stiff dead*. He was placed in this situation by his *master*, to punish him so he says, *for impertinence*.
>
> And what was this punishment—this *poor cripple* was sent by his master ... before daylight (cold and bitter weather, as everyone knows, though Sandiford

says, "It was *not very cold*)," in a paddling boat down the river to get oysters, and ordering him to return before high water, and cut a bundle of marsh. The poor fellow did not return before ebb tide, but he brought 7 baskets of oysters and a small bundle of marsh.... His master asked him why he did not return sooner and cut more marsh.

He said that the wind was too high. His master said he would whip him for it and set to work with a cowhide to him. The fellow hollered and when told to stop, said he would not, as long as he was being whipped, for which impertinence he received 30 cuts.

He went to the kitchen and was talking to another Negro when Sandiford slipped up and overheard this confab, heard Roger, as he says, say, that if he had sound limbs, he would not take flogging from any white man, would shoot them down and turn his back on them. (Another witness, the Negro that Roger was talking to, says that Roger did not say this.)

Sandiford then had him confined, or I should say, murdered.... Even if the fellow had made the speech that Sandiford said he did, and seen worse, I by no means warranted the punishment he received. The fellow was a cripple, and could not escape from a slight confinement, besides, I don't think he was ever known to use a gun, or even know how to use one, so there was little apprehension of his putting his threat into execution.

For these *crimes*, this man, this demon in human shape, this pretended Christian, member of the Baptist Church, had this poor cripple Negro placed in an open outhouse, the wind blowing through a hundred cracks, his clothes wet to the waist, without a single blanket and in freezing weather, with his back against a partition, shackles on his wrists, and chained to a bolt on the floor and a chain around *his neck*, the chain passing through the partition behind him, and fastened on the other side.

My heart chills at the idea, and my blood boils at the base tyranny. The wretch returned to his victim about daylight the next morning and found him, as anyone might expect, dead, *choked, strangled*, frozen to death, *murdered*. The verdict of the jury was, that Roger came to his death by choking by a chain put around his neck by his master—*having slipped from the position in which he was placed*. The verdict should have been that Roger came to his death by inhumane treatment to him by his master.... My individual verdict would be *deliberately* but *unpremeditatedly murdered* by his master.[16]

Chaplin's youthful display of conscience and righteous indignation would recede with the passing of time. Indeed, years later, Chaplin would find himself defending an overseer who killed a slave for stealing some watermelons.

Were an outsider to visit a St. Helena plantation in the years prior to the Civil War, it would not have been unusual for the owner to justify slavery by showing off one of his prized slaves, one who exhibited unusual intelligence, one talented in mathematics, for instance, or good at repairing machinery like cotton gins and presses. He would boast about his superior intellect and trot the slave out to exhibit his appearance of confidence and self-reliance.

He would assure the visitor that "he had witnessed in his own time an obvious advance in the quality of the slaves generally; they were more active, less stupid, employed a larger more exact vocabulary, and were less superstitious, obstinate and perverse in their habits of mind."

In the same breath he would compare his model slave to the rest of his "moping field hands" delivering a heartfelt soliloquy protesting his good intentions by providing for a race of people unable "to understand and to speak the language of human intelligence any more than a horse."[17]

Thomas Chaplin's model slave was his driver, Robert. Chaplin had received Robert as a gift from his mother, Isabella Baker, after a New Year's visit in 1852. In his memoirs after the war he wrote Robert "did very well." Chaplin's biographer Theodore Rosengarten commented that

> no one got more work out of his field hands than Robert.... He was a religious authority and seer, a giant of learning among the Negroes. He could talk to white people without losing his dignity. He could count and figure. Furthermore, Robert could read. How useful this made him to his master! He did not have to be there to give orders. He could leave written instructions with Robert while he went off the plantation.[18]

In the end, however, Chaplin would feel betrayed by Robert. Chaplin fled his plantation in November 1861 after the battle of Port Royal and the capture of Beaufort and St. Helena Island. Robert, however, stayed on, presumably to watch over the plantation. After the battle the newly liberated slaves pillaged the homes of their former masters. Chaplin bitterly complained that when he left Tombee, Robert "was not faithful to his trust.... I left everything in his hands, and he never saved a single thing for me." Chaplin would never understand that while his loss of the plantation was a calamity for him, it was a miraculous event for Robert: Freedom!

After the war many blacks, now freedmen, would reconnect with their former masters, developing new relationships, even friendships, that would last the rest of their lives. Not so Robert. "He has always kept out of my way since peace," Chaplin wrote years later, after his last contact with Robert, embittered by the rejection.

After the Federal occupation of St. Helena Island, the Union occupiers were concerned by what they observed as a backwardness and culturally inferior behavior of St. Helena's slaves when compared to slaves in the South Carolina interior. The missionaries from the north who had never witnessed slavery on this scale characterized the St. Helena slaves as "the lowest grade of Negroes in America." Their unique Gullah dialect sounded crude to them. Some of these observations were part of their own cultural biases and racial attitudes.[19]

There were good reasons for the St. Helena slaves' backwardness. They were arguably the most isolated groups of slaves in the country. Over half of them had never been off the island, indeed, had never been on an adjoining plantation. The Sea Islands were a formidable barrier to life off island, and only a select few would have been able to experience life in even the most modest of towns.

In time, after the liberation of Beaufort and St. Helena by Union forces and given the opportunity to earn their first wages working on the former plantations or working as laborers in the army camps, many of the freed blacks took advantage of the new, economic freedom they had gained with emancipation. Some with an entrepreneurial bent sold chickens, fish and garden "truck" to the occupying soldiers.

Added to this was their excitement that as they saved money, the old plantations were being divvied up into small plots and put on the market for sale by the federal government. Now they would be able to buy their own plots of land to farm with their savings and become landholding citizens. If they could not afford to buy land individually, they formed clubs to pool their funds and buy land. The transition from slavery to freedom and its attendant opportunities and responsibilities would shape and transform many of them into motivated, independent citizens and change the course of Southern history forever.[20]

Three

"He die but he die for doin' de right"

Fear of slave insurrections in the St. Helena Parish was a constant fact of life, compounded by the fact of a slave population far exceeding that of the whites, and the persistent occurrences of slave resistance common in the decades prior to the Civil War.

In February 1860 St. Helena Parish planters—reacting to rumors of a secret cache of Sharps rifles being discovered and rumors of roving bands of abolitionists stirring up discontent among the slaves—ramped up the number of slave patrols across the island. Then in July it was heard an overseer was murdered by his slaves.[1]

Slave murders of plantation overseers was not new to South Carolinians. A newspaper reported in 1824 of the murder of an overseer in Chesterfield County and the swift and brutal punishment of the slave accused of the murder: "The negro was immediately taken, condemned, hanged, and his head cut off, his body burnt, and his head stuck up on a pole and carried about as a terror to other slaves."[2]

In the 1820s and 1830s, fears of slave conspiracies and insurrections reached such a level of paranoia that South Carolina Senator James Hammond described the state as a state in turmoil. In 1837, William Harper published the widely circulated *Memoir on Slavery* in which he characterized Southern slaves as a "barbaric tribe pressing on the frontiers of a civilized nation." [3]

In 1830, William Aiken, a wealthy Charleston businessman and planter, promoted investment in a railroad project, touting it as a way to transport troops quickly from the interior to the coastal areas "to repel ... domestic insurrection." [4]

In 1849, future Confederate General James Pettigrew described Charleston as a town gripped by anxiety and in siege mentality for fear of slave unrest. Curfews were imposed, and armed guards roamed the streets. "The watchmen here are not provided here simply with alarming weapons, such as rattles, etc., but are accoutered as soldiers, with muskets, uniform and bayonet, all of which you may rightly conjecture is for the Black population.... Such precautions are absolutely necessary in a city of which more than a majority of the population are slaves [liable] ... to be corrupted and tampered with [in] every possible manner."[5] Fear of slave conspiracies and insurrections were driven not just by rumor. From South Carolina's earliest colonial history, the fabric of its historical memory was embedded with some of the most frightening and explosive instances of slave insurrection on the North American continent. Not the least of these was the Stono slave rebellion of 1739 in the rice plantations south of Charleston.

The world of the eighteenth-century Charleston slaves was especially barbaric. Their white masters punished them for minor offenses including maiming through castration, nose slitting, chopping off ears, hands or toes, or branding. Charles Wesley, brother of Methodist Church founder John Wesley, described in his journal an especially egregious example of cruelty by a Charleston dancing master:

> Mr. Hill ... whipped a female slave so long that she fell down at his feet, in appearance dead; but when, by the help of a physician, she recovered and showed some signs of life, he repeated the whipping with equal rigor, and concluded the punishment by dropping scalding wax upon her flesh; her only crime was overfilling a tea-cup! These horrid cruelties are the less to be wondered at, because the law itself, in effect, countenances and allows masters to kill their slaves by the ridiculous penalty appointed for it. The penalty is about seven pounds, about a half of which is remitted if the criminal informs against himself.[6]

With the expansion of rice cultivation in the early decades of the eighteenth century, South Carolina's planters prospered through the labor of 30,000 slaves, already the majority population with whites numbering about half that number.

The work was grueling and often demanded a fourteen-hour workday for slaves. The horrid working conditions and the prospect of an unlimited term of slavery was a powerful incentive for slaves to try to escape. Many slaves were aware they could find freedom in Spain's colony to the south, Florida. Spain welcomed runaway slaves. In 1738, seventy slaves fled South Carolina and reached St. Augustine, having traveled nearly 300 miles for their freedom.

Without slaves, rice cultivation would never be a profitable enterprise; but with slaves, no planter ever rested totally secure in his bed. Ominous reports emerged regarding black unrest in the Carolinas. A ship captain named

Von Reck wrote about the situation in the South Carolina colony in his journal in 1724:

> There are computed to be 30,000 Negroes in this province, all of them slaves. They work six days in the week for their masters without pay and are allowed to work on Sundays for themselves. Being thus used, there lays amongst them a foundation of discontent; and they are generally thought to watch an opportunity of revolting against their masters, as they have lately done in the Island of St. John and of St. Thomas and it is the apprehension of these and other inconveniences that has induced the honorable trustees of Georgia to prohibit the importation and use of Negros within their colony.[7]

There was increasing emphasis on the use of public punishment as a necessary form of deterrent which grew as slave numbers increased. Masters were fined for failing to whip unruly slaves. The heads or bodies of slaves were often left on public display as a grim warning to other blacks. In 1732, planter Charles Jones reported having killed a black runaway who had robbed him. Jones told a justice of the peace he had felled the slave in self-defense with a blow of his musket butt, and the justice accepted his story, ordering him to cut off the victim's head "fix it on a pole," and set it up on a road near the Ashley River Ferry.

It was hoped by the whites that dramatic public punishments would have a repressive impact, forcing slaves into patterns of docility. It certainly had that effect for many slaves. Nonetheless, this strengthened system of controls could not deter black resistance. There were incidents reported of slaves who, out of desperation and fury, lashed out against whites despite the consequences. In August 1733 the *Carolina Gazette* reported, "a Negro man belonging to Thomas Fleming of Charlestown took an opportunity and kill'd the Overseer with an axe. He was hanged for the same yesterday."

Such explosions of black rage were usually suicidal, but patterns of black resistance evolved and increased in ways that were terrifying to whites. In 1751, the Reverend William Cotes of Dorchester expressed alarm about the slaves in George's Parish, a "horrid practice of poisoning their masters. For this practice 5 or 6 in our parish have been condemned to die." In 1761, the *Gazette* reported that "the negroes have again begun the hellish practice of poisoning."

Another form of resistance was arson. In 1754, a slave named Sacharisa was sentenced to burn at the stake for setting fire to her owner's house in Charleston. In 1797, two slaves were deported and several others hanged for conspiring to burn down the city of Charleston

The greatest concern was the fear of slave uprisings, and there were numerous attempts as well as conspiracies, real or imagined. The first major conspiracy was uncovered in 1720. A Charleston resident wrote that "very lately we have had a very wicked and barbarous plot of the Negros rising with a design to destroy all the white people in the country and then to take the town in full body."

But it was in the late summer of 1739, in a super-charged environment of suspicion, anger, and paranoia among whites and growing discontent among the slaves, that the bloodiest slave rebellion in South Carolina's history erupted.

In the early morning hours of Sunday, September 9, some twenty slaves gathered near the western branch of the Stono River within twenty miles of Charleston. The slaves proceeded to the Stono Bridge and broke into Hutchinson's general store where they captured small arms, gunpowder, and axes.

Over the course of the ensuing two day rampage through the white settlements south of Charleston, the number of slaves swelled to between sixty and a hundred. It was only after a pitched battle with a hastily organized group of white colonists was the rebellion put down. But not before twenty whites had been killed.

In the days following the battle a desperate and intensive manhunt was staged. The entire white colony was ordered under arms and guards posted at key ferry passages. The Ashley River militia company set out from Charlestown in pursuit.

During the coming weeks accounts varied as to how many slaves were killed in the manhunt. One white resident wrote several weeks later that within the first two days of the manhunt, twenty rebels were killed outright, and forty altogether were immediately either shot, hanged or gibbeted alive.[8]

The opening decades of the nineteenth century brought with them an ever-increasing drumbeat of slave conspiracies and revolts in South Carolina. In 1816, a group of slaves in Camden, South Carolina, conspired to ignite a slave rebellion. During the American Revolution Camden and the surrounding area was the site of many military engagements between British and American forces. The British sought to sow trouble with the slaves in the area, promising them freedom if they would desert their masters and join the British cause.

Slaves were exposed for the first time to the Revolution's ideals of independence and liberty. A contemporary commentator on the conspiracy later wrote on the rebels' motives, "A few appeared to have been actuated solely by the lust of plunder, but most of them by wild and frantic ideas of the rights of man."[9]

Ironically, the conspirators chose July 4 as the date for the revolt. Holidays both religious and secular were often the times slaves would flee their masters, so it made sense to use the diversion of Fourth of July celebrations to launch a revolt. Later, during the trial, Camden attorney Francis Dellesseline described the conspirators' plan:

> The scheme had for its object the conflagration of a part of the town—the massacre of all the white male inhabitants, and the more brutal sacrifice of the female. Their plan was entrusted to a few only, and they left its development and consummation to chance; relying on the presumed disposition to rebellion on the part of the blacks of every description.
>
> To strengthen the possibility of success, the Negroes from the adjacent country were invited, under various pretenses, to Camden that night.[10]

Authorities got word of the plot when a slave of Colonel James Chesnut named Scipio warned his master of the plot in mid–June. Chesnut instructed Scipio to continue to attend conspiracy meetings to gather more information. Chesnut alerted the governor, and quietly, Camden authorities made a thorough investigation of the plot. They were surprised to learn that the slaves most deeply involved in the planning all belonged to prominent Camden citizens, and all of whom were quickly arrested. On July 3, a special court made up of two justices of the peace and five landowners convened to try the cases of fourteen slaves. After deliberating for two weeks, all six of the original plotters were found guilty, condemned to death and hanged in front of the town jail.

The most chilling slave conspiracy was that of Charleston freedman, Denmark Vesey. Originally the property of former sea Captain Joseph Vesey, Vesey purchased his freedom with $600 from a $1,500 lottery he won. At the time of his manumission in 1799 he was about thirty years old and was among the approximately 1,000 freedmen living in Charleston. Freedmen in Charleston generally chose a skill as an artisan, and in the 1790s there was a demand for carpenters, the trade Vesey decided to pursue.[11]

Vesey's work took him to places outside of Charleston, and he saw for the first time the situation of enslaved blacks on plantations. How this experience informed his thinking we do not know, but it is certain this activity enabled him to form a wide network of contacts in the slave community that would be useful when he later planned his slave revolt.

In 1822, Vesey could claim to be successful as any free black in Charleston. His carpentry business was thriving, and his estimated worth was $8,000. He had earned the respect of the white community and the envy of many of its blacks. Yet with all these attainments, he felt deeply the inequities with which he and his race were subjected.

He formed opinions as to what rights and liberties he should be accorded and rejected the whites' patronizing notion that being free should be satisfaction enough for slaves. If whites enjoyed substantially more of the fruits of liberty than free blacks, they should be more than happy with the rights they had. He bridled at the obsequious behavior whites expected of the black freedmen, and openly criticized other freed blacks for their servile behavior.[12]

In 1818, he began to voice his views in church meetings and by 1821, he began to talk about the need for action. By then he had achieved a certain eminence and respect among Charleston's blacks for his bold views, and he struck a chord with many of them. Negroes in Charleston, he said, were living an abominable life and their situation was so bad that he did not know how they could endure it. The time was at hand that they should not be slaves of "damn white rascals" any longer but should fight for liberty.[13]

Vesey began to hold conspiracy meetings in his home, sometimes with as many as thirty conspirators packed into the dwelling. At these meetings a painter, Jack Glenn, would often read the scripture then "pass the hat" for donations to pay for weapons. Vesey would remind the men of how the Israelites were led out of Egyptian bondage by Moses, and that they too, had the right to be free. They were also told that refusal to join meant death.

Estimates vary as to the size of Vesey's army, some as high as 9,000 men. Whatever the size, it had the potential to be a formidable force. The conspirators vowed to be ruthless in their work. Once they controlled Charleston, they would torch it, then massacre both whites and blacks who refused to join them. When their work was done, they would pirate ships in the harbor and sail them to Saint-Domingue (current day Haiti) where thirty years earlier slaves had rebelled and taken over the Island.

Vesey set the date of the rebellion for July 14, a time when many white Charlestonians had left town for the summer for cooler climes on the Sea Islands. Blacksmiths began making pike heads and bayonets that could be attached to poles. Many would be armed to the gills with their own swords and long knives. They would use these crude weapons to capture unguarded stores of muskets on King, Queen and Meeting Streets. The plan had each of Vesey's lieutenants leading forces that would attack and secure different areas of the town.

Then, on May 22, one of Vesey's conspirators, William Paul, made a critical mistake. While talking with a mulatto slave named Peter he was trying to recruit at the Market Wharf, William revealed there were plans for a rebellion. Would he like to meet the leader and join the effort? The astonished slave refused, then alerted his master, Colonel John Prioleau. At about the same time, another slave told his master a slave rebellion was brewing and he immediately shared the news with Charleston's mayor.

The reaction of the white community was swift and ruthless. Within a month Vesey was captured. He was brought before a makeshift tribunal and was sentenced to hang along with other conspirators a week later. On the morning of his execution he and five other conspirators were loaded onto a cart and taken to a makeshift execution site. Before a large crowd of blacks and whites, they were hung. Mayor Hamilton later recorded they "met their fate with the fortitude of Martyrs." In all, 131 conspirators were arrested; thirty-five were hanged, thirty-seven sent to Cuba, twenty-three acquitted, and most of the remainder released without trial.

By 1850, if memories of the Stono rebellion and the Vesey conspiracy had faded among South Carolinians, other jarring events rekindled slave insurrection paranoia. Rumors were rampant of roving abolitionists fomenting unrest among slaves. Newspapers urged that more aggressive slave patrols be dispatched to monitor slaves and ran fear-of-insurrection news items.

South Carolina Congressman Laurence M. Keitt was shaken by the murder of his brother by slaves on his Florida plantation and became caught up in slave insurrection hysteria, writing South Carolina Senator James H. Hammond, "If northern men get access to our negros to advise poison and the torch, we must prevent it at every hazard."

These fears were further fueled by a Beaufort native who, more than any other South Carolinian, would drive the state to secession.

Four

"We can make one long, last, desperate struggle, for our rights and honor"

Robert Barnwell Rhett Sr., was the rock star of the Southern secessionist movement. No one could match him for the virulence of his rhetoric and the urgency of his cause. Born in Beaufort in 1800 and raised for a time in the substantial tabby house of his grandmother, Elizabeth Barnwell Gough, on Carteret Street, he grew up during a cotton boom and one of the most prosperous periods in Beaufort's history. Although his own family was of limited means, he was surrounded by Beaufort's elite families—the Elliotts, Barnwells, and Heywards—heady with wealth and power.

While the privileged children of these families were sent to Harvard and Yale, Rhett received much of his schooling at the local Beaufort College. Except for a brief stint in Washington, DC, as a congressman for the Beaufort/Colleton district and as a senator, he seldom left South Carolina, resulting in a narrow, provincial outlook that instilled trust in his Lowcountry neighbors and buttressed the loyalty and consistent popularity that he would inspire through the thirty active years of his public life.

Rhett studied law in Charleston in the office of Judge Thomas Grimke, who was, ironically, brother to two of the most prominent abolitionists in the United States, Sarah and Angelina Grimke. Rhett opened his own law practice in Beaufort in 1822, then moved to Walterboro to be closer to the District Court of Colleton. It was at Walterboro on the steps of the Colleton County Courthouse that he would be thrust into the national limelight as "the father of secession."

There he delivered a fiery speech in 1828 fulminating at the Tariff of 1828, the so-called "Tariff of Abominations." To the distress of Southern states, tariff rates had been rising steadily since the first tariff law was passed by Congress in 1816. The tariff policy protected Northern manufacturers whose commodities' prices were being undercut by foreign competition. The 1828 tariff set a substantial 38 percent tax on 92 percent of imported goods, and from the South's point of view, it was doubly odious with its higher rates on imported goods and the additional burden of an *ad valorem* tax on its exports of cotton. Rhett's speech on the Colleton Courthouse steps was a call to action, a dramatic challenge to Lowcountry planters and South Carolinians to resist the actions of the federal government—one of the first clear and uncompromising steps toward secession.

Rhett's speeches were enthusiastically published in Beaufort by the *Beaufort Gazette* owned by his brother-in-law, John A. Stuart, and William Grayson. During its brief publication history between 1828 and 1833 it was a strong propaganda machine for states' rights.

Stuart's partner, William Grayson, began his career as an instructor at Beaufort College. He read law and established a law practice at the Coosawatchie Court House the same year as Rhett. Grayson became the owner of Frogmore on St. Helena Island, one of the largest plantations in the Beaufort District, supporting 170 slaves. During the nullification crisis years, he aligned himself with Rhett's views, became an avid supporter of states' rights, and vigorously expounded nullification in Congress representing the Beaufort/Colleton District.

As time went on his views on states' rights moderated, and he aligned himself with the Unionists. While Unionists were fully supportive of states' rights views and the preservation of slavery, they wanted to accomplish these goals within the legal framework of the United States government without seceding.

Rhett was decidedly anti–Unionist, and during the years leading up to the "Secession Oak" speech he earned the reputation as a fierce and vocal advocate of nullification. The concept of nullification was, ironically, a legal concept articulated and promoted by South Carolina's pow-

Robert Barnwell Rhett was the rock star of the secessionist movement. No one could match him for the virulence of his rhetoric. Engraving from a photograph by Cook, Charleston, South Carolina (Library of Congress).

erful senator, John C. Calhoun, to save the Union. (Calhoun's ambitions for the American presidency had their effect on tamping down his enthusiasm for secession.)

Calhoun's nullification position was a constitutional means to assure the South's control over tariffs, resist federal overreach, and maintain slavery. Calhoun maintained that the Constitution provided the right of individual states to organize a convention that could declare a federal law null and void. The Constitution does provide for conventions of states to collectively amend the constitution by a majority of two-thirds of the states. But what it does not provide for is for an individual state to unilaterally void the law within its own borders, a concept Calhoun appeared to support.

This was a radical concept, and one that Southern interests kept alive as leverage against what they felt were onerous tariff policies. Its test came in 1832 with a new tariff law crafted by John Quincy Adams, the former president and newly elected congressman from Massachusetts. As chairman of the Committee on Manufactures, Adams thought he saw a way to mollify Southern representatives who looked at tariffs as anathema. Adams introduced a bill that decreased overall tariff rates modestly as a nod to Southern interests, while maintaining adequate levels of protection on key commodities such as iron and cotton textiles to mollify Northern manufacturers. In an especially conciliatory gesture toward the Southern planters, Adams included in the bill a statute slashing the tariff rate on cheap woolen materials used to clothe slaves from 45 percent to 5 percent. The Adams Tariff of 1832 passed both the House and Senate by comfortable margins and was hailed by most Southerners as a significant compromise to their interests.[1]

Not so South Carolinians—at least the ones who counted. The Lowcountry plantation owners of the Beaufort district dominated both houses of the South Carolina legislature through property qualifications and custom. Between Calhoun's nullification supporters and states' rights radicals like Rhett, a two-thirds majority was reached, enough to approve voting for a statewide nullification convention, one whose members were overwhelmingly in favor of nullifying the 1828 tariff.

Why this obsession with tariff policy by South Carolinians? Was it simply economics, the belief that high tariffs would undercut Southern prosperity? It was a fear much more profound and fundamental: The tariff controversy was a convenient way to mask the other great concern of the southern plantation owners: maintaining the engine of its economic prosperity, slavery. With 50 percent of its wealth invested in the human capital of slaves, and most of its population enslaved, Southerners saw a linkage—real or imagined—between slavery, tariffs and economic survival. At the same time, there emerged another threat: the strident voices of northern abolitionists calling for the end of slavery. Threats like these to the institution were, from their point of view, existential.

Thus, on November 24, 1832, South Carolina held a nullification convention declaring the 1828 and 1832 federal tariffs unconstitutional and null and void in South Carolina effective February 1, 1833. Furthermore, any attempt by the federal government to enforce the tariffs would be met by resistance. Preparations began to raise 25,000 militia men. For the first time in its young history, the United States was threatened by a major internal revolt.

There was one major roadblock to the success of nullification: President Andrew Jackson. Though a slaveholder, nothing was more energizing to the president than defiance to his authority. His Southern address and support of slavery were counterbalanced by his self-image as an antiestablishment defender of the common man and Republican values. These values easily positioned him in antagonism to the Southern slaveholding aristocracy and its rebelliousness.

Jackson made his point of view crystal clear, warning a South Carolina congressman, "If one drop of blood be shed ... in defiance of the laws of the United States, I will hang the first man of them I can get my hands on to the first tree I can find!" When South Carolina Governor Robert Hayne suggested to Missouri Senator Thomas Hart Benton that Jackson would not really carry through with his threats, Benton replied, "I tell you Hayne, when Jackson begins to talk about hanging, they can begin to look for ropes."[2]

Jackson combined forceful rhetoric with legislative flexibility by joining Senator Henry Clay in crafting the Force Bill of 1832 that brought the crisis to a peaceful resolution. He displayed political acumen by compromising on new tariff legislation that did away with some of the more substantial concessions made to the south in the 1828 tariff legislation, but at the same time lowering by increments the overall tariff for eight years, guaranteeing cuts amounting to a substantial 20 percent by 1842.

The other Deep South states failed to come to the support of the South Carolina nullifiers, considering the Force Bill a palatable way for all parties to avert a crisis. The bill passed the house with over a three-quarters majority and the Senate with only one dissenting vote, though nine Southern senators abstained including both South Carolina senators.

The nullification crisis was just one of the factors churning secessionist controversy. With the 1831 launch of the anti-slavery newspaper, *The Liberator*, abolitionist William Lloyd Garrison and the paper's co-founder Isaac Knapp began thirty years of intensifying abolitionist activity resulting in the

Four. "We can make one long, last, desperate struggle..."

establishment of the American Anti-slavery Society, a growing influence on Northern opinion.

South Carolinians found Garrison's rhetoric galling and the incendiary tone of *The Liberator*'s first issue especially threatening:

> I am aware that many object to the severity of my language; but is there not cause for severity? I will be as harsh as truth, and as uncompromising as justice. On this subject, I do not wish to think, or speak, or write, with moderation. No! No! Tell a man whose house is on fire to give a moderate alarm; tell him to moderately rescue his wife from the hands of the ravisher; tell the mother to gradually extricate her babe from the fire into which it has fallen;—but urge me not to use moderation in a cause like the present. I am in earnest—I will not equivocate—I will not excuse—I will not retreat a single inch—*and I will be heard.*

As the years approaching 1842 ticked by, Northern industrial interests became increasingly concerned that the decreasing tariff rates were driving new threats of European competition that would undercut American prices. To counter this trend Congress passed the Tariff of 1842, or the Black Tariff as it became known in the South, placing into law a more protectionist schedule of tariffs, one whose longer-term impacts resulted in a 20 percent decrease in exports, a potentially devastating impact on Southern exports of cotton.

The Black Tariff and the threat it represented was too much for the South Carolina Lowcountry plantation owners to bear. The planters formed an *ad hoc* committee and called on their Congressional representative—at that time Robert Barnwell Rhett—to address these new developments and suggest remedies. Invitations to meet and discuss the situation were sent out to newspapers, planters, and many of the most prominent Beaufort and Sea Island families—families that would provide the future members of the Beaufort Volunteer Artillery during the Civil War.

A date was set for the meeting, July 31, 1844, at the resort village of Bluffton, just south of Beaufort. The day's activities would begin under a huge oak tree in Bluffton, where Rhett would address the attendees.

Rainy weather and limited steamboat service from Charleston, Beaufort and Savannah might have discouraged some attendance. Nonetheless, more than 200 aggrieved and angry plantation owners and their families drew up their carriages around a temporary platform built at the base of the tree. A special delegation from St. Helena Island led by Rhett's brother Edmond attended. At around 2:00 PM, Rhett ascended the platform, having passed through the crowd to cheers and much shaking of hands. For the next ninety minutes, he harangued his audience with a high-pitched voice and volatile rhetoric.

In his speech the tariff controversy took a back seat to slavery. Fueled by the fanatical ravings of abolitionists, the North intended to abolish slavery. The tariff issue was simply a stalking horse for more hideous designs of subjugating the south and destroying its economy. It was time to act, and from Rhett's standpoint, the South had just two alternatives: nullification or secession. The South was once great, and it could be great again, but it must act decisively. To thunderous applause he called for a state convention to take measures to nullify the hated Black Tariff of 1844.[3]

Here, for the first time, a credible movement was launched in the south with the express purpose of defying federal laws and, if necessary, seceding from the United States. Rhett followed his Secession Oak speech with appearances and dinners around the state, his rhetoric becoming ever more radical and inflammatory. "If abolition proved triumphant," he declared, "we must slaughter or be slaughtered." The only hope for the South is in resistance.[4]

As time went on, it became apparent that Rhett's radical views were being embraced by a younger generation of planters in the Beaufort district and in Charleston under the banner of the Young Democracy. His followers were soon labeled "The Bluffton Boys," and their cause, "The Bluffton Movement." They became synonymous with secession and unswerving devotion to states' rights, nullification, and the preservation of slavery. From this time on this movement would stand at the vanguard of the march toward the Civil War and be an active force in the movement to secede.

The movement's ardent supporters were among the most influential planter families in Beaufort and St. Helena Island: Hutson, Chaplin, Jenkins, Barnwell, DeTreville and Stuart, families would fill out the roster of the Beaufort Volunteer Artillery. In 1850, Rhett was hosted at a banquet organized by the elite planters of St. Helena, and his remarks were essentially those of 1844. It was old news, but its message was emboldened by the knowledge that the other Deep South states were slowly coming around to the idea of secession through the efforts of numerous "Southern Rights Associations" that were being formed throughout the South.

Indeed, by 1850, and the emergence of the Beaufort District Southern Rights Association, it was clear that the populace of the Beaufort District had arrived at the conclusion that secession was inevitable.[5] Events in 1850 accelerated secessionist sentiment throughout the state. Alarm bells went off in the Beaufort District with the introduction in the United States Congress of the Wilmot Proviso. If passed, the Proviso would ban slavery in the massive territory the United States had acquired from Mexico in the aftermath of the Mexican War.

Four. "We can make one long, last, desperate struggle..."

The death of John C. Calhoun in March 1850 and his moderating views on secession emboldened the radical wing of South Carolina's secessionist leadership which demanded immediate secession regardless of whether other Southern states would join the state. Secessionists made up most of the state's newly elected General Assembly which elected a secessionist governor, John Means, and sent Rhett to the U.S. Senate. Taxes were passed to fund appropriations for military ordnance and other military activities.

Countering the outright secessionists were the "cooperationists," no less committed to secession but only with the cooperation of the other Southern states, worrying that independent action by South Carolina would bring about financial ruin to the state. Both positions had powerful organs of propaganda. The pages of the *Charleston Mercury* sounded a constant drumbeat of secessionist sentiment for its readers, while the cooperationists' newspaper, the *Southern Standard*, was no less strident in its support for the cooperationists' bandwagon.[6]

In November 1850, leaders of the Beaufort Southern Rights movement convened an organizational meeting at the district courthouse in Gillisonville. Attendees included the most extensive collection of Lowcountry planters ever assembled at one time, including Edmund Rhett, John Barnwell and Richard Reynolds representing the cotton planters of St. Helena Island as representatives were chosen from each of the Beaufort District parishes.

The convention drafted a preamble to the constitution of the newly minted Beaufort District Southern Rights Association. This statement was the definitive expression of the Sea Islands planters' views on secession and its link to slavery. Ten years later it would provide a blueprint for South Carolina's Ordinance of Secession.

> We, the people of the Beaufort District, in this our primary assembly, do declare: That we believe Abolitionism, in common with Socialism, Communism, and Agrarianism, is the natural fruit of infidelity, rejecting the order of God's providence and the teachings of Revelation. That we regard domestic slavery as the great safeguard of political freedom. That without it Republican institutions have never long existed, and in the nature of things never can. That it is the only social arrangement capable of reconciling labor with capital, and protecting us from the inevitable tendencies of the free labor system towards the terrible alternatives of absolutism and barbarism. That is our duty to maintain it at all hazards.[7]

In the fall elections of 1851, secessionists and cooperationists battled aggressively for the hearts and minds of the electorate. In the end, six of the seven Congressional districts voted for delegates representing the cooperationists and only one, representing the Beaufort District, voted in the majority for the secessionists.

The struggle continued in April 1852, when a statewide convention was called and convened in Columbia. This was the kind of state gathering that Rhett had called for in 1844, one that could codify state resistance through secession. The secessionists campaigned across the state to push the Beaufort District's hard line on secession. But again, they were rebuffed at the convention, with no resolutions passed designed to actively resist the United States government. Many of the delegates were having second thoughts about the wisdom of radical initiatives and where they would lead.

This was a stunning blow to Rhett and the radicals in Beaufort and put Rhett's leadership in question. He resigned from the Senate to the dismay of his secessionist supporters and would never again play a leading role in the secession movement. Other hard-line secessionists found themselves marginalized as well.

It was events outside of South Carolina that would reignite secessionist fervor and bring the struggle between South Carolina and the federal government to the tipping point.

The "Bleeding Kansas" struggle erupted in the Kansas-Nebraska territory in 1856. With slavery's status in the territory undecided, armed bands of pro-slavery gangs fought "free stater" immigrants, terrorizing settlers. An armed band of men calling themselves "The South Carolina Bloodhounds," participated in the "sack of Lawrence," a Kansas town made of anti-slavery settlers. On May 20, 1856, Lawrence was burned and destroyed by Southern sympathizers, and during the raid the Palmetto flag was raised over the town.

Responding to the raid, fanatical abolitionist John Brown with his sons and other men slipped into the small, pro-slavery community of Pottawatamie and brutally murdered five men in front of their families. This massacre incited further raids and attacks across the state.

In South Carolina, planters were alarmed by the emergence of the Republican party and its embrace of abolitionism, and the realization that more and more Northerners were becoming sympathetic to the abolitionist cause. Indeed, some Southerners feared that the continuous, abolitionist agitation they perceived coming from the North was becoming "a burning, religious conviction."[8]

But all these developments paled against the hysteria and rage that spread through the Beaufort District upon hearing the news of John Brown's raid on Harpers Ferry on October 16, 1859. Fear of slave rebellions was rekindled and reinforced by the planters' self-deception that their slaves were essentially loyal but were being "tinkered with" and poisoned by abolitionist propaganda. The psychological impact of the attack for many South Carolinians was the melding of slave insurrection, abolition and Republicans into parallel evils.

The coming cataclysms—the rupture of the Democratic Party into Northern and Southern factions, the election of Lincoln, and the attack on Fort Sumter were now unfolding with the stark inevitability of a Greek tragedy.

South Carolinians were especially united in their belief that the election of a "black" Republican for president in the 1860 election would be intolerable, leaving them no choice but to secede from the Union. Since 1856 they had been following the speeches of Lincoln, Seward, and other leaders of the Republican Party, speeches that confirmed their worst fears that the Republican Party's core mission was the eradication of slavery at all costs.

In their eyes the 1860 election would be a referendum on the future of the Union. They would lay back and let the North make the fateful decision on how South Carolina and the South would proceed. Thomas Simons, Charleston's representative in the state legislature laid out the consequences in the darkest terms: "Should a Black Republican President be elected it is the necessary sequence of reason that the majority of the people of the country have endorsed his principles and raised a banner on which is inscribed—death to the institutions of the South. In that event it is my solemn judgement we can no longer with safety remain in the same confederacy."[9]

Many South Carolinians were profoundly ambivalent toward these stark choices, and a certain apathy and fatalism set in discouraging action. Congressman William Boyce voiced the concern that the breakup of the Union was now a certainty, but feared Southerners were unprepared for the consequences of secession. Others worried that if South Carolina were to secede, it would find itself out on a limb with no support from other southern states.

Some, like Beaufort planter William Lawton were less conflicted. Lawton jokingly offered several hundred dollars to be sent to the Republican campaign fund if it would result in "a plan to *drive, whip,* or *kick,* two, three or more of the Southern states out of the Union."[10]

In the end it was Lincoln's maneuverings that forced the hand of South Carolinians to make those first, fateful cannon shots at Fort Sumter in the early morning hours of April 12, 1861. One of those shots, was ignited by Stephen Elliott, the Captain of the Beaufort Volunteer Artillery.

Five

"The dissolution of the Union is the next step in the path of our glory"

The Fourth of July celebration in 1850 in Beaufort, South Carolina, was like that of hundreds throughout the United States on that day, celebrated with "great pomp" as described by Henry Middleton Stuart: "The parade was formed at 10:00 o'clock in the morning. The old negro drum corps at the front.... There was ... a most splendid dinner furnished by the ladies of the town. Punch, champagne and other wines flowed like water. I remember one particular dinner in 1850—such men as the honorable R. B. Rhett, Albert Rhett, William Tabar, Hon. W. F. Colcock, Honorable W. H. Trescott and others. The theme was then separate State Action of the State to leave the Union."[1]

Among the dinner guests was fire-eater Robert Barnwell Rhett, one of the most outspoken and radical secessionists of his generation; W. F. Colcock, former Speaker of the South Carolina House of Representatives and a key figure in organizing state support for secession, and William Henry Trescott, a Charleston attorney and future United States diplomat.

Earlier in the day Trescott had addressed the military pride of Beaufort, the men of the Beaufort Volunteer Artillery. His message was clear and uncompromising; the United States was now two different nations, North and South, with fundamental issues dividing them: "The most hopeful believer in the stability of the country must acknowledge that while our forefathers framed a government, they failed to create a nation.... In the American Union, there are two peoples, differing in institutions, feelings and in the basis of their political faith."[2]

Trescott's bleak message characterized these conflicting interests as so irreconcilable that the nation was on the brink of dissolution: "It has resulted in the developing of two popular wills—northern and a southern—and

Five. "The dissolution of the Union is the next step..."

these two wills stand opposed in undisguised and inextinguishable hostility.... When, then, in any country you find two populations characterized by different institutions, preserving their natural characteristics, and yet so resolutely opposed that a surrender of the one to the other is necessary to national unanimity, the time for the departure of those two people is at hand."[3]

He declared an uncompromising challenge to the North: "While it is impossible for us to foresee our national future, we can yet see enough to warrant us in believing that if the alternative placed before us be the abandonment of the institution of slavery or the dissolution of the Union ... the dissolution of the Union is the next step in the path of our glory."[4]

Trescott could hardly have had a more sympathetic audience for his remarks than the men of the Beaufort Volunteer Artillery. Its roster was unusual for a volunteer Civil War unit. "Ours is a gentlemanly company," mused Milton Maxcy Leverett, a private in the BVA. Leverett was representative of a more modest social status. His father, the Reverend Edward Charles Leverett, was rector of Prince William Parish Church not far from Beaufort. The majority of the BVA men were members of the elite planter aristocracy of the South Carolina Lowcountry with revered family names such as Barnwell, Rhett, Elliott and Fripp.

They took pride in the BVA's historic pedigree extending back to the American Revolution. On February 21, 1776, the Provincial Congress of South Carolina passed a resolution calling for "a company of artillery of one hundred men, with proper officers."[5] With the passing of this resolution what became known

Charleston attorney William Trescott addressed the Beaufort Volunteer Artillery on July 4, 1850. His message was clear and uncompromising: the country was now two different nations, North and South (Library of Congress).

as the Beaufort Volunteer Artillery was initially organized as the Beaufort Independent Company of Artillery joining the Continental Army as the 4th Company of Artillery, 4th South Carolina Regiment.

Trained and drilled by its first captain, William Harden, its baptism of fire came in 1779, under its second commander, Captain John Laboularderie deTreville. Garrisoned at Fort Lyttelton on the Beaufort River, the Beaufort Artillery was assigned to protect Beaufort and the Port Royal area from British attacks. In January 1779, the British Major Valentine Gardner led an expedition of approximately 200 soldiers with orders to capture the Port Royal Ferry on the Whale Branch River near Beaufort.

William Moultrie, the general in command of American Continental troops in the area, hurried toward Beaufort with 300 soldiers including the Beaufort Artillery. His force met the British in the Battle of Port Royal Ferry on February 3, 1779, near Grays Hill. During the battle the Beaufort Artillery held a position on the right wing of the American line. The hotly contested engagement ended in stalemate with the British withdrawing from the field. The American artillery units including the Beaufort Artillery played a crucial role in the battle, raking the British lines with a damaging fire of solid shot and grapeshot.[6]

Later in the War, in 1779, the Beaufort Artillery fought in the unsuccessful attempt by the Continental troops to capture Savannah, Georgia, occupied by the British. The unit was among the American defenders of Charleston, South Carolina, besieged and surrounded by British forces under British Lt. General Henry Clinton. On May 12, 1780, the city was surrendered by the Americans, and the battery was among 4,500 Americans captured and held prisoners until the end of the war.[7]

In 1820, the Beaufort Artillery's name was changed to the Beaufort Volunteer Society. It continued to maintain its identity as a functioning, volunteer military unit in the decades prior to the Civil War drilling on the grounds of the Beaufort Arsenal where its cannons and equipment were stored. In 1843, the unit was merged with the Beaufort Volunteer Guards and reorganized as the Beaufort Volunteer Artillery.[8]

By 1850 when Trescott made his oration to the BVA, Beaufort and the South Carolina Lowcountry around Beaufort had become the epicenter of secessionist sentiment.[9]

For the men of the BVA, the stakes were high. In 1850, the plantations located in the Beaufort district averaged approximately thirty-four slaves per plantation. St. Helena Parish, one of the four parishes that made up the district, was among the wealthiest regions in the United States. With an African American population of 8,261 slaves populating 151 plantations,

Five. "The dissolution of the Union is the next step..." 51

10 percent of the plantations in this parish maintained more than 100 slaves.[10]

The 1862 roster of the BVA included dozens of men who were the beneficiaries of the slave economy. During the course of the Civil War, six Chaplins related to one of the wealthiest Sea Island planters, Benjamin Chaplin Sr., served on the BVA. In 1850, Chaplin owned 272 slaves on a plantation valued at $30,000. Relatives of Dr. Thomas Fuller—with a plantation of 1,000 acres and 145 slaves—provided two sergeants and a corporal for the BVA.[11]

In 1857, the South Carolina Legislature passed a resolution approving funds to reimburse members of the BVA for expenditures for improvements of Beaufort's Arsenal, the headquarters of the BVA. The resolution suggested that the expenditures were made from an excess of zeal in the belief that South Carolina was about to secede from the Union.

> The Committee on the military ... find that the state owns an old dilapidated building known as the arsenal, in the town of Beaufort.... They further find that in the year 1852, the petitioners, a patriotic volunteer artillery company, expended of their own means the sum of $2,835 in erecting on the foundations of the old arsenal a building capable of accommodating a garrison of 250 men and a battery of six guns. That at the time of the said debt was incurred the petitioners were governed by motives of patriotism, believing that the state of South Carolina was about to secede, separate and alone, form the Union. Your committee appreciating the motives of the petitioners and satisfied that they should not be the sufferers from the mistake ... into which they were hurried by a zeal for her welfare, and they therefore recommend that the prayer of the petitioners be granted.[12]

The following year, during the Beaufort celebrations on the anniversary of George Washington's birthday, the marshal spirit continued as the Company's colors, recently sewn by women of the community, was presented to the BVA's Robert Barnwell Fuller. In an article in the March 4 edition of the *Charleston Mercury*, the editor waxed enthusiastically describing the day's festivities.

> The Beaufort Volunteer Artillery, in their new and brilliant uniforms, were out in "full feather" and imposing numbers, to join in doing honor to the day; and the ladies, ever mindful of what is appropriate and tasteful, selected this as a suitable occasion to present to the "Artillery" the rich and imposing order for this ancient corps.
> The inhabitants of the town—citizens and soldiers—assembled at noon under the branches of the Old Oaks upon "The Green," and thither our young men and maidens, "blithe of foot" old men and matrons in their carriages, and youngsters on horseback, all repaired to witness the pleasing ceremony of the presentation.
> The gentleman ... came forward, bearing aloft the Banner, which he presented

The Beaufort Volunteer Artillery's "colors" were severely damaged during the Battle of Port Royal, leaving a large hole in the center of the flag from a cannonball, patched with the phrase "An Unsurrendered Flag" (courtesy South Carolina Relic Room and Military Museum, Columbia, South Carolina).

> on behalf of the ladies of Beaufort, to the Beaufort Volunteer Artillery, in an elegant, tasteful and appropriate address. The Banner was received by Ensign R. B. Fuller, who, on behalf of the Company, made an eloquent and soldier like response—brief, and to the point.
>
> We do not remember to have ever witnessed more spirit and military ardor than was evinced by the Artillery on this occasion. New blood has been infused into the veins of the old company, and a new military enthusiasm has kindled in the ranks. With their new guns, their showy uniforms and splendid banner, they were as ornamental on this gala day, as we hope they will be effective in actual service.[13]

Six

"A grand show of war"

Below the elegant summer residences of St. Helena planters, perched on the crest of the bluffs along Beaufort's Bay Street, the Beaufort River flows south into a majestic body of water: Port Royal Sound. Among the most scenic and spacious harbors on the Eastern Seaboard of the United States, in 1861 it attracted the attention of Union military planners more interested in its strategic importance than its beauty.

By the fall of 1861, the Civil War had gone badly for the Union. The bombardment of Fort Sumter in April of that year was followed by a disastrous defeat at the First Battle of Bull Run in Virginia. To stem the Confederate momentum, planning began in Washington, DC, to establish a naval blockade of Southern coastal cities and ports to halt southern trade with European markets and disrupt its communications. President Abraham Lincoln was himself poring over charts of Southern coastal areas looking for a base of operations for the newly minted South Atlantic Blockading Squadron.[1]

Lincoln appointed a task force to flesh out the tactical details for a naval invasion of the South. Comprised of some the leading naval military theorists of the day, during the summer of 1861, the Blockade Board set about identifying potential locations for a Southern naval port and a plan for invasion. Meeting in secrecy in the red sandstone Smithsonian Building, they considered locations in South Carolina including Bull's Bay, St. Helena Sound, and Port Royal Sound.

In the end it was Port Royal Sound near Beaufort that attracted their greatest interest. Their final report summed up its advantages: "It is the finest harbor south of Chesapeake Bay, which it resembles in capacity and extent. It is approached by three channels, the least of which has seventeen feet of water.... Several of our screw frigates of the first class can pass the bar, and when the entrance is once made a whole navy can ride at anchor in the in uninterrupted health and security.... The entrance is over two miles wide; there is fine anchorage under Bay Point."[2]

One of the most influential members of the Blockade Board was Captain Samuel Francis Du Pont, the senior officer of the U.S. Navy. Commissioned a midshipman in the Navy in 1815, he was easily the most experienced officer in the Navy, with much of his service at sea and commands around the world. Du Pont came of age during the advent of steam powered vessels necessitating an understanding of new technological developments and their strategic and tactical impacts on naval practice.

At fifty-eight years of age, Du Pont could have easily ridden out the war at a comfortable vantage point from behind a desk in Washington. But he felt compelled to serve his country in its crisis, writing his wife, Sophie, "I had been content to remain where the war had found me and where I was doing quite as much good as I could blockading—probably a good deal more—but since the affair at Bull Run I have not been comfortable, and felt that every man who could be doing anything in addition ... this hour required him to do so."[3]

He impressed Secretary of the Navy Gideon Welles, and on August 5—just three months before the expeditionary force would depart for Port Royal—he was appointed its commander. In addition to his appointment, General Thomas W. Sherman (not to be confused with William Tecumseh Sherman) was assigned the command of a landing force of approximately 12,000 infantry.

To ensure the element of surprise, preparations for the expedition at Fortress Monroe at Hampton Roads, Virginia, were carried out with the utmost secrecy. Even the commanders of the ships in the flotilla were not told the destination of the force. They were given sealed envelopes with the destination they were not to open until the ships were at sea.

Du Pont would lead the flotilla in his flagship, USS *Wabash*, a forty-gun veteran of the Navy and relatively new, having been commissioned in 1856. At 301 feet long and fifty-one feet abeam, it was an impressive and formidable warship. The *Wabash* had served as flagship for the Home Squadron in the Mediterranean, with a seasoned crew that had already seen action in the war in the blockade of Charleston and the capture of Cape Hatteras.

Though no specific timetable was set for the launch of the fleet, Lincoln wanted it commenced sooner than later, anxious for the Union's first major military success. But problems arose. Sherman was having difficulty recruiting the 13,000 men he needed, and Dupont had his own problems assembling a fleet. In addition to the warships, transports were needed for the troops and colliers to carry coal, the fuel of the warships. Du Pont impressed a motley assortment of boats: ferry boats, river steamers, coastal craft and sailing vessels. He chartered merchant ships that had to be con-

Six. *"A grand show of war"*

verted to transports and collier service and fitted with adequate defensive armaments.[4]

The ships at Hampton Roads hummed with activity. Boatswains barked orders to scrub the decks, polish the brass, and secure supplies. On the crowded decks sailors were ready to fix the sails, and below decks coal heavers prepared to stoke the engines. "Powder Monkeys," the young boys that would carry the ammunition to the cannons during battle, nervously rehearsed their tasks in their minds.

As the days ticked by, Lincoln's patience finally ran out. He ordered Welles to get the expedition underway. On Tuesday, October 29, at 5:00 AM in the morning, the USS *Wabash* fired a gun signaling the fleet to heave to and get underway. "Soon," described a sailor, "the black funnels of the steamers' clouds of smoke began to pour and in the rigging of the sail frigates were crowds of nimble sailors. The commands 'All ready! Let fall' and broad sheets of snowy canvas appeared where before were but ropes and spars."

It was an awe-inspiring sight: the largest naval and amphibious expedition ever mounted by the United States Navy comprised of seventeen warships bristling with 157 guns, twenty-five colliers and thirty-three troop transports loaded with 12,000 infantrymen and 600 marines.

Three days out, the fleet sailed into a gale off Cape Fear, North Carolina, its winds gusting to near hurricane force. For the thousands of soldiers packed into the troop transports, it was a terrifying experience. One of them, Harry Kauffman, of the 97th Pennsylvania Infantry, described the wide range of emotions experienced by the soldiers during the ordeal. Some of the men prayed, sang hymns, cursed, or gave away their belongings because they thought they were going to die. Some nervously made fun of other soldiers. Despite the ship's heaving and waves "mountains high," Kauffman made his way to the top deck "and enjoyed the scene very much until a large wave ... drenched me to the skin when I became disgusted with storms in general and storms at sea in particular."[5]

The storm scattered the fleet, and the next morning Du Pont could see the flag of only one of his boats on the horizon. As the ships reassembled, he assessed damage reports. To save the ship the crew of the gunboat *Isaac Smith* had to jettison its cannons. The troop ship *Peerless* sank but managed to safely transfer its soldiers to another ship. Three cargo ships and one troop transport had sunk with a few men lost.

Despite these losses, the flotilla moved on, and on November 4, the *Wabash* and twenty-five ships were anchored near Port Royal Sound. The impact of this development was electrifying to the residents of Beaufort and the surrounding sea islands.

On Saturday, November 2, the people of Beaufort learned that a huge Federal fleet was headed south, possibly for Port Royal. The next day at Sunday service at St. Helena's Episcopal Church, the Rector, Dr. Joseph Walker, suggested to his congregation that they start packing. Parishioner Ann Barnwell described her feelings: "Our hearts were filled with patriotism and devotion while the organ pealed the beautiful hymn, *God Save the South*." Dr. Walker reassured his parishioners "that God was nigh to all who called upon Him." He announced he would ring the church bells the next day and asked families to at that time "gather their households together and hold family prayers." Barnwell remembered "We were subdued as we walked home, but we never dreamed of the fate before us."[6]

The next day, Brigadier General Roswell Ripley confirmed the fleet was heading to Port Royal and advised Beaufort residents to evacuate. All across the town carriages, carts and boats were collected and loaded with every family possession that could be packed in them. Emily Walker fretted about how the family would be able to transport her eighty-two-year-old grandmother, an invalid. Family slaves Daddy Will and Daddy Sam carried her on a chair and laid her on a mattress in a carriage where she and other members of the extended family were sent to safety on the mainland.

Later that night the rest of the family evacuated by boat. Emily described the hectic scene:

> By nine o'clock the rowboat with its six hands had anchored in front of the town.... They carried a mattress and placed it in the bottom of the boat, jerked up a carpet, threw that over the awning, three trunks, I think. Mama sent Betsy and myself and Cousin Sada and her two infants; her husband was at the fort. We carried a pot and food for the negroes to cook. We had three negro women and six negro men aboard. My father steered; a lantern was placed on top of the awning.... Before we landed in the morning, the battle began; we heard the shells explode in the water.[7]

On St. Helena Island planters gathered on the veranda of Dr. Joseph Jenkins home at Lands' End with its full view of the Sound. Their world would be turned upside down before the day was over. Two Confederate forts—Fort Walker on Hilton Head Island, and Fort Beauregard on Bay Point, located across the Sound on St. Helena Island—defended its entrance. Du Pont and Sherman determined the guns at these forts would have to be destroyed before any landing of infantry could be safely deployed.

Among the 640 Confederate defenders of Fort Beauregard were eighty-three men of the Beaufort Volunteer Artillery. In 1858, in anticipation of the outbreak of hostilities with the North, the BVA was assigned to a battalion that included the St. Helena Company of Mounted Riflemen and the Beaufort Beat Company under the command of Colonel Robert G. M. Dunovant, 12th Regiment South Carolina Volunteers. Stephen Elliott, Jr., was its captain.

To characterize Fort Beauregard as a fort was an overstatement. A flat, barren compound of sand hills and earth and a few small buildings—its defenders would be easy targets for guns of the naval flotilla. Its armament included nineteen guns, of which only seven could reach warships in the sound. Some of the guns were equipped to shoot "hot shot" projectiles heated before firing to set fire to the warships.

Earlier in the summer, James Stuart, returning from study in Europe, joined the BVA at Fort Beauregard. He saw engineer Lt. John White Gregorie supervising a gang of twenty slaves working feverishly to finish construction of the fort. Through the summer he and the rest of the men drilled on the beach with muskets.

Writing to his brother Edward, twenty-two-year-old Private Milton Maxcy Leverett could find little to complain about regarding the conditions of camp life:

> "Life down here is not that of prodigality as Ma surmised nor is one of incessant toil, fatigue, starvation and deprivation of everything that is comfortable. It is the life (I speak as regards the Beaufort Artillery) of Beaufort men who always try to make themselves as comfortable as possible.... I have a tent to myself and one other man, sleep on a cot with pillow, sheets, mattress, blankets and clean clothes to put on, plenty to eat and plenty to drink ... and what more can a man wish for?"[8]

In addition to these amenities, many of the men had the attentions of their families' slaves who would accompany them throughout the war, preparing meals, washing clothes and bedding, and foraging for food.

Early on the morning of Monday, November 4, the Union Fleet made its first appearance, crossing the bar and anchoring south and opposite Bay Point. BVA Corporal of the Guard Stuart, standing on the south shore of Bay Point described what he saw: "A column of masts and smokestacks moving slowly along the horizon from the north toward the mouth of the harbor. The harbor bar was twelve miles away from our shore so that the hulls of the ships were invisible below the horizon, but by noon there was a goodly gathering of masts, looking much like a forest of dead trees in a clearing."[9]

Du Pont sent out a squadron of six ships, a reconnaissance in force, to ascertain the strength and firepower of the forts. What happened next was perhaps the most quixotic naval attack in the annals of American naval history. A tiny Confederate fleet made up of a riverboat and three converted tugs (dubbed derisively the "mosquito fleet" by the Federal soldiers) was dispatched to confront Du Pont's force. The Mosquito Fleet was commanded by the sixty-five-year-old flag officer Josiah Tattnall who had had a storied career in his service with the United States Navy. As a young boy, he served on a United States ship during the war of 1812. He fought in the Mexican-American War, receiving honors for his bravery. His sailing career was impressive with assignments throughout the world. But, like many regular officers of the United States Army and Navy, his Southern roots trumped loyalty to the federal government, and he accepted a commission in the Confederate Navy.[10]

Tattnall was fully aware of his ships' perilous situation and tried to hide his boats behind Hilton Head Island. But his position was exposed by the thick black smoke issuing from their funnels. Du Pont's ships flushed him out with a few long-range shots. Tattnall's boats gamely ventured out to confront the Federal juggernaut, but their pluckiness was short-lived, retreating quickly after a few shots by Union guns.

On Tuesday, November 5, Colonel Dunovant made some adjustments to the BVA's position, posting it about 200 yards behind the fort buildings to cover them should the Federal troops land. About 7:00 PM, the fort received its first fire from the fleet, a barrage lasting about two hours. "They opened up on us," recalled Stuart, "and we had our first experience of the 'hell shells.' They hit the parapet and made the mud fly and blew up a caisson shaking up the gun squad pretty severely but wounding no one. We made some very bad practice at them and did not make a hit. In fact we had never fired the guns more than a half a dozen times before."[11]

On Wednesday, high winds prevented the Union fleet from mounting an attack. Captain Elliott, concerned that the Federals might make a landing and overwhelm the fort, took advantage of the lull by sending out a small detachment of men to the edge of the beach to serve as pickets during the night. To increase the small number of troops stationed on Fort Beauregard, Brigadier General Thomas Drayton, overall commander of Confederate military operations, attempted to send reinforcements to the fort on November 7 on the steamer *Emma*. The timing was unfortunate, as the *Emma* sailed straight into the advancing *Wabash* at the head of the fleet, cutting her off and forcing her to turn back.[12]

As jarring as this first bombardment on Tuesday was to the men of the BVA, nothing would compare to the shock and awe of the full attack on Thursday. The winds subsided, not even the slightest ripples disturbed waters of the sound. A bright, clear day, conditions were perfect for the ships' cannons to find their targets on Forts Walker and Beauregard.

The attack came around 9:00 AM, and Du Pont's strategy was simple but devastatingly effective. The ships, following each other in close order, would take a circular course through the harbor, passing and firing upon Fort Beauregard, then sailing left and south toward Fort Walker, firing broadsides as they passed. They would make this circuit three times.

Corporal Stuart described the scene:

> It was a grand show of war, but terrible for us. They came on in column, the Wabash at the head of the line. As they moved within range we fired a broadside, all our guns at once, only to see most of the shots fall short. Then there came a puff of smoke from the bow of the Wabash, another and another along down to the stern and then the shells began howling and bursting around us. And the other ships began firing and we were covered with smoke and flying sand from the parapet. The only thing to do was to tend to business—load up and shoot. Our gunner sergeant, Barnwell Fuller, was a notoriously bad shot with a gun. He proved so today with a cannon. It was hard work to load and then to see it wasted. The whole detachment would groan out loud. And Barney would say, "I'll do better next time boys." But he didn't. He couldn't.[13]

In his official report of the battle, Captain Elliott stated he directed the fire of the fort's batteries be directed primarily at the larger ships in the fleet. He claimed to see the shots hitting ships consistently, but because of the distance, about a mile and a half, could not discern what if any damage they were causing.[14]

On board the *Wabash*, Commander Charles Henry Davis could have enlightened him, commenting on the accuracy of one of the larger guns on Fort Beauregard.

Commodore DuPont's strategy was simple but devastatingly effective. The ships, following each other in close order would take a circular course through the harbor, passing and firing on Fort Beauregard, then sailing left and south toward Fort Walker, firing broadsides as they passed. Fort Beauregard's guns did not have the range to reach the flotilla's ships (*The History of the Civil War in America*, J. S. C. Abbott, 1863).

If I had known the existence and position of that venomous rifled eighty-pounder on the salient of Fort Beauregard, to the fire of which we were exposed as we advanced, and still more, if I had known the rapidity and accuracy with which it served, I should have indulged a little more reflection perhaps. Every shot from that pestilential devil which was, I imagine, directed by a navy officer (resigned) either struck us or went forty feet of the bridge on which Dupont ... and myself were standing. It was evidently aimed, according to Southern custom, at the officers, and aimed, I have no doubt, by some one of our old brother officers turned rebel.[15]

There were many problems for the Confederates. Wooden fuses for the Columbiad cannon were faulty, igniting the cannonballs yards short of the targets. After thirty-two firings, one of the cannons exploded, injuring Captain Elliott in the leg. The hot shot battery, in an exposed position, was effectively silenced after a few rounds. The cannonades from the Union fleet were so intense the men of the battery were driven from the guns. Two men each lost an arm due to the premature discharge of a gun.

After two hours of incessant bombardment, Stuart left his gun momentarily to find his brother Allan in the arms of two men, "white, limp and shattered." "I ran back with them and laid him on the parapet slope. He thought he was dying and said goodbye to Mamma, and told Stuart to tell his mother that 'he had died at his duty.' He had been struck by the recoil of the gun carriage and hurled into the air from the chassis to the ground below, one thigh bone almost wrenched out of the socket and the ligaments badly torn." He survived his wounds, but would never fully recover from them, dying two years later.[16]

At about 3:00 PM, the guns of Fort Walker were silenced. Cheering could be heard from some of the Union ships and a band playing. Colonel Dunovant proceeded to Fort Beauregard and conferred with Elliott. After a brief exchange orders were issued to evacuate the island.

Dunovant, anticipating the possibility of defeat, had asked Elliott to locate a local who could reconnoiter and prepare a route to retreat and avoid capture. Elliott chose his father, Episcopal Minister Reverend Stephen Elliott Sr., who also served as the BVA's chaplain.

There was no easy way to withdraw from the fort. After a four hour hike up the beach, "The only line of retreat," Dunovant stated in his official report, was "across the strip of land known as the 'narrows,' scarce 50 yards wide and 1,000 long, to the main body of Eddings Island ... an extensive swamp, entirely impenetrable save by a trail known to few, and of such extreme difficulty as to preclude the possibility of transporting baggage of any kind beyond what could be borne on the shoulders of the men."[17]

Six. "A grand show of war"

Key to the escape was having flatboats available at the end of the swamp to ferry the men to a place called Jenkins' Landing from where it was a further ten miles to Beaufort. Reverend Elliott arranged for barges to meet them there, and they were successfully ferried to the Beaufort side of the water.

When the exhausted men began to straggle through Beaufort that Friday, what they saw amazed them: a town deserted. "As we drove through it," Stuart commented, "It seemed like a city of the dead. I don't remember seeing a single person in the street, not even a negro." Stuart went to his deserted home on Bay Street. Looking out a window from the fourth floor, he saw the Union gunboats. Beaufort had fallen, and soon all of Hilton Head, St. Helena, Lady's and Port Royal Islands would soon be overrun by the Union troops.

As Federal troops landed and began to occupy the captured fort, some of them were struck by the carnage wrought by the bombardment of Fort Beauregard. A private described entering the fort and hearing, "a scream that would have chilled the coldest heart. In one place there was a man's arm in another a hand in another place ... a shell had struck there was a man's skull and brains."

In a memoir written years later, one of the Federal naval officers, U.S. Navy Rear Admiral Daniel Ammen recounted a close call he had with a booby trap during his inspection of Fort Beauregard soon after its capture.

> The flagstaff was on the gable of a small frame house fifty feet from the fort. I went within, saw some books lying on a table, and went out toward some tents in the distance. In a few minutes an explosion was heard, and on turning, I saw a cloud of smoke where the house had stood. A quantity of power had been put under it, arranged so as to ignite from a friction-tube, and a sailor, in passing along outside, had struck his foot against a small wire attached to the tube, thus causing the explosion. He was knocked over, and partially stunned, but soon revived.[18]

Perhaps the makeshift land mind was assembled by Captain Elliott, who later in the war would become known for his experiments developing torpedoes.

The excitement, even joy, of the slaves of Beaufort and St. Helena Island at the fall of Port Royal could hardly be contained, and they celebrated it in song and in memory. Harriet Tubman, who spent nearly a year in Beaufort after the Federal occupation, recorded the feelings of one of the island slaves.

> I been yere seventy-three years, workin' for my master widout even a dime wages. I'd worked wid my mouf full of dust, but Oh Lord, would not stop to get a drink of water. I'd been whipped, an' starved, an' I was always prayin' "come an' delibber us!" All dat time da birds had been flyin,' and de rabens had been cryin', and de fish had been sunnin' in de waters. One day I look up, an' I see a big cloud; it

didn't come up like as de clouds come out far yonder, but it 'peared to me a big house in de water, an' out of de big house came great big eggs went on trou' de air, an' fell into de fort; an' de bad eggs burst before dy got dar.... Den I heard 'twas the Yankee ship [the *Wabash*] firin' out de big eggs, and dy had come to set us free. Den I praise de Lord. He come an' put he little finger in de work, an' dey Sesh Buckra all go; and de birds stop flyin', and de rabens stop cryin' and' shen I go to catch a fish to eat wid my rice, de's no fish dar. De lord Almighty'd come and frightened 'em all out of de waters. Oh! Praise de Lord! I'd prayed seventy-three years, an' now he's come an' we's all free.[19]

With a certain irony and poetic justice, one of the sea island planters was captured by Union forces and rowed as a prisoner to a Union warship by his own slaves to a song they made up as they rowed.

> De Norfmen dey's got massa now,
> De Norfmen dey's got massa now,
> De Norfmen dey's got massa now,
> Hallelujah.
>
> Oh! Massa a rebel; we row him to prison.
> Hallelujah.
> Massa no whip us anymore,
> Hallelujah.
> We have no massa now, we free.
> Hallelujah.
>
> We have the Yankees, who no runaway.
> Hallelujah.
> Oh! all our old massas run away.
> Hallelujah.[20]

Seven

"The Mosby of the Islands"

In the aftermath of the battle of Port Royal, Confederate and Union strategies in South Carolina were influenced by the strategically important Charleston & Savannah Railroad. The railroad was vital to the Confederate defense of the region, providing crucial mobility for Confederate troops over a large, thinly defended area. It also provided Confederates fast movement of reinforcements and supplies to defend either Charleston or Savannah.

At the time of the defeat, Robert E. Lee, in overall command of the newly created Department of South Carolina, Georgia and East Florida, designed a plan to pull back forward coastal positions on the Sea Islands vulnerable to the fire of Federal gunboats. This consolidation of defensive positions and fortifications was necessary for the protection of the all-important railroad.[1]

Conversely, Union forces began organizing periodic military excursions to capture or destroy sections of the railroad. Small flotillas of gunboats and troop transports plied the inland rivers including the Pocotaligo, Tulifinny, Coosawatchie and Combahee waterways that led to the wooden trestles and earthen causeways upon which the Railroad was built.

In mid-November, the Confederate commander of South Carolina, General Roswell Sabine Ripley, called for volunteers for raids to the abandoned Sea Island areas of Port Royal and St. Helena Islands to destroy cotton, food supplies, and gather up slaves. There were no takers except for one: Stephen Elliott, Jr., captain of the Beaufort Volunteer Artillery.

Elliott's family was among the most elite of Beaufort society. He enjoyed the benefits of this status, owning a plantation on Parris Island and serving in the South Carolina legislature. He received the best education available to a South Carolinian, studying at Harvard College and graduating from South Carolina College in 1850. Since its founding in 1801, South Carolina College was the preferred higher education venue for South Carolina's elite families. Families whose sons attended the college could be assured they would be prepared for public service and leadership positions, and that they would be grounded in accepted states' rights philosophy and its rationale for maintaining the institution of slavery.[2]

Elliott was a descendant of two of Beaufort's most distinguished citizens. His granduncle, Stephen Elliott, played a pivotal role in establishing key, educational institutions such as Beaufort College and the Beaufort Library Society in 1807.[3] His cousin, Stephen Elliott Sr., was a distinguished church leader, first bishop of the Protestant Episcopal Dioceses South Carolina and Georgia and provisional bishop of Florida.[4] Bishop Elliott, himself a large plantation owner, was active in the so-called "plantation mission movement," an effort among clerics in St. Helena Parish to provide religious instruction to slaves with an eye toward encouraging peaceful relations on plantations while justifying slavery on biblical and scriptural grounds.

Elliott's childhood in the South Carolina Lowcountry prepared him for the unique style of warfare he would wage as captain of the BVA. The surrounding low-lying marshes with their tidal waters, long stemmed grasses, small creeks, huge live oak trees and long pine forests held an abundance of wildlife for hunters and fishermen, and Elliott established a reputation as an expert sportsman and yachtsman.

Through the years, Elliott became intimately familiar with these waterways flowing off Port Royal Sound. This knowledge would later enable him to lead small detachments of the BVA and infantry, navigating them expertly to make surprise attacks on isolated outposts of Federal troops. Transported on

Stephen Elliott, Jr., the first captain of the Beaufort Volunteer Artillery. Elliott's family was among the elite of the Beaufort Society. He owned a plantation on Parris Island, served in the South Carolina legislature, and studied at Harvard College (Library of Congress).

Seven. "The Mosby of the Islands" 65

The Port Royal Ferry on Coosaw Island, shown here ca. 1863, was the jumping off point for some of the Beaufort Volunteer Artillery's raids (Timothy O'Sullivan, photographer, Library of Congress).

large, wooden, handmade barges with shallow drafts that could transport ten to twenty men, they could be rowed quietly and quickly to insure the advantage of surprise.

On the night of December 4, 1861, just weeks after the Confederate defeat at the Battle of Port Royal, Elliott led twenty-five men of the BVA in a raid on Beaufort. Many of them, like Elliott, had homes in Beaufort— homes their families had deserted after the battle. Their arrival in Beaufort was bleak. Riding through town, only one light was visible, the quiet broken by the barking of a stray dog. Several men were dispatched to a plantation on Parris Island where they set fire to seventy bales of cotton and a large quantity of corn. Large numbers of slaves were seen escaping their plantations, but the unit was not equipped to capture them.[5]

Resourceful and creative, Elliott would use the Gullah dialect of the slaves to deceive Union pickets.[6] In a night raid on June 6, Elliott and about twenty BVA soldiers rowed across the Coosaw River to the Port Royal Ferry. Elliott called out in Gullah to the Union soldiers guarding the Ferry, a ruse to trick the soldiers into thinking his men were runaway slaves. It bought time for them to land and attack the pickets and burn boats used by the Federals in their operations.[7]

On July 4, 1862, Elliott and a section of the BVA supplemented by soldiers of Company I, 11th South Carolina Regiment, returned to the Ferry. Under Federal artillery fire, a small boat of men carried a barrel of turpentine, taking it ashore and lighting it, burning down the Port Royal Ferry House.[8]

Few engagements of this kind of warfare surpassed the success of the BVA's surprise attack on August 9, 1862, on a company of the 3rd New Hampshire Infantry stationed on Pinckney Island. Located northwest of Hilton Head Island, the island was owned by the family of Charles Cotesworth

Stationed on Hilton Head Island, the 3rd New Hampshire Regiment dispatched its Company H to nearby Pinckney Island to flush out Confederate soldiers sighted in the area. The company was the target of one of the Beaufort Volunteer Artillery's most successful guerrilla-style attacks. With the assistance of several companies of the 11th South Carolina regiment, the BVA captured thirty-six Union soldiers and killed fifteen (*Quarters of Emmons and Handerson, Hilton Head South Carolina*. Third New Hampshire Regiment. Henry P. Moore, photographer, 1862–63, Library of Congress)

Pinckney, a Revolutionary War commander. Pinckney's plantation on the Island produced the high quality, long-staple Sea Island Cotton with the labor of over 300 slaves.[9]

The Island's strategic importance to the Union forces was minor, but its substantial population of slaves required protection and the plantation had value for its produce. As such it was occupied by Company H of the 3rd New Hampshire Regiment assigned to picket duty. The company numbered approximately sixty men under the command of Lieutenant Joseph Wiggins and were quartered in two plantation houses located at the junction of the Broad River and Skull Creek.[10]

Three Union deserters were captured by nearby Confederate forces commanded by Colonel William Walker. Walker had been placed in command of the Confederate 3rd District that included Beaufort, Bluffton and Hilton Head Island. Based on the information obtained by the Union deserters, Walker concluded that less than a hundred Union troops were stationed on Pinckney Island, prime targets for attack and capture.[11]

He ordered Elliott to reconnoiter the position of the Union troops and organize an expedition to capture the outpost with men from the BVA and several companies of the 11th South Carolina Regiment led by Captain John Mickler, who had established his own reputation as an enterprising and daring raider leading the 11th against Union forces in the Beaufort region.

Walker was aware of the dangers of such an expedition. From the Union's encampment on Pinckney Island masts of the Union Gunboats in Port Royal Harbor could be seen plying the Islands—a powerful and extensive military presence through which the Confederate expedition would have to wind its way. But Elliott's extensive knowledge of the backwaters of the Lowcountry and his growing reputation as a daring and effective officer made him the natural choice for this hazardous assignment.

On August 26, Elliott and fifty BVA men under the command of Lieutenant Hal Stuart met Captain Mickler and his contingent of about seventy-five infantrymen of the South Carolina 11th Regiment. Meeting at a remote location on Bear's Island, thirty-six of them would row nine boats carrying the men to Pinckney Island, approximately ten miles away.

At approximately 3:00 AM, the men set out.[12] Near dawn, as a heavy fog was lifting, the expedition landed on Pinckney about 300 yards from the two plantation houses quartering the New Hampshire Company. Mickler's detachment quickly jumped off the boats running through the woods toward the houses in which the New Hampshire men were sleeping. One of them, Daniel Eldridge, ran out of one of the houses and down the path toward the boat landing and was fired at immediately, narrowly escaping injury. Following him Lieutenant Wiggins, without coat or side arms, tried to locate the Union position and was quickly captured by Captain Mickler's men.

As the New Hampshire men ran from the house, they were welcomed by the volleys of Confederate rifle fire. One of the Confederates ran up to the porch, shooting through a window and injuring a soldier. In a few minutes the Union soldiers Mickler's men had captured were gathered in a group near the house. Then from the woods, Elliott's men opened fire on the Confederates and their prisoners, wounding eight of Mickler's men and six Union men. In his report of the engagement, Elliott attributed this friendly fire to the limited light, the inexperience of the men—most of them in combat for the first time—and, "an excess of zeal." On the firing of the volley, Lieutenant Wiggin ran, and was quickly felled by Confederate bullets, dying later of his wounds.[13]

BVA Private Milton Maxcy participated in the attack. However exciting these forays were, his description of guerrilla warfare on the islands from the standpoint of the common soldier were more often characterized by wrong directions, lack of sleep and miserable weather.

> We left about daybreak on Tuesday morning with about forty-five men from our company and travelled by wagons to Boyd's Landing where we launched six boats about 7 o'clock that evening. From there we were to row to Foote Point that night, but having missed the way by going up a wrong creek we were compelled to stop.... about 2 o'clock that night, where the men slept on the wet ground. I slept in the boat I was rowing, with nothing but an overcoat over me in a hard rain, half sitting down, doubled up in as small a space as possible with my head bent and my overcoat hauled over me so as to protect myself and my firearms as much as possible. I was so hungry then that I took a knife and hauled a dirty piece of bacon out the bag I carried with me, cut off one or two slices and them raw with as much gusto as if I was eating wild duck. You have no idea how nice raw bacon is.[14]

By the numbers, it was a successful engagement for the Confederates. Federal casualties were fifteen killed, four wounded, and thirty-six captured. Eight Confederates were wounded, six by friendly fire. The prisoners were marched to the boats and taken back to the mainland, where they were held for the night in a house in Grahamville (near current day Ridgeland). The next day they marched to the Grahamville depot of the Charleston & Savannah Railroad guarded by a detachment of the BVA under the command of Elliott. One of the prisoners, Daniel Eldredge, stated later that the BVA artillerymen were "pleasant and agreeable and treated us more like friends than enemies."[15]

Elliott's nickname as "the Mosby of the Islands," was further enhanced by his ambush and capture of a Union gunboat. Federal gunboats patrolled the Sea Island waterways and were natural targets of interest for the Confederates. While designed to be maneuverable in shallow waters, running aground was a common occurrence, exposing their crews to shelling by Confederate artillery.

The armaments of the gunboats could be substantial, with as many as a dozen cannons of various sizes and uses, including the more accurate 30-pounder rifled Parrott guns and the smaller 24- pounder howitzers. As such they were very tempting and highly prized targets for artillery units like the BVA to supplement their own armaments.

One such opportunity arose for the BVA on April 9, 1863, when Elliott and the BVA set an ambush for the armed steamboat USS *George Washington*. The *George Washington* was well known to the BVA, regularly patrolling the Combahee River past Chisholm Island.[16] The day before, Elliott received a report that the *George Washington* was assisting another steamer, the *E. B. Hale*, which had run aground below the Island. He quickly ordered four guns of the BVA and two guns of the Nelson Light Artillery to a position near the gunboat, which had set anchor for the night after the *E. B. Hale* had been freed and left. At about 5:00 AM the next morning, soon after ship pulled anchor and shoved off, Elliott's batteries attacked. One of the BVA's men, described the chaotic scene:

> Soon the bell aboard the boat marked the hour, and, as she rode just opposite us, we opened fire, gun after gun. It was not long before we saw that she was on fire, with the men aboard her throwing themselves into the water and swimming for dear life to the marshes on the other side. We threw several shots among them, though I remember remonstrating against the needless carnage. It was impossible for us to save the boat, but some of our men got aboard of her and somehow managed to get the bell ashore. Later we set it up in our camp ... and used it to ring reveille.[17]

The Confederate fire was accurate and deadly. One of the shots exploded the ship's magazine ripping up the deck, breaking the ship's steering gear and unhinging its rudder. The ship's howitzer tumbled into the hold, and soon the ship caught fire and began sinking. The helmsman tried to maneuver the ship toward a marsh on the opposite shore of the Confederate guns, and soon the ship's crew were scrambling off the boat and wounded and injured men began accumulating on the bank. Elliott directed the batteries to open fire on the escaping sailors, fire which continued until none were seen.

As the ship's hulk burned at the water's edge, Elliott boarded her and found two wounded men and one dead who were then taken ashore. A detachment of men tried to pull off one of the ship's two 24-pounder howitzers to no avail. Time was of the essence. Someone had informed the crew of the nearby *E. B. Hale* navigating on the Broad River of the George Washington's ambush, and it began to steam to its assistance. Under a flag of truce Elliott met with the captain of the *E. B. Hale* and arranged for his crew to recover the wounded men on the marsh.[18]

Fearing further Union reinforcements, Elliott withdrew his forces. He returned two days later with a more substantial force including artillery, three companies of infantry and three companies of cavalry. Union artillery had been shelling the wreck in the interim to destroy any weapons or supplies that might be salvaged by the Confederates. Despite this, the Confederates were able to salvage one of the ship's 24-pounder howitzers, a few Enfield rifles, and a souvenir of the engagement, the ship's bell.[19]

Something of the flavor of these expeditions is described by a BVA Corporal in a letter to his family dated October 3, 1863, written at the unit's encampment in McPhersonville:

> I just got back late last night from that expedition I told you of and I feel pretty tired and sleepy, having rowed about twenty miles the night before last. We had

Federal gunboats like this one, the USS *Tyler*, patrolled the waterways around the Sea Islands near Beaufort. One of them, the USS *George Washington*, was ambushed by the BVA on April 9, 1863. Confederate fire exploded the ship's magazine, ripping up the deck and disabling the ship's rudder (Library of Congress).

***Seven.** "The Mosby of the Islands"* 71

some pretty rough weather in [the] Broad River and could scarcely manage our boats. We had to stand in the water about an hour, holding our boats, to keep them from striking the marsh, it was pretty cold too. We went to the Big Island again ... but did not find the Yankees we heard of. They failed to come over, but we saw one Yank and some negroes coming over in some boats about twelve o'clock yesterday and fired into them, and about the same number got away. All the men then rushed for the boat immediately except for me, I was left on picket until they got everything ready. Just as we left we fired our guns several times to make them believe we had a large force. We got a large lot of plunder having been detailed for that purpose. We got some fifty chickens and ducks, some cooking utensils—tubs, jugs, jars—some cane bottom chairs, some greenbacks and a little silver money. Everything will be divided today around the crowd between forty men.... We ate our chickens this morning for breakfast. Last night I found the box here that you sent, and I was very glad you sent it especially being pretty well starved. Next time I wish you would send me some towels.[20]

Eight

"The bullets were like hail"

In the months following the Battle of Port Royal, there was pressure from the Lincoln administration for Federal troops to quickly attack Charleston and Savannah.

But Federal troop strength in South Carolina was thin. Newly organized as the Department of the South and covering the states of Florida, Georgia and South Carolina, the majority of the approximately 13,000 Union troops were required to garrison various forts and outposts, leaving just 6,000 troops available for active, military operations. Most of these troops were garrisoned on Hilton Head Island and received reinforcements between December 1861 and February 1862 amounting to about 5,000 additional troops.[1] General Thomas W. Sherman, commanding the expeditionary force on Hilton Head Island felt there was insufficient cavalry or field artillery required for a full-scale invasion.[2]

Lowcountry warfare required new kinds of tactics. Smaller sized troop movements were necessitated by a landscape crisscrossed by dozens of rivers, waterways, and canals. Military expeditions required shallow draft gunboats, large army transports to convey troops, and smaller flatboats to convey individual companies. Groundings on sandbars were frequent in these shallow waters, upsetting timetables, and causing confusion. There were many moving parts, a disruption in any one of which could cause critical delays in the movement and disposition of forces.

The Beaufort Volunteer Artillery had an encounter with a Union gun boat which typified the unique character of Lowcountry combat. The battery was ordered to withdraw from their camp at Red Bluff to a more defensible position four miles inland at Camp Hardee. Several days later, on picket duty at the new camp, Private Milton Maxcy Leverett sighted two Union gunboats "shelling plantations."

> I looked around and saw a white puff of smoke from the side of the boat, and in a second heard the boom of the gun, then in another second, I heard the singing

of the shell in the air high up describing its curve, as it was coming at us, I was behind all others and it came more directly at me, and as I looked up and heard it rushing down thought I, it will hit me right on my forehead and I ought to dodge, but in the first place it was in a bare open field and I could only dodge it by laying down flat but it was coming so direct that I thought it would hit me.... It rolled within twenty or twenty-five feet of me and did not burst, otherwise some of us would have been killed.[3]

Upon orders from Captain Elliott to keep an eye on the gunboats, Leverett climbed a tree and saw Union soldiers cutting a chain drawn across the river to prevent gunboat travel up the river. The gunboats then proceeded to the Confederate fort and shelled it, destroying its wooden ramparts and several houses in the area.

Despite their deficits of manpower, the Union forces had the advantage of a clear military objective: the capture and destruction of the Charleston & Savannah Railroad. The task of cutting the railroad was assigned to an enterprising Brigadier General Isaac Stevens. Stevens, a hot-tempered forty-two-year-old from Massachusetts, graduated first in his 1839 West Point class. Just five feet tall, what he lacked in physical presence he compensated for in self-confidence and a healthy ego.[4]

Since his brigade had landed at Port Royal Island, Stevens lobbied hard with his superiors to make an attack on the Charleston & Savannah Railroad. Carefully studying maps of the region and personally exploring the regions waterways, he saw a way to use the waterways and land to mount an attack on the railroad. Convincing his superior, General

General Thomas W. Sherman commanded the occupying Union forces on Hilton Head Island after the capture of Port Royal Sound. Sherman believed he had insufficient forces for a full-scale invasion of the South Carolina interior (Library of Congress).

Henry Benham to approve the plan, he ordered the 50th Pennsylvania Infantry and companies from several other units to carry out a raid under the command of Colonel Benjamin Christ.

At 9:30 AM on May 29, 1862, a small force of approximately 300 Union soldiers including infantry, artillery and cavalry left Beaufort on twelve flat boats, and began making the crossing at the Port Royal Ferry. The artillery lagged, taking two hours to feed and water their horses, delaying the advance. Thus, it was not until 5:00 AM the next day that the full force had crossed over and began their march inland toward Pocotaligo Station.

Confederate troops in the Beaufort District including the BVA were under the command of Colonel William S. Walker. Born in Pittsburgh, Pennsylvania, Walker was raised by his uncle in Washington DC, Mississippi Senator Robert Walker. A veteran of the Mexican-American War, at the beginning of the Civil War, he was a captain of the 1st Cavalry of the regular army. Resigning his commission, he joined the Confederacy as an infantry captain. Assigned command of the Third District the first week of May 1862, his troops were scattered throughout the district, and depended on the railroad for quick disposition and concentration of forces to meet Federal advances.[5]

Receiving word that Union forces were on the move, Colonel Walker dispatched a small force to engage them including companies from the First South Carolina Cavalry Battalion, the Rutledge Mounted Riflemen, and the 2nd South Carolina Cavalry Battalion. They arrived at Pocotaligo Station at 10:30 AM and were deployed along a causeway through a rice canal that led to a bridge and some woods behind. Half of the

The hot-tempered and aggressive Union Brigadier General Isaac Stevens was assigned the task of cutting the Charleston & Savannah Railroad (Library of Congress).

Eight. "The bullets were like hail"

seventy-six men deployed on the left bank of the canal as skirmishers and the remaining to the right of the bridge into the woods.[6]

When Christ's force arrived soon after the Confederates, he deployed his infantry on either side of the causeway facing opposite their position. For two hours the two sides traded sporadic rifle fire, but neither of their artillery units had yet arrived. In an excess of caution, the Union artillery stopped in its march to the bridge to rest and water their horses, concerned that in the heat of the day they might collapse. This delay forced Christ to attack the Confederate position without artillery support, concerned that too much delay would provide Confederates with time to bring up additional forces.

When the fighting began, the BVA's private Maxcy Leverett described the action:

> Our men were stationed among the live oaks and at the edge of the bushes, firing across at the enemy who were stationed near Mr. Screven's big canal and the bridge over it near the other oaks on the causeway.... Some of our men had been stationed over along the dam in Mr. Screven's rice field but had fallen back to Old Pocotaligo. The enemy would rush up to the bridge and try to get over under cover of the causeway, at the same time attempting to pull up the bridge, they could be heard cursing and damning at their men and trying to incite them.[7]

At 4:00 PM Confederate reinforcements finally arrived including the BVA under Captain Elliott with three artillery pieces and two companies of the 11th South Carolina Infantry. Walker placed the battery in a position to command the road, then soon learned that the Union troops were retreating, just a few miles short of the railroad crossing. Confederate troops followed the Union soldiers, skirmishing with their videttes outside of Garden's Corner at 10:00 PM. Concerned that a Federal gun boat might provide cover to the retreating Federals, and the possibility of a trap, Walker stopped the advance.

The next morning, Walker's troops marched to the Port Royal Ferry and found that the Federals had crossed during the night. There he ordered Elliott and the BVA to batter the ferry house and destroy the flat boats that had been used to transport the Union troops.

Casualties were minimal: The Federals two killed and nine wounded; the Confederates two killed six wounded. On balance, the Confederates could lay claim to a victory, having pushed back the Union incursion, but Isaac Stevens could take some satisfaction in knowing the Union troops came very close to reaching and cutting the railroad, and might have but for its dwindling supply of ammunition and the exhaustion of the troops.

Of more significance was the impact on the enslaved population. As the Union troops retreated, thousands of slaves left their plantations to follow them to freedom on the Sea Islands. Some of these would be recruits for the first black regiments of the war, organized in Beaufort.

The summer months after the Pocotaligo fight were uneventful for the Confederate troops in the St. Helena Parish. Priorities were focused on Charleston and its defense while the Federals consolidated and organized their foothold in South Carolina and launched expeditions on the islands and their defenses surrounding Charleston.

Walker knew the hiatus was temporary, and it was only a matter of time before another attack on the railroad. He kept a close eye on his network of scouts and pickets south of his headquarters in McPhersonville monitoring Union activity. While the Union military presence was modest by the standards of other theaters of war, Walker could rightly assume his forces were outnumbered, a situation exacerbated by Richmond's continuing pull of troops from his command for transfer to Virginia. Artillery was an especially dear commodity. In addition to the four guns of the Beaufort Volunteer Artillery, the only other artillery unit immediately available was the four guns of the Nelson Light Artillery, a Virginia battery temporarily assigned to the First Military District.

The newly appointed head of the First Military District, General Pierre G. T. Beauregard, received intelligence that the Federals were planning another offensive, alerting Confederate troops in and near Charleston and Savannah to be prepared.

Beauregard and Walker's concerns were justified. Soon after taking command of the Union command of the De-

Soon after his appointment as commander of the Department of the South, Union Major General Ormsby MacKnight Mitchel launched an offensive to destroy the Charleston & Savannah Railroad bridges over the Pocotaligo and Coosawatchie rivers (Library of Congress).

Eight. "The bullets were like hail"

partment of the South in October, Major General Ormsby MacKnight Mitchel saw the strategic importance of the Savannah & Charleston Railroad and quickly decided to mount an offensive to attack it. A graduate of West Point class of 1829, Mitchel was an aggressive officer, and had led some successful operations in Florida and South Carolina. He ran afoul of senior military in the Chattanooga campaign for destroying private property and was relieved of duty and sent to Washington. Having friends in high places including Secretary of War Stanton and President Lincoln, he was ultimately reassigned to command the Department of the South.

Soon after he took command, he addressed his restless troops with a fiery speech promising action to capture the Charleston & Savannah Railroad.[8] His plan was a two-pronged assault to destroy the railroad bridges over the Pocotaligo and Coosawatchie Rivers. A squadron of steamships accompanied by warships would transport approximately 4,000 troops to Mackey's Point, the tip of a peninsula between the Tulifinny and Pocotaligo Rivers southwest of Beaufort. From this embarkation point the Federal troops would march nine miles north to attack the Pocotaligo Bridge. A much smaller force would sail up the Coosawatchie River to destroy the railroad trestle at Coosawatchie. The troops making the assault would include units from the 47th, 55th and 76th Pennsylvania; the 3rd and 4th New Hampshire; the 6th and 7th Connecticut; the 48th New York; the 1st Massachusetts Cavalry; the 3rd Rhode Island Artillery, and a detachment of the U.S. Artillery. The large number of transports, fifteen, was very ambitious, and would require an extraordinary degree of coordination and communication. They would be piloted by contraband slaves who had navigated these waters for their former plantation slave masters.

General John Brannan led the attack on the railroad bridges at the Pocotaligo and Coosawatchie Rivers. A brave soldier, he was not known for his tactical competence in the field (Library of Congress).

Under the command of Mitchel's subordinate, General John Brannan, the flotilla would experience problems and delays immediately after its launch at 12:30 AM on October 22. One of its transports ran aground, slowing them down, providing more time for the widely dispersed Confederate forces to consolidate and deploy.

At approximately 9:00 AM Colonel Walker was informed that Union forces were landing at Mackay's Point. Soon after that he received word that a second force was heading up the Coosawatchie River in the direction of the village of Coosawatchie and the railroad trestle there. He urgently wired for reinforcements from General Beauregard in Charleston, General Hagood south of Charleston, and General Mercer in Savannah.

The troops at Walker's disposal were a varied array of forces including artillery, cavalry, infantry, mounted infantry and a unit of sharpshooters—approximately 450 men in all. Though outnumbered, the relatively small size of these units would ultimately work to Walker's advantage, enabling him to concentrate his widely dispersed forces quickly, deploying them nimbly to slow the advance of the union force up the peninsulas.

Walker acted quickly and decisively, directing most of his available troops to the Pocotaligo area. A small unit of artillery including a section of the BVA under Lt. H. M. Stuart was sent to Coosawatchie to support a company of the 11th South Carolina stationed there to protect the town and railroad trestle. Colonel John Colcock, with five cavalry companies and two companies of sharpshooters, was directed to guard the approaches to Coosawatchie. Walker himself led the force to protect Pocotaligo Station.[9]

The imminent battle would be a defining moment both for Colonel Walker, Elliott and the BVA, one that would mark the beginning of a productive military partnership between them in the battle for the Lowcountry. From the outset of the struggle Walker would rely heavily on Elliott.

As his units arrived, Walker directed them to a position behind a stream called Frampton Creek on a plantation owned by Dr. Thomas W. Hutson, about six miles from the Federal landing site at Mackay's Point. To buy time while the rest of his force was arriving, Walker sent out a small detachment to Mackay's Point including Captain Elliott and two guns of the BVA to engage the union force and hopefully stall their advance while he prepared his defenses. With the BVA were Company B of the first Battalion of South Carolina Sharpshooters commanded by Captain Joseph Allston, and two companies of Major Joseph Morgan's 2nd South Carolina Cavalry Battalion.[10]

Morgan's cavalry arrived first, engaging Union skirmishers near Mackay's Plantation then falling back quickly, galloping down the road to join Elliott and sharpshooters waiting in a defensive position coincidentally located

Eight. *"The bullets were like hail"*

on a plantation owned by Elliott's uncle, George Elliott. Elliott chose to position his two Napoleon 12-pounders directly on the road with a clear shot to the advancing Federals, and where he could easily unlimber them and carry out a fighting withdrawal.[11]

Just before noon, the BVA fired its guns at Union skirmishers of the 47th Pennsylvania less than a mile away. The 47th's Colonel, Tilghman Good, saw that the Confederate position was not a strong one, and ordered his troops to charge. The resulting skirmish was a bracing one, and featured the appearance of an unlikely combatant, Elliott's elderly uncle George. In a letter written after the battle Stephen affectionately described his uncle's spirited participation: "Uncle George seems to love me very much. He behaved admirably on horseback during the thicket of the fight. Helped me with my first position. Dashed up to his place … and wanted to pistol whip fellows who were running past who said to him, 'Look here old man you had better get behind a tree, I have seen many a better man get knocked off his horse today.' But the old fellow … got off unhurt."[12]

Elliott quickly saw this position was not a strong one, and withdrew his tiny command, destroying a bridge on the way heading north on the road toward Caston's Plantation. The Confederates retreated in orderly fashion, the sharpshooters and cavalry covering the artillery with a steady fire until a stronger defensive position was established by the artillery about a mile down the road adjacent to an impassable marsh to the left of the BVA. Three

Sketch of the Pocotaligo railroad station (Theodore Davis, artist, Library of Congress).

of the unit's guns found cover in nearby woods, and Elliott placed one cannon on the road behind the bridge which began firing at the Federals.

Good attacked this new, strengthened position, receiving, he described, "a terrible fire of shell from the rear of the woods." Good called up the rest of the 47th troops and attacked in quick time the Confederate line again, with three companies to the right and five to the left of the road and charged into the woods receiving "galling fire" and again the Confederates retreated from the woods.

The 47th halted in the woods and took time to reorganize their line. The BVA and Nelson Light Artillery regrouped and began to fire into the woods. Good described the scene:

> During this time a terrible fire of grape and canister was opened by the enemy through the woods.... We immediately charged directly through the woods, but in consequence of the denseness of the woods, which was a perfect matting of vines and brush, it was almost impossible to get through, but by dint of untiring assiduity the men worked their way through nobly. At this point I was called out to the woods by Lieutenant Bacon [aide-de-camp of General Brannan] who gave the order, "The general wants you to charge through the woods." I replied that I was then charging, and that the men were working their way through as fast as possible.[13]

Reinforcements from the 6th Connecticut, 55th Pennsylvania and the 4th New Hampshire followed the 47th. When they emerged from the woods, they faced a quarter mile of open field to Frampton Creek. Across that creek the BVA and Nelson Light artillery were firing volleys into their ranks. To cover the 47th, General Brannan ordered 10-pound parrot guns from Henry's and Getting's batteries positioned at the edge of the woods. The 47th drove to the edge of the creek just fifty yards from the Confederates before being forced back into the woods to reform yet again. The Union guns continued to duel the BVA and Nelson Artillery, assisted by long-range fire from the Union gun boat *Uncas*. Shrapnel flew over the treetops downing Confederate snipers.

The BVA and Nelson Light Artillery threw a devastating fire into the ranks of the oncoming troops. Elias Bryant, a soldier in the 4th New Hampshire, later described the effects of the barrage: "It made a space in the ranks about eight feet wide, killing one man and wounding two, and knocking down two or three more. The air from such a shot is enough to knock a man down. I have heard of men being killed by losing their breath from the wind of a ball. If these men had only been looking up they could have dodged it by stepping to one side, at least, it seemed so where I stood, since I could see it coming."

Eight. *"The bullets were like hail"* 81

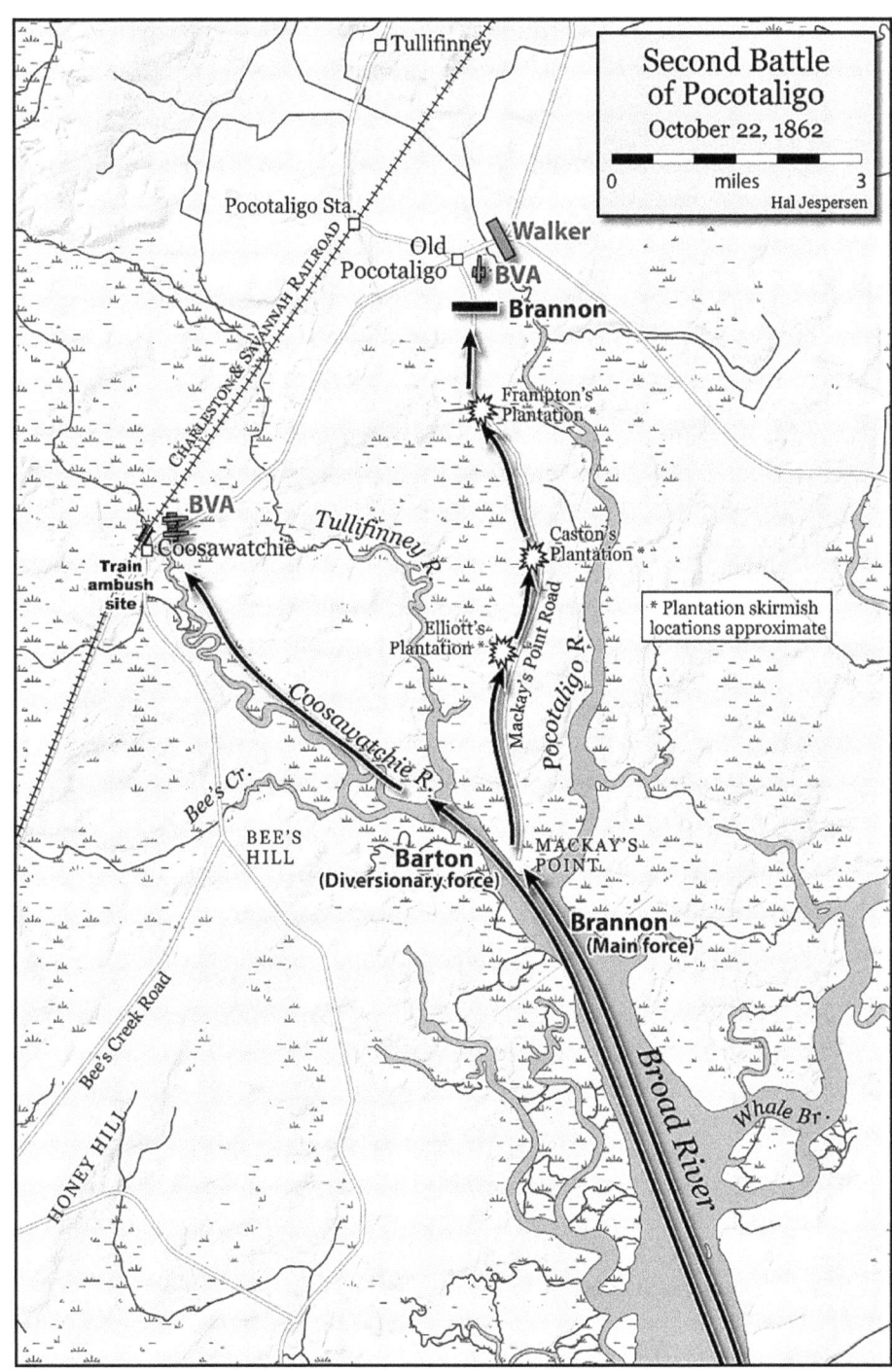

A soldier of the 6th Connecticut described the toll of the confederate fire on his comrades: "John Hassenan had a canister enter his thigh, coming out near the knee.... Henry Heydt ... had his ankle shattered by grape. As he passed by the regiment, borne on a litter, his ghostly face and forbidding wounds attested his suffering. ... W. H. Sherwood and Dennis Burns were shot in the chest. Andreas Provost, arm broken. Robert Wilson wounded in the shoulder. Charles Wood in the head. Joseph Topher in the head. Smith Scofield and Albert W Crooker in the feet."

The toll on the Confederates was high as well. Sharpshooters from the 55th Pennsylvania and 7th Connecticut advanced to the edge of the marsh and poured deadly fire into the ranks of the BVA. Elliott wrote that "the bullets were like hail. The infantry would lie in the grass and behind trees and houses, but my boys had just to stand up and take it, which they did beautifully. Their conduct the whole day was beyond praise. When wounded they would quietly pass off as if nothing was the matter and got on a caisson and jog along."[14]

Two guns of the BVA were silenced due to the injury and incapacitation of the men. Elliott himself received an ankle wound from shrapnel, and his horse was injured as well. By the end of the battle one man, Daniel Campbell, was killed, and thirteen injured. The Nelson artillery also sustained serious losses of dead and wounded men and horses: four men killed and fourteen injured.

In the chaos, Elliott felt the full force of his responsibilities, "Had I not exposed myself and gone to and from every gun and been at them in their critical moments the artillery would perhaps have been lost and with it probably the battle. I will confess that it is no joke to use two batteries in a narrow road while pulling back in retreat during some confusion, but I am glad that they [the Union soldiers] felt the force of it. Some halves of heads and legs bear faithful testimony to the accuracy of our fire.... I don't like fighting a bit.... I always am scared before getting into one and am always willing to stop when in one."[15]

Brannan's men, though exhausted and running low on water and ammunition, continued to press the Confederates. Walker, facing a force nearly eight times the size of his and fearing his force would be outflanked and overwhelmed on both sides of its line, called for his men to retreat and reform in line nearly three miles just outside the village of Pocotaligo. The Confederates retreated with the Federal troops pressing them closely. When Walker and his men reached bridge crossing over the Pocotaligo River the infantry took cover behind houses and trees in the village across the river from the approaching Federals.

Eight. "The bullets were like hail" 83

Men of the 11th South Carolina ran across the bridge, dismantling it behind them. As the Union troops approached the bridge, Elliott's battery sent a volley into them, and they halted at the edge of the Pocotaligo River, fanning out on Walker's front.

Throughout the battle the sound of train whistles coming from the railroad line generated nervous rumors among the Union troops that trains of Confederate reinforcements from Savannah were on their way. Reinforcing this concern was Elliott's placement of a cannon far to the right of the Confederate line and out of view of the union forces, shelling them from a position suggesting new units had arrived. Walker in turn brought forward the Charleston Light Dragoons he had kept in reserve behind Pocotaligo, instructing them to shout the rebel yell vigorously to further signal to the federals that reinforcements had arrived.

Troops from Nelson's 7th South Carolina Infantry Battalion arrived on the train from outside of Charleston, and Walker quickly directed them to the front to relieve his tired troops and strengthen his right flank. Two companies of the battalion attacked the Union left flank but a volley from the 76th Pennsylvania pushed them back. Guns blazed as two more Union companies arrived to hold the Union left flank. The fire continued until Union ammunition ran low.

The Battle of Pocotaligo (*Frank Leslie's Illustrated News*, November 15, 1862).

Finally, at approximately 6:00 PM, General Brannan ordered a retreat to Mackay's Point. Walker sent detachments from the Rutledge Mounted Riflemen and Kirks Partisan Rangers to harass the Yankees to little effect as the Union rear guard destroyed bridges on the return march.

To the west the other Union force under the command of Colonel William Barton had orders to sail up the Coosawatchie River, disembark near the village of Coosawatchie and destroy as much as possible of the Charleston & Savannah Railroad. The detachment included Barton's own regiment, the 48th New York, the 3rd Rhode Island Artillery, and a detachment of the New York Engineers Corps with equipment to dismantle the railroad.

One of the Union transports, a side-wheel steamer, *Planter*, was captained by Robert Smalls, who had famously piloted it out of Confederate hands in Charleston to join Union forces in Port Royal. Gun boats accompanied the *Planter* to provide cover, but the ship ran aground two miles short of Coosawatchie; and Barton's men disembarked, forced to march on very swampy ground lugging a 12-pound howitzer. They finally reached the main road at a point just a mile from the town.[16]

When Colonel Walker learned of this movement, he dispatched Colonel Charles Colcock, commander of the 3rd South Carolina Cavalry, to intercept Barton's 300 men. Colcock ordered Lt. Colonel Thomas Johnson to lead a small force including five companies of his cavalry and two companies of sharpshooters of the First Battalion South Carolina Sharpshooters. Four

Robert Smalls and the side-wheeler steamer he piloted, the *Planter*. In May 1862, Smalls made a daring escape with the *Planter*, carrying fifteen slaves out of Confederate hands in Charleston to freedom behind Union lines (*Harper's Weekly*, June 14, 1862).

miles from Coosawatchie, at Bees Creek Hill, Johnson received erroneous intelligence that Federals had landed a force on Seabrook Island, threatening his rear. Responding to the supposed threat, he divided his command and left three companies at Bee's Creek Hill, and with the remainder of his force headed to Coosawatchie.[17]

About a mile from Coosawatchie, Barton and his men heard a locomotive whistle in the distance creating a stir among the troops. The contraband slave guiding Barton's troops thought it was the "dirt train," delivering sand and gravel to Savannah. Actually, the train was heading north, toward Charleston, and was loaded with Confederate troops to reinforce the Confederates fighting at Pocotaligo. These companies of the 11th South Carolina Infantry and a company of Chisholm's First South Carolina Sharpshooters were traveling up the tracks in an exposed position, sitting in the open on the train's six platform cars.

Union scouts reported the train, which had temporarily stopped to pick up Chisolm's sharpshooters, to Barton. This gave Barton time to set an ambush, deploying his troops and their howitzer a few hundred yards away from the line. "As the train approached," he stated later in his official report, "I directed a heavy and rapid fire upon it with grape and canister and musketry. This fire was very destructive."

At the first volley many were killed or wounded, and about twenty-five or thirty jumped from the train. A flag bearer lost control of his company's colors, and it tumbled off the train to be gathered up by Union soldiers. Major J. J. Harrison and the train's engineer were killed. Many of the men disappeared into nearby swamps, but the majority stayed on the train, which was now being driven by the conductor, J. H. Buckhalter, who kept the train moving on through Coosawatchie.

Now Barton's detail of engineers began to tear up the railroad using claw bars, setting fires to bend the rails and burn cross ties, while the rest of Barton's troops headed to the Coosawatchie train trestle to see what damage was possible to that structure. They had little time to cause much damage. On the far side of the river two guns of the BVA and the Lafayette Artillery covered the approach to the trestle and began firing on the Federals. Formed next to the artillery were the remaining soldiers of the 11th Infantry whose train had made it through the ambush and had hurriedly taken position for battle. The fire they laid down had the desired effect on Barton. Feeling outnumbered and outgunned and worried that Colonel Johnson's cavalry would soon be on the scene, he ordered retreat, returning his men to the safety of the *Planter* and retreat to Hilton Head.[18]

While the Union command on Hilton Head could rationalize the

First Pocotaligo skirmish as a reconnaissance in force, and thus the retreat of their forces excusable, such a characterization was less apt for the Second Battle of Pocotaligo. Union forces outnumbered Confederates by a ratio of approximately three to one. Given the high hopes for this expedition and the enthusiastic support it received from the Union command on Hilton Head, its paltry results—the destruction of a few rails and cross ties—was a far cry from the mission of destroying and securing the railroad.

Lack of coordination and delays in the timely concentration of forces bedeviled the Union command, demonstrating consistent weaknesses in successfully executing combined land and sea operations in this unfamiliar environment. The men on the ground fought valiantly and hard, but against the nimble and fast-moving Confederates, the Pocotaligo trestle was, literally, a bridge too far. Confederate troops commented in the aftermath that they were close to leaving the field and the train line to the Federals when the Union retreat began.

The effective command collaboration between Colonel Walker and Stephen Elliott was a key element of the success of the Confederates' fighting retreat. The role of the cavalry and mounted infantry provided timely, fast response to events unfolding in the field. But arguably, it was the artillery—the BVA, Nelson's Light Artillery, and the Lafayette Artillery batteries that made the difference. Union field commanders attested to the intense pressure the Confederate artillery maintained on their positions, slowing the Union advance.

Nine

"Ours is the gentlemanly company"

On the eve of the Civil War, an Alabama attorney and author, Daniel Hundley, described what he saw as the superior refinement and lifestyle of the "Southern gentleman."

> To begin with his pedigree, we may say, the Southern gentleman comes of a good stock. Indeed, to state the matter fairly, he comes usually of aristocratic parentage; for family pride provides to a greater extent in the South than in the North.... In South Carolina, they were Huguenots—at least the better class of them—those dauntless chevaliers, who ... drained France of her most generous blood to found in the Western Hemisphere a race of heroes and patriots.
>
> Besides being of faultless pedigree, the Southern Gentleman is usually possessed of an equally faultless physical development. His average height is about six feet, yet he is rarely gawky in his movements, or in the least clumsily put together.... We may attribute the good size and graceful carriage of the Southern Gentleman, to his out-of-doors and horseback mode of living.... By the time he is five years of age he rides well; and a little while thereafter has a fowling-piece put into his hands... and so accoutered, he sallies forth into the fields and pastures in search of adventure.
>
> When the Southern Gentleman has fully completed his academic labors—has honorably gone through the University Curriculum—if his means be ample, he seldom studies a profession, but gives his education a finishing polish by making the tour of Europe; or else settles down to superintend his estates, and devotes his talents to the raising of wheat, tobacco, rice, sugar, or cotton.[1]

Of the four services—infantry, cavalry, navy and artillery—the artillery was often considered the most desirable for the Southern gentleman. In general, Confederate artillerymen considered themselves among "the better class of men." Many came out of colleges, both professors and students, in addition to lawyers, merchants, businessmen, politicians, planters and others representing the professional classes.[2]

That is certainly the way BVA private Milton Maxcy Leverett thought

A rare photograph of a Confederate artillery battery (Library of Congress).

about it commenting condescendingly on other units being mustered in in the Lowcountry by giving them derogatory nicknames. "Ours is the gentlemanly company, the others mostly are Crackers. The Hamilton Guards, Minny Stuart's Company from Bluffton are called Goths by us, the Harrison Guards from Wippaw Swamp are called Vandals, Visigoths or Philistines."[3] This bias was reflected with angry disdain as Leverett bitterly complained of the overly democratic election of the 11th Infantry regiment's colonel in the early days of the war when the BVA was still attached to the regiment.

> I can hardly write. The men vowed they would not have gentleman over them and so in exercising their right to vote rejected all who had any pretensions to being considered gentlemen; they elected men of their own stamp—not with reference to their qualifications and fitness for office, but such as they supposed would be lenient, and could be imposed upon. The result is that one of the best officered and best disciplined regiments in the service is virtually demoralized, and will soon be not worth the powder and shot it would take to kill the men. The election has utterly disgusted me with democracy.[4]

One contemporary described the BVA as "an ancient and honorable company of volunteer soldiers, all planters of the Sea Islands, each man capable of being a commissioned officer and each accompanied by one or more body servants."

In other theaters of the war, Confederate units like the BVA, made up of "first families" of the local elite, presented discipline problems. A battery

Nine. "Ours is the gentlemanly company"

commander of the Rockbridge Artillery of Virginia had several of this class in his battery, and in an attempt to rein them in, arrested some of them for desertion. He later recounted, "They became greatly incensed at me.... One of them, a member of a prominent family, became so offensive and insulting that it was with the greatest difficult that I controlled my temper and prevented a personal alteration which I thought he wanted to bring on."

Members of the BVA had their class pretensions, but the record reveals no insubordination like that of the Rockbridge Artillery. Much of the credit lies with their two Captains, Stephen Elliott and his successor Hal Stuart, both of whom were highly respected by the men.

From February through November 1862 the BVA was stationed at Camp Willis in McPhersonville and then through October 1864 at Camp Beaufort, three miles away near Pocotaligo. Their camp's close proximity to their families' homes was an advantage, and they occasionally received homemade food, fresh vegetables and new clothes. Indeed, as Maxcy Leverett wrote home, "Life down here is not that of prodigality ... nor is it one of incessant toil, fatigue, starvation and deprivation of everything that is comfortable. It is the life (I speak as regards the Beaufort Artillery) of Beaufort men who always try to make themselves as comfortable as possible wherever they may be."[5] Though the average diet was often just biscuits and water, soldiers were free to hunt and forage the occasional stray cow or calf.

For most of the men this was their first experience living away from home in tents and temporary quarters, and some became sick. In one of the nearby camps, a member of the Harrison Guard suffered from diarrhea. One of the BVA men sent him tea and biscuits from the BVA mess, but he died, and his body sent home.

Their campsites were "neat as a penny" wrote Leverett, and made up of about twenty cabins, each one with a street lamp. Corporal David Hemphill expressed some pride in their appearance in a letter home. "We have our chimney up, and our house stopped up with moss which gives it quite a romantic appearance."[6]

Like soldiers of every era, the men anxiously awaited letters from home, and boxes filled with delicacies unavailable in the army. BVA Corporal David Hemphill wrote home, "You must try and send us a box for Christmas. We would like to have some sugar if you have any to spare. We are getting a few eggs from our chickens now and are saving them for Christmas. There is no chance to get a furlough until next summer unless you can find a deserter or conscript and let me go after him. Then I can get twenty days. So if you want to see me badly you had better look around."[7]

Writing from Camp Elliott to his mother, Milton Maxcy Leverett described a furlough he had made to Savannah with his body servant, Billy, and another soldier. "I took a trip to Savannah about two weeks ago with Stuart Rhett and made a few purchases ... carried Billy along with a basket to bring along the parcels, gave him money to spend, with which he purchased something for his wife. He seemed quite fond of gazing in the toy shops, looking with admiration at the round jolly figure and laughing face of some... wooden imitation of humanity."

Their creature comforts were especially well served by their slaves, or "boys" as they were called. It was not uncommon for Confederate officers and their men to bring their slaves to cook, forage for provisions, care for the horses, wash clothes, and provide for a variety every day personal needs. With the large number of slaves available to many of the BVA men, they could rotate them between their camps and their homes, bringing food, clothing, letters to the men on a regular basis. One of these slaves, Billy, belonged to Leverett.

> I have Billy with me, so far doing very well, somewhat deliberate though in his movements, he cooks sometimes, waits on table, makes up our beds, cleans our shoes, and attends to my horse, also, a pair of the cannon horses which I have to attend to, washing he does also, the latter he does very well and appears to like it very well inasmuch as it takes him away or he takes it away to a neighboring plantation where with his usual aptitude he has managed to make some acquaintants among the "ladies" got the washing done by one of them, staid and took dinner and brought my clothes back done very nicely.
>
> When I asked him if he intended to court the one he appeared to take a fancy to, he said "donno sir don't think I will hab time."[8]

Several weeks later Leverett writes his mother that he intends to send Billy back to the family home. Billy has apparently married one of the women on the neighboring plantation and is taking every opportunity to sneak away and join her or extend his visits to the plantation beyond what his master Leverett approves. This kind of behavior was always a red flag for slave owners, fearful that their slave might runaway permanently to seek freedom behind Union lines. Especially as the war wore on, and with the close proximity of Union forces on Hilton Head, slaves had greater incentives to escape.

One night in July 1862 Leverett was woken up and informed that Billy had been caught by Confederate pickets "with a bag of grist, flour, and some biscuits going off to see his wife and expecting to be back in the morning." When Billy was returned, Leverett had him tied up and watched by a guard through the night. When he was freed the next day, Leverett hoped Billy had learned his lesson.

Nine. *"Ours is the gentlemanly company"*

Time in camp provided opportunity to attend to uniforms which would be sewn by the women back home, and in some cases by tailors. One of the soldiers needed replacement uniforms due to the wear and tear of battle. One of the women from home came directly to the camp with a replacement shirt, made from a dress and with an interior lining for extra strength.

The *Charleston Mercury* reported that the women students of the Beaufort Female Seminary held a fair for the benefit of "the brave defenders of our beloved State" in October 1861. Funds raised from the benefit enabled them to donate six India Rubber overcoats to the BVA, and a new uniform for one of the BVA's soldiers "who had lost all his clothing in the retreat from Port Royal."

Leverett urgently requested that stockings and three sets of drawers made of homespun be sent. He was a bit fussy. The socks were too short in the toes and tight on the calves. Handkerchiefs that his family sent him were "very unique," but not the kind that he wanted. He sent directions to his mother for a cloak, then thought better of it, ordering one from a tailor. He also requested shirts, but "not too fancy and flashy," and some letters (B, V, and A) for his cap.[9]

Daily camp routine would begin at daybreak with Reveille, roll call, then stable call with slaves watering, feeding and grooming the horses. After breakfast call there was an hour for drill, then horses were put to pasture. The men returned to the campsite to pass the time writing letters, reading, playing ball, cards, chess, checkers or marbles. One of the more literary soldiers penned some patriotic verse:

> Three cheers for the "Stars and the Bars,"
> Oh! the South is the gem of the ocean.
> The land of the noble and free;
> The shrine of secession's devotion,
> Our hearts bow in homage to thee.
> When northmen descended in numbers,
> Proudly waving their "Stripes and their Stars,"
> Our cannons belched forth their war thunders,
> And high roved the "Stars and the Bars."
>
> They have dared to approach Carolina,
> For our rights she has struck the first blow,
> And shall we to the vandals resign her
> And ere her proud cities laid low.
> Our Georgians! then fly to her rescue,
> The foe hoists his "Stripes and his Stars!"
> Their brave hearts forever will bless you,
> And die for the "Stars and the Bars."[10]

Some of the soldiers found smoking a pipe an enjoyable way to while away the hours, despite its associations with vice, especially by the more religious. Cannoneer David Hemphill wrote in a letter home, "I have a new pipe now, and have laid aside my 'old clay.'" Another cannoneer wrote to a loved one, "Sallie, I have not learned to drink and swear like nearly everybody else in the army, but have become a constant companion of the pipe, what do you think of that? I have not resorted to this disagreeable practice for the purpose of drowning my sorrows so much as from a love of the weed, perhaps I will quit it when the war closes."[11]

In the early days of the unit, several shooting accidents were reported. Private Franklin Talbird's rifle accidentally went off while he was cleaning it, sending a load of buckshot in the direction of one of the men, Phillip Murray, who received minor wounds to his scalp. Leverett describes a much more serious incident: "The other accident was the shooting of a little fellow, a mere boy, who had just joined our Company, Richard Reynolds of Beaufort, by Henry Elliott. Henry was playing with a pistol and pointing it at this fellow and said he was going to shoot him not knowing that the barrel was loaded, when pulling the trigger the pistol went off, little Reynolds walked on for a second then clapping his hands to his chest cried out and fell and died in a few minutes."[12]

By the standards of Confederate artillery, the BVA was well armed. A tiny memorandum book kept by the unit's secretary reveals that the BVA's gunnery usually included two 12-pounder Napoleons, two howitzers, one of which was a 12-pounder and one 10-pounder Parrott.

Leverett recorded in his journal that in 1862, prior to the Battle of Port Royal, the unit's field artillery on hand included two 6-pounders and two 4-pounders. Prior to the war, the 6-pounder was the most common field artillery piece in southern arsenals, and most Southern foundries were fitted for this gun.

Its light weight provided the advantage of greater mobility than heavier guns, but it had disadvantages as well. The maximum range was limited to 1,500 yards with solid shot, and Civil War artillerymen wanted a weapon that could throw heavier shot and shells longer distances.

As the war proceeded, 12-pounder, smoothbore Napoleons were the cannons of choice for both sides. The Napoleon could send a 12-pound solid shot 1,700 yards, a substantial advantage over the 6-pounders. Its smooth bore could accommodate all types of standard ammunitions including solid shot, spherical case shot and shells. It was especially deadly using canister at close range (up to 300 yards out) against advancing infantry. It became so popular that Robert E. Lee ordered that the Army of Northern Virginia's 6-pounders be melted down and recast into Napoleons.[13]

***Nine.** "Ours is the gentlemanly company"*

The Southern version of the Napoleon was slightly lighter than the Northern, did not have the muzzle swell of the northern version, and, Confederate cannoneers claimed, jarred less when shot. Charleston's foundry, the Charleston Armory, produced Napoleons used primarily by South Carolina batteries, and it is likely that the two carried by the BVA throughout the war were manufactured there.[14]

Though howitzers were generally less popular with gunners than the Napoleons they had the advantage of being the lighter gun. During the course of 1864 the unit spent more time in target practice with the howitzers than their other gunnery. With a bronze tube weighing 400 pounds lighter than the Napoleon's, and a lighter carriage as well, the howitzer's lighter weight and greater maneuverability had clear benefits in the unique environment of the coastal area with its densely wooded areas punctuated by soft, marshy ground.

They were especially effective with canister at short ranges of 300 yards or less, ideal for the close fighting at the two Pocotaligo battles and Honey Hill, and for the kind of guerrilla fighting in the marshy areas like the attack on the USS *George Washington* gunboat.

The 12-pounder M1857 Napoleon smoothbore was the cannon of choice for both Confederate and Union artillery batteries. The Napoleon could send a 12-pound solid shot 1,700 yards (courtesy Gettysburg National Military Park).

The howitzer's lighter weight and easier maneuverability had clear benefits for batteries in the coastal region with their densely wooded areas and marshes (Library of Congress).

An analysis of the results of two target practice sessions recorded in the BVA's daily record book for 1864 provides insight into the accuracy of the unit's guns. One feature in the data stands out: the importance of distance. A difference of 300 to 400 yards made a considerable impact on the battery's accuracy.

The accuracy of the unit's two Napoleons shooting at a target at 1,000 yards was mixed. Of four practice shots using shot and shell projectiles, one shell exploded approximately fifty yards overhead of the target, and one fifty yards to the rear. In battle conditions these shots would have resulted in negligible damage to the enemy. However, another shell hit the left side of the target, and one ten yards to the left. One can assume both would have caused damage to their targets.

At a range of 700 yards the accuracy of the battery improved substantially. One shot hit six feet right of center of the target, one fifteen feet left of center. Since solid shot was used primarily for fortifications, these results were more than adequate. The two shells burst approximately twenty yards to the front of the target, a proximity that would likely have caused human casualties.

Nine. "Ours is the gentlemanly company" 95

Distance to target continues to be the defining factor in a November 9 practice with the unit's howitzers. At ranges between 1,000 and 1,400 yards, two of the four practice shots fell far wide of the target, and one round failed to explode. Just one shell fell within a distance to the target likely to cause casualties.

At a January 23, 1865, practice using shells fired by a howitzer aiming at a target at 700 yards accuracy was substantially improved. Ideally, shells were aimed to explode close in front of the target, the forward momentum of the shell's fragments hitting soldiers. In this practice, two of the BVA gunners' shells exploded twenty yards in front of the target, a distance that would likely cause damage to the enemy. The other two practice shots hit forty and sixty yards short, presumably too far from the target to cause significant damage.

On that same day the battery practiced using their Parrott rifled cannon. It is not known whether this was a 10- or 20-pounder gun. The Parrott was a rugged, cast iron cannon invented by a West Point graduate, Robert Parrott. It was the only rifled gun used by the BVA. The results of its practice rounds at 700 yards suggested it was the most accurate of the unit's guns, one round striking just three feet from the center of the target.[15]

The Parrott was the only rifled gun used by the Beaufort Volunteer Artillery. The results of the battery's practice rounds indicate it was the most accurate of the unit's guns (Library of Congress).

Parrotts were easy and cheap to produce and could take a beating. They were popular with artillerists, but had a serious flaw, a tendency to burst at a weak point next to the breech band, especially after long service. The guns were originally produced in northern foundries, but the Tredegar Iron Works in Charleston produced fifty-eight copies, one of which was likely used by the BVA.

The BVA's accuracy was further hampered by the generally inferior quality of southern munitions and fuses. In 1861, E. Porter Alexander, then a Confederate battalion commander commented: "Our smooth bore shells and shrapnel would very frequently explode prematurely and our rifled shot and shells would all tumble or fail to go point first, so that they had no range at all and were worse than worthless.... We gradually made improvements but the enemy were far ahead of us in artillery, ammunition of all kinds both in quality and quantity."[16]

The BVA's preponderance of smooth bore cannon with only one rifled gun was not necessarily a disadvantage. Rifled projectiles often became buried, exploding so deep in the ground no damage to the enemy was inflicted. On the other hand, smooth bored cannons seldom buried their shells.

The Confederate States Ordnance Manual of 1863 recommended that the ammunition chest should carry for a Napoleon cannon twenty rounds of shot, eight of spherical case, and four canister shells. For a howitzer, fifteen shells, twenty spherical case and four canisters. Because the BVA had to carry ammunition for three different kinds of guns there may have been challenges keeping the unit adequately supplied.

The BVA battery fielded four guns divided into gun sections. The captain exercised overall command with the assistance of a first lieutenant. Each gun section was commanded by a second lieutenant and a sergeant was assigned an individual gun. Each gun was manned by five cannoneers, each one of which had a specific duty when firing the gun. The individual guns were pulled by a team of fifteen to twenty horses.

Ten

A Glimpse of Total War: The Burning of Bluffton

Major General David Hunter had a problem. Newly assigned to command of the Department of the South, he was responsible for the military operations of a vast swath of territory extending from the Florida Keys to the northern border of South Carolina. When he arrived in March 1862 to take command, the actual extent of the Federal enclave was limited to the St. Helena Parish including Beaufort, Hilton Head and St. Helena Island.

A soldier with a respectable pedigree, his father had been a chaplain in George Washington's army and his grandfather a signer of the Declaration of Independence. At fifty-nine, one of the oldest generals in the army, he died his hair and wore a wig. Since his graduation from West Point in 1822, his career path was typical of other cadets: multiple assignments in remote areas of the country interrupted once by a brief and unsuccessful stint in the private sector. He fought in the Mexican-American War giving him valuable, real time experience in combat, and in 1856 was assigned to duty in the Kansas Territory. There he witnessed firsthand the bloody, guerrilla warfare between pro- and anti-slavery forces, an experience that transformed his thinking, generating avid, abolitionist sympathies.

General Hunter's problem was the small village of Bluffton on the May River. Bluffton had become more than a nuisance to Hunter and his command. An outpost in the no man's land outside of the federal conclave in Beaufort, Confederates maintained a network of pickets there that reported on Federal movements and troop strength. This intelligence network with its lookouts, couriers and pickets moved freely in an out of the town providing valuable reports to Confederate commanders on enemy movements in the Lowcountry. Equally important, it was a potential staging area for attacks on Federal forces.

Since January 1863, Company E of the 11th South Carolina regiment encamped near the wharf in Bluffton placing torpedoes in the nearby Skull Creek to blow up Federal gunboats patrolling the area. West of Bluffton in the village of Pritchardville, a detachment of guns of the BVA protected a bridge overlooking the New River along with Company C of the 11th SC.

It was well known to Union officers that Bluffton contained the summer residences of some of the wealthiest Lowcountry planters. Seven of the homes were owned by members of the Pope family of planters, including Squire William Pope, the titular head of the clan. One of the richest men in America, Pope drew his wealth from the Coggins Point, Skull Creek and Point Comfort plantations on Hilton Head Island, and the Crescent Plantation near Bluffton. Pope owned approximately 200 slaves. Located on the May River and just across the road from the elegant Anglican Church of the Cross built by the planters in 1857, Pope's summer residence was one of the largest in Bluffton.

Members of the powerful Seabrook family owned five residences in Bluffton. The Seabrooks owned multiple plantations on the Edisto River south of Charleston and on Hilton Head Island. There were others. Three members of the Kirk family maintained homes there including the Rose Hill plantation and its elegant, Gothic Revival mansion owned by planter physician John W. Kirk. There were also homes of senior officers of the Confederate army, most prominently, Brigadier General Thomas F. Drayton, commander of Fort Walker during the Battle of Port Royal. Middleton Stuart and Henry Middleton Stuart, Jr., of the Beaufort Volunteer Artillery also had homes there.[1]

Added to this was the memory that Bluffton was the epicenter of secessionist sentiment, the place where Robert Barnwell Rhett stoked the fires of secession with inflammatory speeches. Might an attack on Bluffton be an appropriate response to the guerrilla attacks on Federal forces like the raid on Pinckney Island that resulted in the deaths of many Union soldiers?

At this stage of the war, the military destruction of civilian property was not a generally accepted practice. But might it not be poetic justice that these slave owners and their trophy homes in Bluffton suffer some consequences? Hunter's abolitionist sympathies might have tended that way. We don't know for sure. Bottom line, the town's destruction would not have been an event likely to generate much criticism in the north or by Hunter's military superiors. Although Hunter's motives in ordering this action are not documented, his reputation as an ardent abolitionist may have been a factor in targeting the town.

For whatever reasons, on May 27, 1863, Hunter made a request to Rear Admiral Samuel Francis Du Pont for naval assistance in mounting an attack on Bluffton. His plan called for 1,000 infantry troops to be transported on four naval vessels that would also provide artillery support for the landing party. The force was made up of six companies from the 48th New York Regiment, fifty infantrymen each from the 3rd Rhode Island Artillery and the New York Volunteer Engineers, and three companies from the 115th New York Regiment. The troop convoy would be launched late in the evening and land early next morning at Hunting Island (not actually an island, but part of the mainland two miles downstream from Bluffton).[2]

The troops would be under the command of Colonel William Barton, the boats under Lieutenant Commander George Bacon. After hasty preparations the convoy embarked on June 3 and immediately had problems. One of the army gunboats, the *Mayflower,* ran aground, and could not be freed. Bacon assured Barton that the guns on the remaining gunboat, *Commodore McDonough*, would be more than adequate to provide the infantry with cover and the convoy continued.

In the early morning hours of June 4, the Federal troops disembarked from the ships and began to make their way north to Bluffton. The convoy then proceeded on and ultimately anchored at a point about a half mile from Bluffton where they could provide artillery support to the infantry.[3] Confederate troops in the area were stationed Camp Pritchard located near present-day Pritchardville, approximately eight miles from Bluffton. These troops included companies A, B, and G, 3rd South Carolina Cavalry, and company B, 4th South Carolina Cavalry. Company E of the 11th South Carolina was camped in Bluffton near the wharf.

Three Confederate lookouts stationed on the May River sighted the convoy sometime in the early hours of the morning. One of them left immediately to alert the 11th South Carolina in Bluffton. For reasons that are unclear, he never made it to the South Carolina unit to warn them. At 6:15 AM, one of the two remaining soldiers, a Private Savage of company B, mounted his horse to notify the Confederate cavalry units at Fort Pritchard. He reached the Fort at about 7:00 AM, and the bugler sounded the call to arms.

Federal troops landed without opposition at Hunting Island Plantation, quickly formed, and entered Bluffton at approximately 7:30 AM. As they swarmed through the abandoned town, they set fire to several homes on the east side of Heyward Cove near the May River. They were unopposed in Bluffton because the 11th had left and taken a defensive position west of the town about one mile away. Colonel Barton of the 48th New York had no intention of moving west of the town to engage Confederate troops. Thus, as Smith's Confederate troops were filing out of town, Barton's 48th were streaming in unopposed.

The Anglican Church of the Cross was one of the few Bluffton buildings that Union troops did not torch (photograph by the author).

Federal troops fanned out through the town in squads with specific orders to torch specific homes. Soon the entire town was engulfed in flames. Lt. Colonel Thomas Johnson, commander of the South Carolina cavalry units, arrived about this time just ahead of his command, met Lt. Smith, and directed him to return to Bluffton and engage the enemy with forward elements of the cavalry. The confederate force amounted to 238 men opposing 1,000 Federals and gunboats. Throughout the morning Confederate and Union troops exchanged fire, but the artillery salvos from the Federal gunboats proved decisive. The intensity of the bombardment of the Confederate troops severely hampered their ability to make headway against the Federals. Lieutenant Commander Bacon aboard the largest gunboats described the scene:

Ten. A Glimpse of Total War

> The enemy advanced down the street leading to the wharf through the town, expecting no doubt to sweep off in the general rush the [rear guard] who were covering the embarkation, as they were in considerable force by that time. They charged with cheers to within a short distance of the steamers, when, from their repeated volleys, we got their position ... when we opened with shrapnel and shell in the direction of the enemy. The effect was instantaneous, as I have since been assured by the commander of the land forces that our shrapnel and shell passed directly over the heads of our men, exploding in front of the ranks of the enemy, causing them to break and retreat in disorder.[4]

As billowing clouds of smoke could be seen rising over Bluffton, the Confederates continued to press the Union rear guard, but the guns of the *Commodore McDonough* held them at bay as the Federals quickly re-embarked their transports. By 12:00 PM, all the Federal troops had been loaded on the boats and were on their way back to Ft. Pulaski and Hilton Head Island.

Twenty-seven buildings, over half of the known forty-eight structures of the town were destroyed. The burning of Bluffton alarmed and outraged the Confederate senior military staff. A month after the attack, General P.G.T. Beauregard, the Confederate commander in South Carolina, was still seething. Beauregard sent a scathing letter to the new Department of the South commander, Brigadier General Quincy Gillmore, complaining, "In the interest of humanity, it seems to be my duty to address you, with a view of effecting some understanding as to the future conduct of the war in this quarter."

Somewhat hyperbolically, Beauregard compared Bluffton's burning to the British rampage against American property in the War of 1812. Would Gilmore adhere to the generally accepted norms of warfare in the future, he asked? Or did he consider destroying private property a "legitimate measure of war"? Gillmore quickly responded he would adhere to generally accepted standards if Beauregard would. That said, there was little doubt that something new and chilling had been added to the vocabulary of war as they knew it and with it the specter of Sherman's concept of total war.

Eleven

"Freedom is sweeter than life"

On paper, Thomas Wentworth Higginson was the perfect man to command the United States' first black regiment. His abolitionist credentials were impeccable. Born in Massachusetts, a Harvard graduate and Unitarian minister, the resume of his youthful causes read like that of a radical reformer: abolitionist, advocate for women's rights and champion of the working class and temperance.

His passion for the abolitionist cause was especially intense. On a Sunday in 1848 he proclaimed from the pulpit he would be remiss if he "let one Sunday pass in the professed preaching of Christianity, and [left] the name of slavery unmentioned."

The following year his radical pronouncements drove his more conservative parishioners to force his resignation. Undaunted, he turned to lecturing and writing to support himself, and slowly, found an audience for his speeches and essays. He became a regular contributor to the *Atlantic Monthly*, a prominent pro-abolitionist magazine and made friends with such literary lights as Emerson, Longfellow and Whittier.[1]

While most northern abolitionists like William Lloyd Garrison advocated politics and persuasion as the desired strategies for change, Higginson was not averse to more forceful means

Harvard graduate, Unitarian minister and abolitionist Thomas Wentworth Higginson was the first colonel of the 1st South Carolina Regiment (Library of Congress).

Eleven. "Freedom is sweeter than life" 103

when necessary. In 1854, he led a mob that attacked a Boston court house where a fugitive slave was being held for return to the South. The Fugitive Slave Act had long been a flashpoint for violence between pro-slavery and anti-slavery forces since its passage in 1850. The act permitted Southern slaveholders to find and reclaim their escaped slaves.

That same year Congress decreed that the future of the Kansas Territory—whether it would be a slave or free territory—would be decided by the settlers there. This resulted in a torrent of pro-slavery Southerners and anti-slavery Northerners descending on the territory. Soon "Bloody Kansas" (as the newspapers called it) was rife with violence, including John Brown's murdering of five proslavery settlers. Brown's crime left Higginson unfazed as he purchased and sent revolvers, rifles and ammunition to Kansas "Free Soilers." He became Brown's friend and a member of the Secret Six, a cabal that supported and funded Brown's plan to incite a slave insurrection in the entire South.[2]

During the early and middle years of the Civil War, Higginson served as Captain in the 51st Massachusetts Regiment. Then, in November 1863, a friend of his, Brigadier General Rufus Saxton, Commander of the Union's Department of the South, wrote Higginson asking him to consider taking the command of the Union's first black regiment. Higginson readily accepted and reported for duty within the month at Camp Saxton. Located four miles south of Beaufort on Port Royal Island, Camp Saxton was the headquarters of the 1st South Carolina Regiment.

Brigadier General Rufus Saxton, Mitchel's successor as commander of the Department of the South, wrote Higginson asking him to consider taking command of the 1st South Carolina Regiment (Library of Congress).

The genesis of this improbable site for an African American regiment began after the Battle of Port Royal when the Sea Island planters abandoned their plantations fleeing inland. Remaining behind were most of their slaves whose numbers would swell over the months as runaway slaves from the South Carolina mainland found their way to the Union enclave. Many of them were starving, thirsty, and had been fleeing their former masters through swamps, dodging Confederate patrols and bloodhounds. They were now the responsibility of the occupying Union forces and referred to as "contrabands."[3]

A term coined by Brigadier General Benjamin Butler in Command of the Department of Virginia, in May 1861, the concept of contraband would have historic consequences in the South Carolina Sea Islands. Early in the war, slaves were considered a nuisance by Federal forces and were typically sent back to Confederate authorities. But Butler had an idea. Why not put them to work for the Union Army? Why should the enemy be given the benefit of their labor? Thus, when a Confederate officer under a white flag came to claim three slaves that had escaped to his command, Butler informed him he was going to keep them as "contrabands of war."

Lincoln and his cabinet liked the idea and approved the practice for use in all theaters of war including the Beaufort District after the Battle of Port Royal. Major General David Hunter, commander of the Department of the South headquartered in Hilton Head was in desperate need of troops to defend his far-flung command that included Georgia and Florida in addition to South

Major General David Hunter wanted to recruit 50,000 blacks to his command in South Carolina, Georgia and Florida (Library of Congress).

Carolina. An ardent abolitionist, he took advantage of this expanded status of contraband and boldly made a request of the War Department in April 1862. Would the government authorize him to recruit 50,000 blacks from throughout the Department of the South?

Hunter understood that his request would be a political hot potato for the Lincoln administration. Elected to office by the slimmest of margins, this was an administration that could not afford to antagonize slaveholding border states still in the Union and the moderate base of the Republican Party. This fear of alienating loyal Southerners was famously memorialized in a quip attributed to Lincoln: "I would like to have God on my side, but I must have Kentucky."

Hunter was determined to have his black regiment. Having received no authorization from the Lincoln administration for the 50,000, but no denial either, Hunter made one of the most consequential passive-aggressive directives in the history of the United States military: He ordered his troops to bring to Camp Saxton all able-bodied black contrabands between the ages of eighteen and forty-five.[4] When Washington finally got word of this, Hunter's order was quickly countermanded by the administration, and Hunter was ordered to disband the blacks recruited thus far. Most went home, except for one: Company A stationed on St. Simon's Island off the Georgia coast. Company A did not receive the order.

This fortuitous oversight would benefit Saxton when he later took over the Department from Hunter in August 1862. Sensing an opportunity, he shrewdly requested from the War Department permission to enlist and arm blacks in his department, but careful not to refer to them as soldiers nor as members of a formally organized regiment. His political savvy was further demonstrated in his request for just five thousand men that would be used strictly for defensive purposes to guard Federal property from Confederate attacks.

Secretary of War Stanton approved the limited mission in a letter dated August 25 but added significantly that the troops *could* be considered full-fledged Army. Saxton chose to interpret Stanton's tacit recognition of the blacks as soldiers with the widest possible latitude and proceeded to use Company A under the command of Charles Trowbridge as the nucleus for a black regiment. Saxton then proceeded to fill the regiment's ranks with relish, personally traveling through the Sea Islands to recruit until the command's roster included about 500 men, and then securing his trusted friend Higginson as the regiment's colonel.

When Higginson reviewed his new command and its ten companies, he saw mostly teenagers and men in their twenties, but there were also sub-

The only known photograph of the 1st South Carolina Regiment (Library of Congress).

stantial numbers of soldiers in their thirties and forties, even older. Most had toiled in the cotton fields on plantations, and some were former house servants, carpenters and other craftsmen.[5]

As he talked to his men, Higginson learned many of them were from the mainland, or "main" as they called it. This was a powerful incentive for them to fight, to liberate their loved ones they had to leave behind. Some expressed a desire to help free their race from its bondage and were grateful to the Union for fighting for their freedom. Many took pride in their soldiering, and few were motivated by money.

One of the regiment's black laundresses attested to this.

> The first colored troops did not receive any pay for eighteen months, and the men had to depend wholly on what they received from the commissary, established by General Saxton. A great many of these men had large families, and as they had no money to give them, their wives were obliged to support themselves and children by washing for the officers of the gunboats and the soldiers and

Eleven. "Freedom is sweeter than life"

making cakes and pies which they sold to the boys in camp. Finally, in 1863, the government decided to give them half pay, but the men would not accept this. They wanted "full pay" or nothing. They preferred to give their services to the state, which they did until 1864, when the government granted them full pay, with all the back pay due.[6]

Revenge on their masters was not usually a motivation, but one of the men could not resist the temptation to offer up a prayer describing the sins of his master while forgiving him with the caveat, "Oh God, shake him over the brink of hell, but don't let go of him." Another soldier, private Cato Waring, was less charitable toward his former master, asking the regiment's surgeon, Seth Rogers, if he knew the name of a Confederate officer killed in the regiment's first action on St. Mary's River in Florida. When Rogers replied "no," Cato glared at him saying, "Oh, I hope to God it was my young master who went down that way."[7]

The horrors of Cato's story were carefully recorded by Dr. Rogers and were not atypical of those of other men in the regiment. In his sixties, private Cato was likely the oldest man in the regiment. Because of his age, he was assigned duty as a nurse and deferred from any combat action. Raised on a plantation somewhere in the South Carolina Lowcountry, he was sold to another plantation to pay off his master's widow's debts.

Cato described his new master, a Dr. Waring, as "a bad man, but not so bad as his wife." Cato was made overseer of the plantation, a status he held for sixteen years until his escape. The enslaved house servants were daily expected to have all the brass shined and furniture dusted before sunup. Dr. Rogers recorded Cato's description of what happened next.

> When she [Mrs. Waring] arose in the morning and examined the furniture with her white handkerchief for dust there were usually one or two victims selected for the lash. It was Cato's business to wait at the door for orders to apply from one hundred to five hundred lashes every morning before going out to the plantation. If the victim was male, he was stripped and cords were fastened to his fingers and then drawn over a horizontal pole above his head, till his toes only, touched the ground; then the master would stand behind Cato with a paddle and knock him over for any delinquency on his part. The same treatment was applied to women, except that instead of stripping off the clothing, the skirts and chemises were drawn up over the rear. When the parlor was filled with visitors, the mistress would wind a towel around the end of a stick, and have it thrust into the throat of the victim and it would come out all covered in blood—thus the screams of the tortured would be smothered. These statements would seem exaggerated to me if I had not, over and over, in my medical examinations of this regiment, found enormous horizontal scars around the body, and, on inquiry been told "Dat's whar my ole marsa had whipped me."[8]

As time went on after the occupation of Port Royal by Federal forces, the Warings increased their slaves' work vowing, Cato described, to "work de niggers to deat' before the damned Yankees should have them." Cato resisted these orders, and before his master could exact punishment for his insubordination, he fled the plantation in a dugout canoe. Making his way slowly, rowing by night and resting by day, chased and attacked by dogs, he went days without food.

His luck changed when he found a black he could trust and informed him a Yankee gunboat was about twenty-two miles away and making its way upriver. The captain of the boat was on an expedition to find contrabands and recruit them to the Union cause. Making his way slowly to try to locate the boat, he awoke one morning in a house garden with the unwelcoming sight of a rebel taking aim at him. His gun dampened by the rain, would not fire, and Cato escaped.

Finally, after wandering in his canoe for six weeks, he caught sight of the gunboat and hauled up a "white rag" to hail the boat. When he boarded, as he described it, he thought he was in heaven.

Higginson became especially attached to a sergeant in Company A: Prince Rivers. Rivers held one of the most exalted positions in the regiment, the colors-bearer. Approximately forty years old, he had been the carriage driver for wealthy Beaufort family. When the family fled for the mainland after the occupation by the Federals, Rivers remained and found work in Beaufort. He left this job to enlist in General Hunter's new black regiment and continued on after its reincarnation as the 1st South Carolina Regiment.

Higginson came to recognize Rivers's unique constellation of assets, most prominently, his literacy. He soon assigned him to write his daily reports and perform tasks that in today's parlance would characterize him as high-level executive assistant. His innate oratorical skills were soon put to good use as a recruiter, making speeches throughout the islands exhorting Sea Island liberated blacks to join the 1st South Carolina. He demonstrated leadership skills that enabled him to discipline the men while retaining their respect.

Naturally media savvy and articulate, he was the informal spokesman for the regiment's blacks on various issues. To the *New York Independent* correspondent he commented: "This is our time. If our fathers had had such a chance as this, we should not have been slaves now. If we do not improve this chance, another one will not come, and our children will be slaves always."[9]

A strict disciplinarian, he gradually earned the respect and devotion of his men. The burden of his responsibility as the leader of the first black regiment weighed on him. He entertained doubts about his ability to lead these men under the microscope of intense political scrutiny and national attention. These doubts led him to undertake a frank inventory of his weaknesses and strengths and accepting the understanding that he would have to adjust his management style.

Any hint of paternalism in Higginson's attitudes was morphed into an empathy and intuitive understanding of his men that earned their trust. Higginson sensed the damage slavery inflicted on the blacks' dignity and self-worth, and he set about to address this as best he could in military terms. He insisted that they not raise their caps obsequiously to their officers and stop addressing them as "Massa." He drilled them to stand erect and proud, to make a crisp salute and to expect the same in return. Furthermore, he forbade them the use of "nigger" referring to themselves.

He learned that the typical negative stereotypes of blacks were uninformed. While they were illiterate for the most part, they were not ignorant, and hungered for knowledge that would improve their lives. Dozens of the men enthusiastically attended the regiment's chaplain's reading and writing lessons. They were not lazy, nor were they hard to manage. They responded well to orders and were not as prone to vices typical of white solders: theft, drinking, gambling and swearing. They were not inclined to feign illness to avoid guard duty.[10]

He was careful to check any racial attitudes lurking in his behavior or that of his white officers. The racism that pervaded society in general was prevalent among Union troops as well. A New York officer stationed in South Carolina, Lt. Colonel Charles Halpin, published some doggerel verse titled *Sambo's Right to be Kilt* with the less than subtle message that the blacks' only worth was to stop Confederate bullets aimed at white soldiers.[11] White officers assigned to General Hunter's original Company A of the black regiment were subjected to the taunts and insults of the other white regiments. Higginson and General Saxton fought with Army supply departments for tents, muskets and medical supplies manned by men unwilling to service the "nigger regiment."

To address this problem, Higginson took aggressive steps. He recruited only those white officers who had specifically volunteered to lead black troops. They were to return salutes of their men respectfully and avoid any abusive language when addressing them. While none of these men could be characterized as civil rights advocates, they *were* looking for opportunities for promotion that service in the black regiment would provide them. Some were keen to be on the ground floor of this historic experiment and enthusiastic to play a role in producing good soldiers.

One of these, Captain Charles Trowbridge of Company A of the regiment, would soon become Higginson's right-hand man. The two could hardly have been more different. Brilliant and precocious, Higginson entered Harvard at thirteen and graduated Pi Beta Kappa at sixteen. Trowbridge on the other hand was born and raised in Brooklyn and worked as a bricklayer. Unschooled, with a muscular build, Brooklyn accent and little previous contact with blacks, he was an unlikely candidate for fame as the first Union officer to command black troops in combat.

Recruited into the 1st New York Engineers Regiment, he arrived with that unit as part of the Port Royal invasion in 1861. Reassigned captain of Company A, he and his men were dispatched to defend St. Simon's Island, Georgia, and its 400 armed black residents from possible Confederate raids from the mainland. There was reason for concern. A Confederate general had suggested that the Island's blacks "be hanged as soon as possible at some public place as an example." [12] Thus, Higginson had reason to put his faith in Trowbridge: The young captain was the only officer in the Sea Islands with experience—limited as it was—commanding black soldiers.

* * *

General Saxton reviewed again the August 25 letter from Stanton authorizing him to recruit black soldiers but with no specific permission to engage them in combat. He noted some ambiguous language in the letter to the effect that he could engage the enemy with efforts "consistent with civilized warfare to weaken, harass, and annoy them."[13]

This was enough for him to feel authorized to make raids on the mainland with soldiers of the 1st. These defensive raids could conceivably draw Confederates into combat accomplishing two goals: giving his troops experience under fire and demonstrating to the public that black soldiers could fight.

There were significant risks. The troops were green with insufficient training. But they knew how to load and fire their rifles, and they were eager to prove themselves. Thus, on November 3, 1863, sixty-two men of Captain Trowbridge's Company A under the command of Colonel Oliver Beard (Higginson had not yet arrived to take command) boarded the Federal transport *Darlington* and set out to patrol the mainland and harass the rebels.

Eight days the *Darlington* prowled the coast and rivers of Georgia and St. Mary's River in Northeastern Florida, making numerous stops for troops to disembark quickly, destroy Rebel saltworks, burn or seize supplies, and most importantly, free slaves and bring them back to Beaufort.

Ambushed three times by Confederate troops concealed along the shoreline, the men responded effectively, taking cover on deck and firing back. When the expedition returned 150 bullet holes were found on the *Darlington*, and four black soldiers had been wounded. Lt. Colonel Beard reported his troops "behaved bravely, gloriously, and deserve all praise."

Ten days later another contingent of the 1st set off from Beaufort on the *Darlington*, again under the command of Beard. Much greener than the first expedition's troops (they had been issued their rifles just four days before), on November 18 they reconnoitered the coastal waters of Southeastern Georgia for a place to land. Beard led a detachment of thirty-four men that quickly ran into a force of dismounted Confederate cavalry. Taken by surprise and flanked on both sides by the rebels, some of the men panicked, and some of them ran. But Beard quickly rallied them and led them back to the boat in a fighting retreat that was performed competently with four of the men wounded.

Though modest in scope, these excursions did wonders for the men's morale. Here, for the first time, they tasted combat, and performed well. One of them commented, "I feel a heap more of a man."[14]

Their performance encouraged their newly arrived colonel Higginson who realized they had a powerful incentive to perform well not shared by white troops: If captured they could be hung, returned to their masters, or re-enslaved elsewhere. Later in the war at the Battle of Olustee in Central Florida it was reported that after the battle roving bands of Confederate soldiers indiscriminately killed injured black soldiers and prisoners. The same threat loomed over the regiment's white officers. Confederate President Jefferson Davis made a proclamation denying white officers of black regiments prisoner of war status. In other words, the green light was given to summarily execute them.

Now with some real-life combat experience, Higginson thought it was time to up the ante and lay the groundwork for approval of a full-fledged military raid with the entire complement of the regiment's 850 men. In preparation he decided to stage a full-dress military drill in Beaufort near the Arsenal for the benefit of the public and the white Union troops stationed there. In the early afternoon of Sunday, January 17, 1864, with their spit and polish muskets and fixed bayonets, the regiment assembled on the parade ground of Camp Saxton for the march to Beaufort.

Just after 1:00 PM Higginson gave the order to move out. It was a splendid sight, one that could not have been imagined in the heart of the most rabidly secessionist locale in the Confederacy. With Sergeant Rivers at the head of the column, the colors flying to the stirring strains of "John Brown's Body" sung by the men, the regiment marched to Beaufort and was welcomed there by the band of the 8th Maine playing a martial air and leading it into the town. Men, women and soldiers lining the streets or ogling from house windows hailed the men, some with taunts and some with measured cheers. If the welcome was lukewarm it didn't matter to the men. They were excited and proud on this red-letter day. Prince Rivers smiled exuberantly at Colonel Higginson exclaiming: "When dat band begin for play, good heaven, I lef dis world altogether!"[15]

At the end of the day the regiment's major, John Strong, wrote glowingly, describing an incident emblematic of the challenges that would dog the regiment throughout the war.

> This has been a triumphant day for our regiment. We have marched to Beaufort and back in such style as to turn jeers into admiration, and tonight our men are full of music and delight. The Colonel, not content with marching the whole length of the front street, actually stopped on the parade ground and drilled the regiment an hour or more and then they marched home to the music of their own voices.
>
> The different encampments at Beaufort had large delegations by the wayside, as we entered the town, and we were greeted with such language as pertains to vulgar negro haters. Our men were apparently indifferent to it and the officers could afford to wait in silence.
>
> I fell back to the rear with the major and was constantly delighted at the manly bearing of our soldiers. Not a head was turned to the right or left, not a word spoken. At length a white soldier struck a black man, not of our regiment the poor fellow appealing to us, we wheeled our horses upon the rabble, and Major Strong, with drawn sword pursued the offender, with the point of hat instrument a little nearer the fellow's back than seemed wholesome.... The effectiveness was magical, no more audible sneers.[16]

Soon after the parade Higginson and Saxton met with Hunter. The time was right they, they said, for the full regiment to take the field and show the country what it could do in real war conditions. Hunter agreed, granting them permission to organize an expedition.

Higginson and Saxton wasted no time organizing a raid. Just a few days after their meeting with Hunter three navy troop ships—the *Ben De Ford*, *John Adams* and *Planter*—arrived at Camp Saxton and began taking on supplies and boarding men. The *John Adams* carried heavy artillery giving the flotilla some potent firepower. On January 23, the expedition set out.

Its target was the St. Mary's River along the Georgia-Florida border. Navigable up to forty miles into the interior, its location had the added benefit of being the area where color bearer Robert Sutton had been born and raised, giving Higginson the benefit of Sutton's intimate knowledge of the River. Engine problems with the *Planter* and the *Ben De Ford*'s large size—

too large to navigate the river—forced Higginson to rely entirely on the *John Adams* to carry men and limiting the force to 200 men.

Progress up the river was slow. "It is very crooked and sluggish and black and got us aground so many times," the regiment's surgeon Dr. Seth Rogers wrote. "Again and again we had to turn points at right angles, and we were never more than two rods from one or another shore. Often the sides of our boat were swept by the boughs of the mournful looking trees. The shores are generally low and marshy and the moss droops so low as to give the appearance of weeping willows."[17]

On the night of January 26, the *John Adams* set out to find Confederate cavalry thought to be camped at a place called Township Landing, upriver ten miles on the Florida side of the river. Higginson's plan was to surprise and capture the rebels in their camp. Just outside of the town, Higginson and a small detachment of men disembarked and secured the town, allowing none of its residents to leave to tip off the Confederate cavalry. The *John Adams* soon arrived, and the rest of the troops landed. Fortuitously, Sutton found a local black who knew the location of the rebels and agreed to guide the men directly to their camp about five miles away, perhaps motivated by the distinct pleasure of learning that he was now a free man.

For an officer with no previous experience leading a guerrilla style attack, Higginson demonstrated exceptional skill. Whittling down his attack force to about a hundred men, he left behind the rest to guard the landing and protect the ship. After cautioning his men not to talk and to move as quietly as possible, they moved out at midnight, their vision aided by a clear night and bright moon. Slowly they snaked their way through the forest down a narrow path. Suddenly, two miles down the path, shots rang out.

A bullet through the heart instantly killed a soldier standing next to Higginson. Mounted Confederate cavalry attacked the head of the Union column. Higginson quickly ordered his men to take cover and return fire. Easier said than done. Where were the Confederates? Confusion and near panic gripped the men as they faced their first encounter with a deadly enemy. Sheets of flame bellowed from the muzzles of the Confederate's rifles and pistols pierced the black night, seeming to surround the advanced elements of Higginson's command. The men's officers yelled orders, "Hold your ground!" and despite the terror of the surprise attack, they did.

It is said that soldiers in war age rapidly, and the men of the 1st now had their first opportunity to experience this adage. In the heat of battle, minutes can seem like hours, so it was hard to tell just how long the rebels pressed their attack. But the guns of Higginson's regiment answered that of the rebels without pause as its officers yelled encouragement to the men. In time, Confederate fire slowed, then abated entirely.

It soon became clear that the Confederates were retreating, and the men, excited by the action, wanted to pursue. Higginson was not so sure. The mounted Confederates had the mobility to do further harm, and without the ability to follow their movements, Higginson decided not to take undue risks. Besides, his men could claim their first victory, one that would be a first step in establishing the credibility and reputation of black troops as fighters and competent for battle.[18]

The troops gathered up the seven injured men, then made their way through the forest to the *John Adams* for the trip back to the deserted village of St. Mary's at the mouth of the river. Among the wounded was Robert Sutton, who had been hit by bullets in three places. After the skirmish he hid his injuries, saying nothing about them until he arrived at Dr. Seth Rogers makeshift infirmary on the *John Adams*. As Dr. Rogers treated the wound, Sutton quietly described his experience to the surgeon. "He quietly talked of what they had done and what they yet can do.... He is perfectly quiet and cool but takes this whole affair with the religious bravery of a man who realizes that freedom is sweeter than life."

Meanwhile, something at St. Mary's had caught Higginson's eye: a substantial pile of lumber on the wharf that would be useful back in Beaufort. When his command arrived at St. Mary's, Higginson knew there was some risk in stopping to secure the lumber. The troops would again be subject to a surprise attack. Nonetheless, he thought the risk worth it, and the troops disembarked to load the lumber.

Sure enough, just as the *John Adams* pulled away from the wharf, "a regular hailstorm of bullets" as Higginson later described it pummeled the ship. More than a little annoyed at this ambush, Higginson ordered the ship back to the dock and ordered the *John Adams*'s four big guns to bombard the town. While a detail of men cleared the surrounding woods of rebels, exploding shells lit the landscape and the town in bursts of surreal, unnatural light. Higginson ordered his men to torch the town. As the ship pulled away from the dock the men watched in awe as the fire spread quickly, destroying all but a handful of the town's buildings.

Soon after arriving at Fernandina Harbor at the mouth of St. Mary's an officer informed Higginson of a large stockpile of bricks located in the village of Woodstock, forty miles up the St. Mary's River. These bricks would be useful reinforcing Union fortifications at Fernandina. He also got wind of a rumor that a Confederate blockade runner was docked somewhere near Woodstock.

Eleven. *"Freedom is sweeter than life"*

And there was one more thing: Robert Sutton's former master lived in Woodstock, a Mrs. Alberti. Might not a visit to her plantation with Sutton be of interest? Higginson's motives for the visit are unclear, but what was eminently clear when they arrived at Mrs. Alberti's doorstep was that she was not amused—unable and unwilling to conceal arrogant posturing as a Southern aristocrat and her contempt for her former slave.[19]

Sutton found the keys to the Alberti's "slave jail" and gave his colonel a tour. Higginson was appalled at what he saw. Heavy chains used to constrain slaves were strewn across the floor with stocks used to punish women and children. In another building Higginson saw an odd-looking apparatus. To his horror he realized it was used to torture slaves by binding them in painful, unnatural positions. He ordered his men to gather the stocks and chains. He would take them back to Beaufort and show General Saxton.

Sutton scrubbed the search for the blockade runner when he learned from local blacks that it was in such bad condition it was unusable for service. Satisfied at the accomplishments of the expedition and the performance of his men, he decided it was time for the regiment to return to Beaufort.

Not long after they started back, the Georgia shoreline erupted in intense gunfire. The Confederate ambush rained bullets into the hull of the *John Adams*, but Higginson's men kept calm. Most of the soldiers were confined below decks, but as many as could scrambled to the portholes returning fire. While the *John Adams*'s guns poured shells into the shoreline, Higginson's men implored him to allow them to go to shore for a standup fight with the rebels. Higginson refused thinking it too risky.

The Confederates kept up their fire for a while, moving down stream following the ship. Eventually they withdrew, but not without inflicting a major Federal casualty: a bullet through the head of the ship's captain, killing him instantly, jeopardizing the ship's safe return to Fernandina. But Sutton piloted the boat back to Fernandina and safety, despite sporadic gunfire by Confederates near Township Landing.

There the men were transferred to the *Ben De Ford* for the voyage back to Beaufort and Fort Saxton. On board Higginson wrote his official report for Saxton praising the men and their performance. The opinions of the white soldiers on the expedition were quite different. Refusing to bunk with the blacks below decks, they opted instead for an uncomfortable trip back exposed to the elements unsheltered on the main deck.

In his report Higginson could not claim that the expedition captured any major stores of material or men. Besides the bricks, lumber, railroad ties and a few horses, sheep and steer, they returned with just a few contraband slaves. But that was not the point. They did not pillage nor mistreat civilians.

They followed orders without complaint. And most importantly, for the first time in the War, black soldiers had demonstrated their competence. They did not shirk combat. "The men have been repeatedly been under fire," he proudly declared, "and have in every instance come off not only with unblemished honor, but with undisputed triumph showing a fiery energy about them beyond anything of which I have read."[20]

The men themselves were satisfied as well, regaling each other around campfires with their stories and experiences of their first taste of combat. They could be excused for exaggerating some. After more than 200 years of experiencing the cruelest oppression a race could be expected to endure at the hands of slave masters against whom they could not retaliate, it is not much wonder they were jubilant. Higginson was further gratified at the sight of the men's newfound confidence in themselves, a confidence that significantly, was shared by their officers.

As a result of their success, Higginson and Saxton hatched a daring plan to send the full regiment of 775 officers and men and elements of the newly formed 2nd South Carolina on an expedition to capture and permanently occupy Jacksonville, Florida, using it as a base of operations for ongoing incursions into the Florida mainland. In making their case to General Hunter, they emphasized the critical shortage of troops in many of the theaters though out the country, and their deeply felt belief that full-scale recruiting of black troops in Florida could represent a major source of manpower.

Hunter was not unsympathetic to this argument, but felt black troops were best used in garrison duty, freeing up white soldiers for combat. Besides, racial attitudes of the public continued to push back on the idea of a full mobilization of black soldiers, and the Lincoln administration, ever attuned to the Republican middle, was not yet ready to lead on this issue.

Even in the hotbed of abolition sentiment of Boston, a February 13 editorial in the moderate *Boston Daily Advertiser* stated darkly that those who would propose a massive recruitment of black soldiers "forget the ignorance and mental darkness, which generations of oppression have fastened upon the mass of the slave population.... Those who hope that we are to finish this with black levies are falling into a dangerous error."

Higginson and Saxton continued to press their case. Jacksonville was an ideal choice to attack. One of the largest towns in Florida, it had excellent harborage for Federal warships, and the U.S. Navy's dominance of St. John's River was unchallenged. While technically the rebels controlled the Florida mainland, there hold on it was tenuous at best. Troop presence there was weak, and to its commanding officer, General P. G. T. Beauregard, headquartered far away in Charleston and tasked with the responsibility of defending Charleston and Savannah, it was strictly a sideshow.

With newly arrived reinforcements of 10,000 troops to bolster his campaign to take Charleston, Hunter felt he could spare the black troops for a Florida incursion, and he approved the St. John's expedition. After Hunter's approval, things moved quickly.

On March 5, from his headquarters in Beaufort, Saxton issued the formal orders for the expedition to Higginson.

> Colonel, —You will please proceed with your command, the First and Second Regiments South Carolina Volunteers, which are now embarked upon the steamers John Adams, Boston and Burnside, to Fernandina, Florida.... The main object of your expedition are to carry the proclamation of freedom to the enslaved; to call all loyal men into the service of the United States; to occupy as much of the state of Florida as possible with the forces under your command; and to neglect no means consistent with the usages of civilized warfare to weaken, harass, and annoy those who are in rebellion against the government of the United States.
> R. Saxton
> Brig.-Gen.,Mil. Gov. Dept. of the South.[21]

On that same day Higginson asked one of his company commanders, Captain James Rogers, how long it would take for his men to break camp and board ships. "About an hour," he replied. Rogers later recalled the excitement of men. "Knapsacks were paced, tents struck, and everything was ready for moving. All that afternoon my men were on board the Boston waiting for the vessels to be loaded.... About nine p.m. they relieved another company which had been hard at work all the afternoon, and from then till nearly one they worked with a will, wheeling and carrying, rowing and 'toting' goods."[22] By sunrise the next day the troops were ready to cast off, and on the morning of March 10 they occupied Jacksonville without opposition.

Most of the town's homes were deserted with about only a quarter of the town's 2,000 prewar residents remaining. On the outskirts of town, they cleared areas to provide an adequate field of fire, burning the homes occupied by the families of Confederate soldiers. Soon Confederate cavalry began to appear daily, trading fire with Union pickets and reporting any movements to Brigadier General Joseph Finegan, commander of the Confederate District of East Florida.

A laundress for the regiment, Susie King Taylor, described one of the first skirmishes with the rebels, one that turned deadly:

> The regiment landed and marched up the street where they spied rebels.... They were hiding behind a house ... their faces blackened to disguise themselves as negroes, and our boys, as they advanced toward them, halted a second, saying,

"They are black men! Let them come to us or we will make them know who we are." With this, the firing was opened and several of our men were wounded and killed [and] the rebels had a number killed and wounded. It was through this way the discovery was made that they were white men. Our men drove them some distance in retreat and then threw out their pickets.[23]

To some of the men of the 1st and 2nd regiments, this was distinctly disagreeable territory, having been enslaved here prior to the war. Higginson wrote in his diary, "many [of his men] were owned here and do not love the people." As such "they fear ... black troops infinitely more than they do the white soldiers." Many were outraged by the presence of black troops. Captain Rogers, assigned provost marshal and responsible for law enforcement, received an unusual request from one of his men.

He told Rogers that one of Jacksonville's residents owned one of his daughters. Could he find her and get back his daughter if possible? Rogers agreed to accompany him and when they located her, found themselves in the presence of one of the most disagreeable and rabid secessionists in the state. "I know what you are after you dirty Yank," she said after they confronted her. "You are after that nigger's girl. Well, she is safe beyond the lines where you can't get her. I expected you Yanks would want to steal her, so I sent her off yesterday. You are too late."

As it happened, a young boy approached them, and Rogers asked the woman whether he was her son. When she replied yes, Rogers calmly instructed one of his black sol-

Susie King Taylor was one of the laundresses for the 1st South Carolina Regiment (Library of Congress).

diers to secure the boy and take him to the guard house. As he walked off with the boy, Rogers recounted the woman's enraged reaction: "The 'lady' gave me a volley of abuse which I will not repeat, nor did I stop to hear the end of the tirade. Finding she should get no satisfaction from the colonel she was advised to hunt up the provost marshal and get a pass [through the lines]. Imagine her chagrin and disgust when she found I was the man she was seeking. She asked for the pass."[24] Rogers then made sure she was accompanied four black soldiers through the lines.

The Confederates were thoroughly alarmed by this new incursion of black troops into Florida. In his distress General Finegan wildly overestimated the number of black troops that had landed. It was his worst nightmare, rightly if after occupying Jacksonville powerful Federal gun boats and troopships packed with armed, black soldiers would advance up the St. John's River and foment a slave rebellion the likes of which Florida had never seen.

"Intercourse will immediately commence between negroes on the plantations and those in the enemy's service.... This intercourse will be conducted through swamps and under cover of the night and cannot be prevented. A few weeks will suffice to corrupt the entire slave population of East Florida."[25]

Indeed, with the white 6th Connecticut and 8th Maine regiments just arrived to secure the town, the 1st South Carolina was poised to set out and make life very miserable for the Confederate inhabitants of East Florida. But only five days after the landing, the unthinkable happened. Orders came from department headquarters in Beaufort to abandon the town and the operation and return immediately.

Higginson and his men were stunned. On the threshold of the first major military operation by the black United States soldiers, they were reigned in for reasons beyond their understanding. But General Hunter, having been rebuffed by the War Department, was desperate for troops needed to launch his grand strategy to capture the "Holy City," Charleston. He would have to find the men from his own command, so it was "all-hands on deck" back at Beaufort, and the 1st was recalled.

From that time on until the end of the war, the 1st regiments active combat duty was desultory at best. The 1st was relegated to picket duty on the northern shore of Port Royal Island, across from the mainland and a detail of Confederate pickets.

After Hunter was relieved from duty on July 9, the regiment participated as part of a larger campaign under his successor, Major General Quincy Gillmore. Gillmore organized his own campaign to capture Charleston in which the 1st and the more recently organized 2nd South Carolina regiment would, predictably, be relegated to a minor role.

Higginson and a select group of 200 men were loaded on three troop ships assigned to move up the South Edisto River and at a point about halfway between Port Royal Sound and Charleston disembark and attack the Charleston & Savannah Railroad line, destroying its bridge across the river.

The next morning, they were floating through rice plantations about twenty miles upstream. After routing a small confederate garrison, the expedition was blocked from further progress by pilings sunk across the river preventing his boats from continuing. While some the men pulled up the pilings, others torched store houses of corn and rice and destroyed the sluice gates that controlled water to irrigate the rice fields.

As the tide began to flow, the small flotilla got underway only to stall again when two of the boats ran aground. These delays gave the Confederates a chance to place six guns near the bridge making attack suicidal. Just when Higginson thought things couldn't get any worse, the rain of fire from the Confederates killed the first engineer of the ship he was on, then wounded the second.

While the troops below decks maintained order, the crew above was half crazed with fear. "We were perfectly helpless," Captain Rogers later wrote:

> We could not use our guns. One [paddle] wheel of the boat was plying through the mud and high grass of the river bank, and we pushed and rolled the vessel for some time.... I remained on the upper deck with the colonel and pilots and did what I could to make the latter do their duty and to keep the captain of the boat away from them, for he was so frightened that he was almost crazy. Once when the steam nearly gave out ... the firemen were all so scared that they were lying on their faces on the floor and not until I had thrown the wood at them did they turn and go to work.... The only thing to keep her from falling into the hands of the rebs was to burn her, and accordingly it was done after spiking the guns and taking off all we could of value.[26]

Despite the debacle the retreating troops somehow managed to free two hundred slaves during their retreat, but the bridge remained unharmed.

While the sum of the military impact of these expeditions was modest at best, their political impact was incalculable. Normally such minor engagements would not have attracted the attention of major northern newspapers. But the notoriety and daring of black troops fighting to liberate slaves was a story line they couldn't resist.

During the weeks of the Georgia and Florida expeditions the *New York Times*, *New York Herald*, *Boston Daily Advertiser* and *Chicago Tribune* among others followed events in those states closely, generally reporting favorably on the mission. Black news publications like the *Christian Recorder* of the

African Methodist Episcopal Church were ecstatic, reporting on March 28 that "our colored soldiers prove themselves to be men.... The expedition into Florida has proved a complete success."[27]

No less than President Abraham Lincoln sent Hunter a congratulatory note commenting on the black soldiers. "I see that the enemy are driving at them fiercely.... It is important to the enemy that such a force shall *not* take shape, and grow, and thrive, in the South; and in precisely the same proportion, it is important to us that it *shall*.... The enemy will make extra efforts to destroy them; and we should do the same to preserve and increase them."[28]

President Lincoln, needing hard evidence that black troops could fight, now, with the achievements of the 1st South Carolina, had it. On March 24, his Secretary of War Edwin Stanton summoned the adjutant general of the Army, Lorenzo Thomas, to his office. The decision had been made, he told Thomas, to begin full scale recruiting of black men to the Union army and to do so with the utmost speed.

This was a pivotal decision in the Civil War and initiated one of the most massive recruiting efforts in the history of the United States. By the end of the war 180,000 blacks had been recruited and served in the Army, plus an additional 24,000 in the Navy. They paid a heavy price for their service with 30 percent of them dying in combat or of their wounds or disease. Fifteen black sailors received the United States' highest military award for valor, the Medal of Honor.[29]

* * *

In the pantheon of legendary Civil War regiments, 1st South Carolina Regiment deserves an especially high level of veneration. Not for its military prowess, but for its momentous impact on the course of the war: for its courage and perseverance in the face of the suspicion and disdain of white soldiers, the disrespect and bigotry of the public that couldn't believe they could fight, and a timid, coddling Lincoln administration unwilling to give them the chance. Like the black Civil Rights heroes of mid–twentieth century, they had to do it alone, and do it they did. These 700 men opened the door for the approximately four million African Americans who served in wars for the United States since then.

Although they could never know the long-term significance of their service, they were profoundly aware of the importance of their active participation of the liberation of their race. In a moving tribute to their achievement, one of their own, Corporal Thomas Long of Company C gave a Sabbath message on March 27, 1864, to his comrades that described compellingly why it was important and what was at stake:

> We can remember, when we first enlisted, it was hardly safe for we to pass by de camps to Beaufort and back, 'lest we went in a mob and carried our sidearms. But we whipped down all dat not by going into di white camps for whip um; we didn't tote our bayonets for whip um; but we lived it down by our natural manhood; and now de white sojers take us by de hand and say Broder Sojer, Dat's what dis regiment did for de Ethiopian race.
>
> If we hadn't become sojers, all might have gone back as it was before; our freedom might have slipped through di two houses of Congress and President Lincoln's four years might have passed by and nothin' been done for we. But now tings can never go back, because we have showed our energy and our courage and our natural manhood.
>
> Another thing is, suppose you had kept your freedom widout enlisting in de army; your chilen might have grown up free, and been well cultivated so as to be equal to any business, but it would have been always flung in dere face—"Your fader never fought for he own freedom"—and what could they answer? Neber can say that to di African race any more. Tanks to dis regiment, never can say dat anymore, because we first showed 'em we could fight by dere side.[30]

Twelve

"Never have I seen such terrible havoc"

On Monday, February 15, 1864, a brief notice appeared in the *Charleston Mercury*.

> THE RE-ENLISTMENTS
> Camp of Beaufort Vol. Artillery
> February 8, 1864
> At a meeting of the Beaufort Volunteer Artillery held this day, it was unanimously *Resolved*, Whereas a nation of fanatics is seeking the destruction of our liberties, and it remains to be expelled from the sacred soil of our country, therefore, *Resolved,* That it is a duty we owe, alike ourselves and to the memory of the noble dead, who fallen in our defense, to meet the foe readily and never to return to the homes we have until they shall have been driven from our borders. *Resolved,* That we will, at the extension of our present term of service re-enlist for the war, however long it may last.
> E. B. Cuthbert, Chairman
> S. T. Baker, Secretary

This commitment by the BVA to reenlist until the end of the war was quickly relayed to all the soldiers of the Confederacy's 3rd Military District in an official bulletin issued by its commanding officer, Brigadier General William S. Walker. His statement had a ringing, martial quality to it meant to stir patriotic sentiments and bolster morale for a cause that was becoming increasingly desperate.

> Hd. Qtrs. 3rd Mil. District
>
>   Pocotaligo Feby. 13th 1864
> I take great pleasure in announcing to the troops of this District that the Beaufort Volunteer Artillery 150 strong, Captain H. M. Stuart commanding on the 8th and without a dissenting voice resolved as a body to volunteer for the [rest of] war. I commend the example of these gallant corps to their comrades. Let us

respond cordially and with unanimity to the invitation of General Beauregard and let the men on the sea coast stretch out their hands to their brothers on the Rappahannock and the Tennessee and swear to fight out this great battle while there is a hope left to cheer them.

We are now suffering only as all men in past ages have suffered who fought for their liberties against a powerful oppressor. But the battle is now more than half over. By perseverance and determination we shall secure a victory which will emblazon the names of our fathers and brothers and sons who have fallen in the fight as heroes and martyrs through all time. If we falter they will be stigmatized as rebels and the blood shed on many battlefields will have been expended in vain. Our great leaders whom we admire, and reverence will be blackened as the Arnolds of the Great Rebellion. Our children will be called the sons of traitors and take a lower stand in the social scale than the greedy ravagers who divide their inheritance.

Let us leave despondency to the old men and women, to the skulkers and speculators. The courage and spirit of the South is in the army. The army is the people—its will is the peoples' will. Let us illustrate the devotion of our buried comrades and resolve to give our services to the country for the war be it long or short.[1]

Two months later, Walker was relieved of his command of the 3rd Military District and ordered to North Carolina to command a brigade of South Carolinians in the Department of the North Carolina and Southern Virginia. Private Milton Maxcy Leverett described his emotional farewell to the BVA. "General Walker has left us, and also a pleasant little note to the BVA in which he begs Capt. Stuart to assure the gentlemen of the B. Vol. Artillery that during my continuance with their command they have been linked to me by ties which may never be broken and connected with me by associations which I trust will never be forgotten. He shed tears the morning he was leaving."[2]

Since the Second Battle of the Pocotaligo in October 1862, the BVA continued its assignment defending the Charleston & Savannah Railroad from Federal incursions out of Hilton Head or Port Royal. While 1863 was a relatively inactive year for the battery, it did include an important change in command. Stephen Elliot was promoted to Major and reassigned to the command of Fort Sumter. In his place, Lt. H. M. Stuart was promoted to captain of the battery.

Son of a prominent St. Helena planter of the same name, Henry Middleton Stuart studied engineering at Harvard from 1853 to 1855, then transferred to the Medical College in Charleston, graduating with honors in 1857. Dr. "Hal" Stuart established his practice in Beaufort prior to the War then joined the BVA as a second lieutenant. Stuart would prove to be an extremely able captain, gaining the respect and trust of his men, leading them through the rest of the war until the final surrender.

In the first months of 1864, Stuart circulated the battery between make shift camps—Camp Beaufort and Camp Wilderness—near Pocotaligo and the vital Charleston & Savannah Railroad. By December, along with other Confederate batteries the BVA's two 12-pound howitzers were stationed in Grahamville, and its two 12-pound Napoleons on the Coosawatchie River covered the approaches to the railroad trestle at Pocotaligo.[3]

The unit's relative inactivity would now come to an end, as William Tecumseh Sherman's 60,000 Federal troops arrived at the doorstep of the Lowcountry in Savannah, poised for a final drive through the Carolinas. As he paused in front of Savannah, Sherman wired General-in-Chief Henry Halleck in Washington. He worried that the approximately 10,000 Confederate troops in South Carolina (including the BVA) commanded by Lt. General William Hardee might be sent south on the Charleston & Savannah Railroad to reinforce the Confederate defenders of Savannah. Might he order a force of Federal troops stationed in Hilton Head be dispatched to threaten the railroad, thus diverting Hardee from any move toward Savannah?

Major General John Foster, commander of the Union Department of the South headquartered in Hilton Head, was happy to oblige. Foster could muster an expeditionary force of about five-thousand men to support Sherman and make another attempt to breach the C&S Railroad.[4] The force, a cobbled together conglomeration of troops stationed in Florida, Georgia and South Carolina would be led by Major General John Porter Hatch. A West Point graduate, Hatch had commanded both artillery and infantry brigades in the Army of the Potomac and a division at the Battle of Antietam. Transferred to the Department of the South in 1864, he had the reputation as a brave and aggressive soldier, but not one known for superior tactical skills.[5]

With the added support of a naval brigade, his force would assemble at Hilton Head, be transported up the Broad River in naval transports and land at Boyd's Point near the present-day town of Ridgeland. From there, they would march approximately ten miles to Gopher Hill in Grahamville and tear up tracks of the Charleston & Savannah. Hatch had just two days to prepare his troops, and they were hurriedly issued cartridges and five days' rations.

The division was divided into two brigades. Brigadier General Edward Potter, a New York City lawyer commanded the First Brigade with elements of seven regiments including the 34th and 36th Colored Troops. For the first time, BVA soldiers would face African American soldiers in combat, some of whom were former slaves recruited from their own plantations on St. Helena Island.

The Second Brigade under the command of Harvard graduate Colonel Alfred Hartwell included African American troops of the 54th Massachusetts, veterans of the disastrous assault on Battery Wagner where it suffered a 40 percent casualty rate and the death of its martyred commander, Colonel Robert Gould Shaw. The expedition also included a naval brigade of 493 men led by Commander George Henry Preble.

At 2:00 AM on the morning of November 29, twenty-eight Union transports carrying the troops set out from Hilton Head Island in a dense fog, heading for Boyd's Landing. Very soon the combination of fog and incompetent piloting resulted in a substantial number of the transports becoming lost, while others were grounded in the Lowcountry mud. The delays were costly in time and men, and it was not until 4:00 PM that enough of Hatch's troops had landed to begin the march to Grahamville and the railroad.[6]

Confederate forces to contest the Federal landing were sparse, most them further inland to assist in the resistance to Sherman's advance. The few units immediately available to confront the Union force happened to be artillery batteries, among them the BVA, stationed at McPhersonville. The Confederate commander of the Third Military District, Colonel Charles Colcock, was fifty miles away supervising the construction of field works along the Savannah river. He planned to leave the next day to marry his fiancée in Robertville near Charleston when his second in command, Major John Jenkins, informed of the Union landing sounded the alarm, urgently requested reinforcements. Colcock replied that the 47th and 32nd Georgia regiments would be sent quickly.

In the meantime, a detachment from Company C of the Third South Carolina encamped in Grahamville was dispatched to shadow the Federal force as it marched along Boyd's Landing Road toward the railroad.[7] Two fortifications protected the approaches to Grahamville and the railroad. Two miles east of Grahamville, a ridge called Honey Hill overlooked a marshy, narrow creek with two earthen lunettes and trenches. Another set of fortifications near the junction of Bee's Creek and Grahamville Road guarded the approaches to Coosawatchie and Grahamville. Jenkins ordered the BVA to occupy the Bee's Creek Hill entrenchments, while other units were dispatched to Grahamville and toward Boyd's Landing to intercept the Union troops.[8]

As the morning progressed and Federal intentions became clearer, the BVA's position would change several times. After surveying the ground in

Twelve. *"Never have I seen such terrible havoc"*

and around Grahamville, Major Jenkins ordered three of the BVA's guns to leave the Bee's Creek entrenchments and reposition in Grahamville, closer to the railroad line. When Colonel Colcock arrived and assumed command, he sent the three guns to a new position on the right flank of a line of defense he was organizing on Honey Hill where they would help protect the Confederate right flank from being turned.

Meanwhile, confusion and disorientation plagued the Union march to Grahamville. Though pushing back Confederate cavalry skirmishers with ease, the Federals took a wrong turn heading south, missing the Bolan's Church road that led to Grahamville. Finally, at 2:00 AM the morning of the 30th, the exhausted troops found their bearings, but were too tired to continue. Beginning their march, the next morning, the delays provided the Confederates with valuable time to strengthen their position, and more time for reinforcements from Georgia and Charleston to arrive.

There were problems within the Confederate ranks as well. With only 600 soldiers on hand to oppose Hatch's 5,000, any hope for successfully holding back the Union incursion until the Georgia regiments arrived depended upon the timely appearance of 700 men of the Georgia Militia State Line troops under the command of Major General Gustavus W. Smith.

Smith's men were among the Confederate forces fighting Sherman in his march through Georgia. The unit had suffered grievous casualties, approximately 25 percent of its men and some of its best field officers. Arriving in Savannah on the 28th with his exhausted troops, Smith fierily resisted orders to proceed into South Carolina insisting Georgia militia were not permitted to fight outside of Georgia.

It was only with the intervention of General Hardee, overall commander of the Southern Department, that Smith relented. Hardee convinced Smith that the situation in Grahamville was desperate, and without reinforcements the C&S Railroad would be cut and dismantled, depriving Confederate forces of an effective means of transporting troops to resist Sherman. Savannah would be lost.[9]

Smith relented, and with only two, battered, old passenger cars available to transport his troops, he loaded as many as he could on the cars and headed to Grahamville. He was met there by Colonel Colcock who directed them quickly to positions on Honey Hill where he was consolidating his small force. Colcock ordered Stuart to rush all available guns of the BVA to entrenched positions on Honey Hill. After a brief meeting between Stuart, Jenkins and Colcock, Stuart was put in command of all confederate artillery units on the field including two guns of the Furman Artillery and a battery of the Lafayette Artillery which he positioned atop Honey Hill.[10]

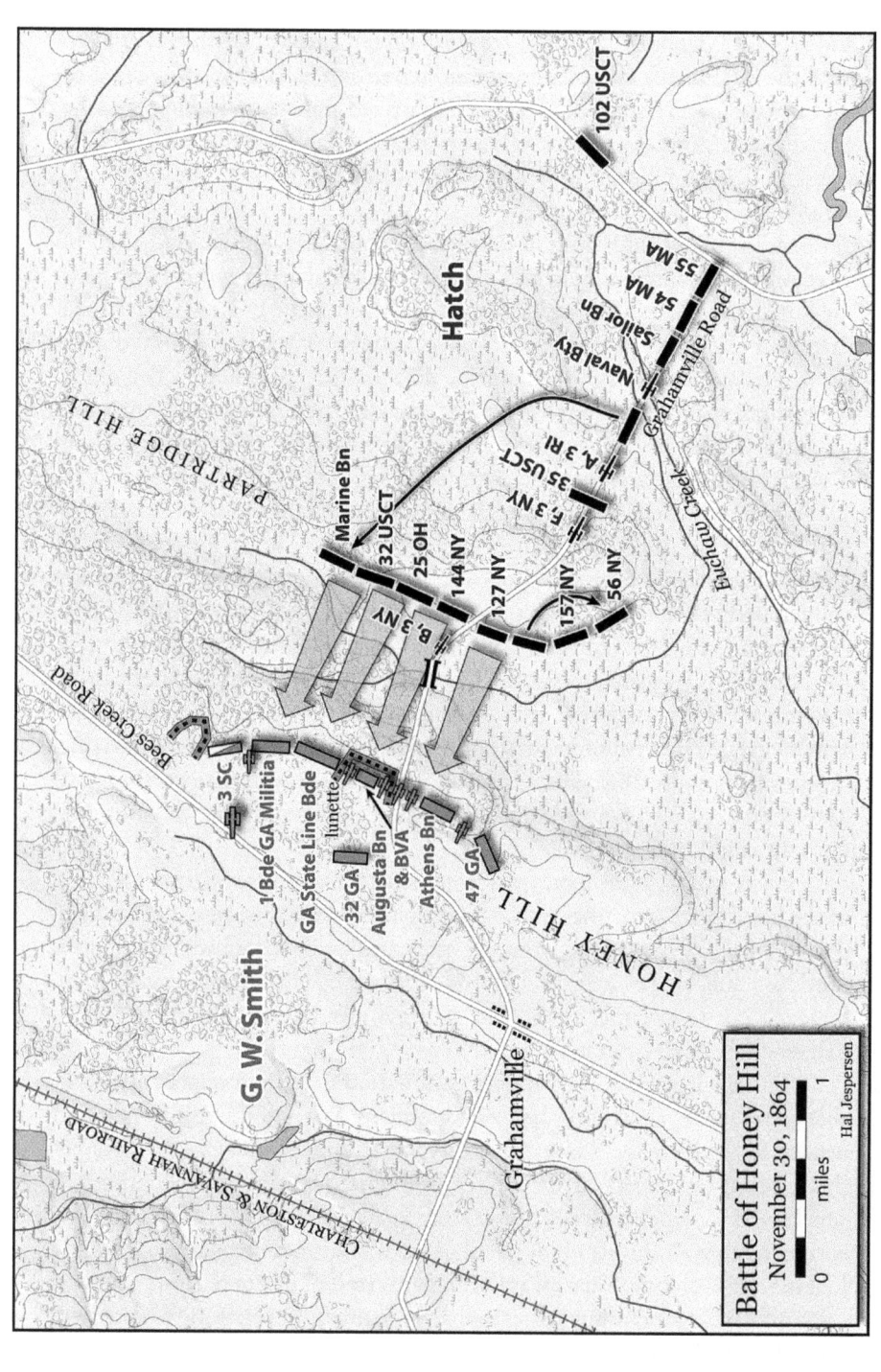

Twelve. "Never have I seen such terrible havoc"

Elevated defensive positions were always the preferred battlefield arrangement for artillery, enhancing its range and accuracy. Despite the modest size of the Confederate force at Honey Hill, about 2,000 men, the hill provided a formidable barrier to Union troops, strengthened further by the marshy stream troops would have to cross to assault the position, slowing them down and providing Confederate gunners with more time to rake their positions with deadly rounds of canister. As Hatch's troops approached, Stuart methodically paced off the distance from the cannons to the creek, computing the time to set the fuses of the case shot so that it would detonate in the ranks of the attacking Federals.[11]

The first assault of the Confederate position was made by the 35th U.S. Colored Troops led by Colonel James Beecher, brother of Harriet Beecher Stowe, author of *Uncle Tom's Cabin*. The 35th was one of the African American regiments recruited after President Abraham Lincoln's issuance of the Emancipation Proclamation on September 22, 1863. Like most of the African American regiments, they had been used primarily as laborers, kept out of combat due to doubts their white officers had about their fitness for battle.

That concern vanished for the 35th based on their performance in their first engagement of the war at the Battle of Olustee in Florida, in February 1864. The unit suffered an extremely high level of casualties with 230 men killed, wounded or missing, one of the highest of the war. (The high casualty rate was due in part to a brutal practice by some Confederate troops of killing wounded and captured African American soldiers. Letters and recollections of Confederates engaged at the Battle of Olustee suggest Confederates killed most of the black prisoners that were captured.)

As the 35th approached Honey Hill, buoyant and cheering as they readied for the assault, they were easy targets for the concentrated fire of the BVA and the other Confederate cannons. The guns' compact position in the line heightened the intensity of their fire. Major George Jackson, commanding the Augusta Reserve Battalion in position next to the BVA, described the impact of the first round of artillery fire on the 35th: "The enemy marching in fours appeared ... and the order was given to fire. I watched the effects of the shot. If the guns had been aimed at a painted target, and the shot had struck the bulls eye it would not have been any better. It was loaded with canister ... and did fearful execution."[12]

Captain Stuart gave detailed instructions to his gunners, ordering them to prepare five loads of double canister: "I ordered the artillery only to fire when they thought they could make a shell tell.... I had the men pile canisters under each gun. They were to be fired when I gave the command and loaded with double shot cannister and fired as quickly as possible.... The command to fire was given.... The six guns fired together, and the slaughter began."¹³ (Canister was the deadliest artillery fire for use against infantry at close range. Basically, a tin cylinder filled with iron balls, it had the effect of a giant shotgun, ripping large holes in the lines of approaching soldiers.)

The artillery, supplemented by rifles, mowed down the black troops in swathes. Colonel Beecher was hit in three places, his horse killed beneath him. Advised to leave the field by a surgeon, he refused, finally ordering his shattered regiment to retire. As the 35th retreated, the 55th Massachusetts USCT formed its lines for an attack. Colonel Hartwell led the regiment on his horse, yelling out to it "Follow your colors!" A soldier of the 55th later described the attack "like rushing into the very mouth of death up that road."¹⁴

A Confederate gunner near Stuart also described the scene:

> Suddenly there burst through the myrtle bushes a battle line of negro troops followed closely by another line in furious charge, all yelling like demons. Captain Stuart waited until they were about 100 yards distant, when he sent the full charge of canister from all ... guns into their ranks.
> I've seen wheat and oats go down before the scythe or mowing machine and that is the way the ranks, both first and second, fell beneath the hail of bullets.... The Negroes, as usual, formed the advance, and when the batteries opened ... this threw them into confusion, but ... order was quickly restored.... Thus the battle raged ... till dark.¹⁵

Colonel Hartwell described the chaos and devastating lethalness of the Confederate guns:

> The grape and canister became unsupportable. Captain Crane, acting aide, was killed, with his horse; Lieutenant Hill, second acting aide, was knocked off his horse by concussion; and my own horse was killed and fell on me. The road seemed to be swept of everything. I was pulled from under my horse and back by an officer and a man of the 55th Massachusetts, and during the time was hit in the boot heel by a shot that burned my ankle, and in the side by a spent grape shot that knocked me down and partially stunned me, and lodged in the coat; also, by a spent musket ball in the back, that lodged in the shirt; in consequence of which, I regret extremely to say, I was unable to give further orders ... and was taken to the rear.¹⁶

The fighting was chaotic, desperate and deafening a Confederate soldier later recalled: "The noise of the battle at this time was terrific, the artillery crashing away in the center, while volley after volley of musketry ran down both lines and were reverberating from the surrounding forests."¹⁷

As the 55th attacked the center of the Confederate line on Honey Hill, the 127th New York moved to the left of its line, crossing the creek in front of the hill. It was slow going on the soft, boggy soil through one-foot puddles of standing water, but gradually, the regiment gained a position that threatened to turn the Confederate's right flank.

Just as the regiment was ready to make its move against the flank, the 47th Georgia Regiment, whose train was delayed near Savannah, arrived on the field after a hurried march from the Grahamville and slammed into the oncoming Union regiment, forcing it back. As the fighting intensified, General Smith and Colonel Colcock were keenly aware their force was outnumbered, by over two to one. Though reinforcements from Augusta and Charleston had been promised, only a small detachment of the 32nd Georgia had arrived from Charleston. But although the Confederate line was thin, Union troops were never able to penetrate it. General Smith credited the firepower of the South Carolina batteries for the hardening of the Confederate line in his official report stating, "It was due to the South Carolina artillerists that I should say I have never seen [artillery] pieces more skillfully employed and gallantly served upon a different battlefield."[18]

Additional probes and thrusts were made by the Federals through the course of the day, but the Confederate lines on Honey Hill held. Then, at dusk, Union forces began to withdraw, ordered back to Boyd's Landing where they reformed in defensive lines until troop ships arrived to transport them back to Union lines.

On the morning of December 1, Confederate troops flooded over the battlefield. The devastation of the Confederate artillery was everywhere evident from the mutilated bodies, some missing heads or disemboweled, black soldiers piled on one another five deep in places.[19] A local resident described the grisly scene several weeks after the battle:

> They left their dead and dying scattered promiscuously from the church to the hill, numbering about eight hundred, something near half of them have been prepared to have been buried, the remainder are still lying upon the field as deserted by their comrades rendering the more frightful by their spectral appearance. The already dismal and gloomy swamp of this fatal section, the fit abode of alligators and other horrid monsters. There are more signs of bullets and shell to be seen here than ever I beheld before, every shrub, and tree from top to bottom were completely lacerated. The old church which was used by the yanks for hospital a slaughter house more than a church, great streams and puddles of blood are still there cold and clotted, with feet, legs, kneecaps, hands and arms lying scattered in and around its once consecrated walls.[20]

The Southerners stripped the dead soldiers of much needed rations and equipment. They found haversacks filled with pickled meats, sugar, coffee, clothing, dozens of rubberized blankets and ponchos, and 175 Enfield rifles.[21] Among the more desirable items left behind was Union Colonel

Harwell's saddle. The saddle was presented to Captain Stuart in appreciation for his exceptional management of Confederate artillery.

The presence of so many dead black soldiers was not lost on the Confederates and they could not resist a disdainful gesture to express their contempt for them. While the white soldiers were buried in shallow graves, the blacks were stripped of their clothes and belongings and left to rot unburied. Planters brought their slaves to the battleground to view the dead black soldiers and what could happen to them should they run away and join the Union army. There were three black prisoners from the 54th Massachusetts. Two were summarily executed, and the remaining one spared because of his claim to be from South Carolina and his desire to return to his home.[22]

For the BVA, the battle of Honey Hill represented the high-water mark of its service for the Confederacy. Captain Stuart had excelled in his management of the Confederate artillery, and the BVA was the cornerstone of the firepower of the Confederates in one of the most hotly contested battles in South Carolina.

Thirteen

"It is now a question of very few days"

Against the backdrop of William Tecumseh Sherman's army's epic and irrepressible march through the Carolinas, the Confederate victory at Honey Hill was little more than a minor skirmish and the last engagement in the Carolinas that the Confederates could claim a victory.

Under Sherman's command were 60,000 soldiers divided into two wings—the Army of Georgia under the command of Major General Henry Slocum and the Army of the Tennessee led by Major General Oliver Howard. The men were seasoned veterans, many of them having been in Sherman's command since the early years of the war and who affectionately referred to Sherman as "Uncle Billy." They would, and did, follow him anywhere.

To resist this juggernaut the Confederate President Jefferson Davis called upon General Joseph E. Johnston to replace John Bell Hood as commander of the army of the Tennessee. Johnston cobbled together all available units for a final rally near Charlotte, North Carolina. Johnston was not optimistic, writing to Robert E. Lee, "In my opinion these troops form an army too weak to cope with Sherman."[1]

Now facing the sobering reality of its deteriorating military position and the growing numbers of desertions, at least one desperate if fanciful measure was proposed. Colonel Ambrosio Gonzales, the Cuban revolutionary who served as the Department of South Carolina, Georgia and Florida's Chief of Artillery, floated a plan designed to defend South Carolina by using the Charleston & Savannah Railroad to insulate the state east of the railroad, including Charleston, from attack. In his plan, the BVA played a crucial role.

Gonazales estimated it would take as many as 30,000 men to adequately defend the coastal areas and Charleston and Savannah, a number far beyond Confederate means. Instead, he maintained, a much smaller force, as few as 2,000, could do the job if centrally located and "capable of moving rapidly along the lines of defense, and in time to meet any attacks, which can be done with proper arrangements, would meet all the requirements of a general defense and with great economy of men and means."²

And how would this rapid movement be achieved? By means of a "flying column," made up of 2,000 Georgia Infantry and two handpicked artillery batteries including the BVA. They would be transported along the Charleston & Savannah Railroad on fifty open platform cars which would carry their equipment at all times and move the troops rapidly where needed. The soldiers would be encamped at a Central location and drilled to respond quickly. Gonzales stated, "At a given signal, this body of 2,000 men with two batteries would be moving in half an hour ... upon any point between Charleston and Hardeeville, either of which, at both extremes, could be reached in two hours and of course the intermediate ones in proportionately less time." Gonzales's vision for this unit had all the markings of an elite guerrilla unit, and his choice for one of the two artillery units was the BVA which he described as one of "the two best armed and the two best companies in this State."³

Nothing ever became of the plan, and as it became clear to Gonzales the state would fall to Sherman, he urgently wrote to his mother-in-law to gather what belongings she could and leave her home quickly.

Confederate President Jefferson Davis called General Joseph Johnston out of retirement to replace John Bell Hood as commander of the Army of the Tennessee (Library of Congress).

> The So. Ca. R. R. [the Savannah & Charleston Railroad] will be in running order tomorrow evening. Thence forward everything can go and shall go at once that is to go that way. You have not one minute to lose for things material or immaterial. To move from here is now a question of very few days. I want Hattie and the children and nurse here at once, with whatever bedding and indispensable crockery and utensils they can

Thirteen. "It is now a question of very few days"

bring. It will relieve the house by that much and the movement of the rest will be more rapid and certain as well as much less troublesome. The balance of the family should follow as soon as possible. If you are not needed at Oak Lawn you had better come with Hattie, for here you are on the way to any point and in case of a miracle like that of the parting of the Red Sea might go back to Oak Lawn.[4]

Panic spread through the Lowcountry. In a letter to her sister, Gonzales's wife went so far as to suggest the family may have to seek refuge in a swamp.

> My dear Emmie,
> You will see when such matters as these are calmly discussed in what a condition our affairs are. The truth, the melancholy truth is ... that we have no troops to crush Sherman, that we have not heard of one word of help from Virginia and that the whole State is at the mercy of Sherman who is in the heart of it and can make raids as it pleases him. Gonzie has left us to see what we shall do. I have told him that I cannot remain here if the city is to be taken. Charleston is not Savannah, and I don't believe that there will be law and order.
> There is a place called "Marion" somewhere in the swamps where we may get shelter, but you have no idea of the difficulty in finding any place. The up country is crammed and no place can be said to be safe.[5]

A woman named Leila living in Robertville, South Carolina, northwest of Charleston, noted in a letter to her future husband, John Heidt of Savannah, that the planters in the area were relocating their slaves in anticipation of Sherman's army's inevitable arrival. She flailed out at Beauregard in reaction to a rumor he planned to abandon Charleston. "How can Gen. Beauregard entertain the idea for an instant? Surely he must know nothing about the topography of the country; and ignorance in him is criminal. He must intend to give up Charleston for how would it be possible to hold the city when the Yankees shaved the surrounding country? What makes him so blind."[6]

The BVA was among the remaining Confederate units making up an independent artillery battalion that with five-thousand infantry, were all that was left under the command of Lt. General William J. Hardee and his Department of South Carolina, Georgia and Florida. They were hurrying north to join Johnston and the remnants of the Army of the Tennessee.

Hardee was an ideal soldier to lead the retreat into North Carolina. Commandant of West Point for four years before the war, he authored a highly influential and widely used book on military tactics, *Rifle and Light Infantry Tactics*, more commonly referred to as *Hardee's Tactics*. Commissioned early in 1861 as a major general in the Confederate Army, he went on to serve with distinction commanding a Corps in the Army of the Tennessee, participating in significant battles including the battles of Perryville, Stones River, Chattanooga, and under Johnston in the Atlanta campaign. He was known for his reliability, good judgment and steady leadership. His expertise in tactics enabled him to manage the tactical retreat of his depleted army with skill, limiting casualties, maneuvering to slow Slocum's corps while keeping his army intact.

The BVA was one of the few battle ready veteran units among this army. Most of the rest of the soldiers—garrison troops from Charleston, heavy artillerymen from the coastal areas, and Georgia militia—had not had battle experience. There were a few depleted but experienced units on loan from the Army of Northern Virginia. Nonetheless, this force had seasoned leadership including the BVA's former captain, Stephen Elliott, now brigadier general, commanding a brigade and veteran cavalry led by South Carolinian Lt. General Wade Hampton and Major General Joseph Wheeler commanding the remnants of the Army of the Tennessee's cavalry.

As Hardee's two divisions headed north to join Johnston and the remnants of the army of the Tennessee, they were closely followed by part of the left wing of Sherman's army commanded by Major General Henry Slocum: approximately 20,000 men of the Slocum's 14th and 20th army corps. Hardee's force reached the area south of Fayetteville on March 9. That afternoon, Hardee met with General Johnston in the Fayetteville Hotel. Johnston initially thought that Sherman was heading directly north in the direction of the state capitol at Raleigh. Indeed, Sher-

Lt. General William J. Hardee commanded what was left of the Confederate Department of South Carolina, Georgia and Florida. The Beaufort Volunteer Artillery was among his 5,000 men desperately hurrying north to join Johnston and the remnants of the Army of the Tennessee (Library of Congress).

Thirteen. *"It is now a question of very few days"*

man sent Slocum's army in that direction to divert Johnston's attention from his actual objective, Goldsboro. In any case, Johnston needed Hardee to continue his holding action, buying Johnston more time to consolidate his scattered units of the Army of the Tennessee for a final confrontation with Sherman.

Time was working against Hardee as desertions continued to mount and state governors were panicking, recalling their states' units from Hardee's command. On the morning of the 10th of March, he abandoned his positions south of Fayetteville and marched his force into the town. It was a fortuitous move for the sake of his soldiers' morale. As Hardee's men marched through the town, many of the women of the town opened their doors, providing hot meals and tables stocked with food.

One of them, Sarah Tillinghast, recalled later, "Footsore, weary, dirty and hungry they came.... No time for them to cook rations.... So on that memorable 10th we all went to work as cooks for Hardee's army."[7] Some of the women made quick mends of uniforms, and two young sisters handed out sandwiches to the soldiers of the cavalry to grab as they rode by. Their mission of mercy was jarred by the sound of gunfire, as advanced elements of Sherman's army pushed into the outskirts of the town. A cavalry officer rode up to the girls telling them to return home as quickly as they could.[8]

The respite was short-lived for Hardee's men. Leaving Fayetteville on March 11 and marching north along the Raleigh Plank Road, they halted at Smithville at the junction of Raleigh and Goldsboro Roads to try to ascertain the direction of Slocum's advance.[9]

It is likely that some of the BVA's men used the time to write letters or perhaps, like the commander of their division, General McLaws, have their clothes washed and mended by their slaves.[10] Hardee later claimed he decided to make a stand there due to its position between the Cape Fear and Black rivers, natural protections of his flanks. He would force Sherman to show his intentions.

He needed to engage Sherman while he still had a command. A full brigade was recalled by Governor McGrath of South Carolina to return to their home state, and the rate of desertions had reached near catastrophic proportions. By March 15, the day of the Battle of Averasboro, the number of effective troops, about 6,500, were just half of the number available just one month ago.[11]

Hardee placed Wheeler's depleted corps of cavalry south of the main body of Hardy's troops to scout any advance of Slocum's army. It did not take long. Early in the morning of March 15, Hardee's cavalry commander, Lt.

General Wade Hampton, notified General William Taliaferro that Wheeler's men were being driven back by a substantial force of Federal cavalry. These were advance units of the second brigade of Major Judson Kilpatrick's Third Cavalry.[12]

Kilpatrick was a colorful if controversial cavalry commander with a record of as many defeats as victories and a penchant for recklessness. But he earned Sherman's confidence in the operations around Atlanta and was now leading his unit as a reconnaissance in force in advance of Slocum's wing of the army. To meet the threat Taliaferro moved Colonel Alfred Rhett's brigade forward to occupy a position straddling the Raleigh Plank Road. To provide artillery support to Rhett's right flank he ordered up one 12-pounder Napoleon gun of the BVA, and two 12-pounder howitzers of Le Gardeur's Battery.

As the BVA unlimbered, its former captain, Stephen Elliott, now brigadier general, deployed his brigade in line about 200 yards behind Rhett's brigade. Taliaferro's intention was to withdraw and reposition Rhett's men next to Elliott's line as soon as his supply train was safely behind the Confederate lines. Taliaferro was surprised when Hardee arrived on the field and ordered Rhett to maintain his position and push his skirmishers forward to actively contest the field.

Hardee was keenly aware that the troops in Taliaferro's division were largely untested in battle, and his move may have been motivated by a combination of reasons: a desire to provide his inexperienced soldiers with some battlefield experience in anticipation of a decisive battle after they had joined Johnston's Army of the Tennessee; and the more immediate necessity of buying time to establish a strong fallback position with McLaw's division of veterans.[13]

When Kilpatrick's full brigade came forward, the BVA cannon and those of LeGardeur's battery poured shells into the Federal line, answered by the cannons of Atkins section of the 10th Wisconsin Battery. Nightfall and heavy rains brought an end to the artillery duel that day and the battlefield quieted quickly. The rain continued through the night, creating conditions for the next day's battle that would have fatal consequences for the BVA. But for now, as the men of the BVA settled in for the night, the pleasant music of a brass band could be heard, that of the 2nd Massachusetts, just a few hundred yards away, serenading the men of both sides.

Rain and its attendant mud are the bane of Civil War artillery batteries, and on the gray, overcast morning of March 16, there had been plenty of both, with more to come. The most valuable asset of light artillery is its ability to move quickly, a benefit lost in the mud as the gun carriages and caissons mire in it and the horses and men strain to move the equipment forward. At those times, success in forward progress is measured in feet, not miles.

The BVA's lone 12-pounder Napoleon and LeGardeur's battery of two 12-pounder howitzers were in position protecting the right flank of Rhett's brigade, and in a perfect world, had they been able to maintain that position through the course of the battle, they might have been able to save men and equipment. But as it turned out, their little spot would be under the most intense and savage fire as any place on the battlefield.

Rhett's infantry on their left, now under the command of Col. William Butler (Rhett had been unceremoniously captured by the Federals the day before while scouting his troops' position) began the morning gamely, its skirmish line reinforced and pressing the 8th Indiana Cavalry of Colonel Thomas Jordan's brigade. Despite their repeating Spencer rifles, the 8th was soon pushed back, then quickly reinforced by Jordan with the 9th Pennsylvania Cavalry and the 2nd and 3rd Kentucky Cavalry regiments.[14]

The South Carolinians continued to press Kilpatrick but were pushed back. The tempo of the fighting on the Federal right continued with such intensity that Kilpatrick called up a full division to relieve Jordan, arriving just as Jordan's men were running out of ammunition.

The ground directly in front of Butler's position and that of the BVA was open fields, and remained unoccupied by Federals only briefly, until 9:00 AM, after which the remaining brigades of the 20th Army began to fall into line across the field. Six brigades from Major General William Ward's and Brigadier General Nathaniel Jackson's divisions poured onto the field and into position across from Butler—approximately 12,000 men facing the 1,051 men of Butler's brigade and the artillery battalion of the BVA and LeGardeur's batteries.

They were not on the battlefield long when Kilpatrick's cavalry on their right broke and retreated with Butler's South Carolinians in close pursuit. A volley of fire from a brigade on the left of Jackson's line stopped the South Carolinian's charge immediately, sending them back to their original position in disorder.

The battle quickly heated up as the Confederate batteries flung continuous volleys of shells into Slocum's corps on their front. With no protection from the Confederate artillery, Colonel Daniel Dustin ordered the men of his brigade to avoid artillery shells by flattening themselves on the ground. It was a chaotic and frightening scene. The shells "whizzed and burst dangerously ... close at hand" according to William McIntosh of the 22nd Wisconsin.[15]

For a while, the Confederate artillery was able to maintain a steady, deadly fire, but that was soon to change. By mid-morning, three of Slocum's 20th Corps batteries lumbered onto the fields and orchard of the Smith farm just south of the Confederate line, taking position on a rise less than 500 yards from the Confederates. With a clear line of fire, twelve Federal batteries slammed dozens of rounds of solid and exploding shot into the center and right of Butlers's line.

The effect on the BVA and LeGardeur's batteries was devastating. The screams and agony of their horses rose above the gunfire as all but one of the BVA's horses were killed and nine of LeGardeur's.[16] A Federal shell hit one of LeGardeur's limber chests filled with ammunition. The explosion killed or wounded many of the three batteries' men including BVA Private Wilson Hall, who lost his foot. (Hall joined the BVA when he was just sixteen years old. His mother tried to keep him out of the army, but she finally relented. Over the next four years, Hall participated in every major engagement of the BVA, from the Battle of Port Royal to the Battle of Honey Hill. His loss of blood was severe, and family members attributed his early death in 1873 to tuberculosis to a weakened condition from his war wound.)

The intensity of the fire and the explosion soon silenced the battalion, which in any case had exhausted most of its ammunition. It remained in its position in the South Carolina line until Butler's brigade was attacked on its right flank by an infantry brigade commanded by Colonel Henry Case. Case's movement to the right was masked by woods just 200 yards to the right of the BVA's position. Emerging from the woods and charging the Confederate flank on the run, his attack took Butler's brigade by surprise. Soon after that Dustin's brigade of Ward's division attacked Butler from the front. The Confederates responded with rifle fire so heavy it forced Dustin's regiments to make an oblique left march into the cover of woods and buildings of the nearby Smith farm. The delay was temporary, however, and soon the flank and the frontal attacks overwhelmed the Confederates, abandoning their position retreating quickly toward Hardee's second line of defense behind them.

But the retreat was not so simple for the BVA and LeGardeur's batteries. The few horses that had not been killed were quickly mired in the soft muddy ground as they struggled desperately to free their cannons and caissons amidst the bodies of the dead and injured men and horses littering the field. As time ran out the men were forced to abandon two of their three cannons: the BVA's 12-pounder Napoleon, and one of LeGardeur's 12-pounder howitzers. As soon as the Federals captured their position, they turned the cannons around and began firing on the fleeing Confederates.

As they attacked, the federal troops were surprised that they had re-

Thirteen. *"It is now a question of very few days"*

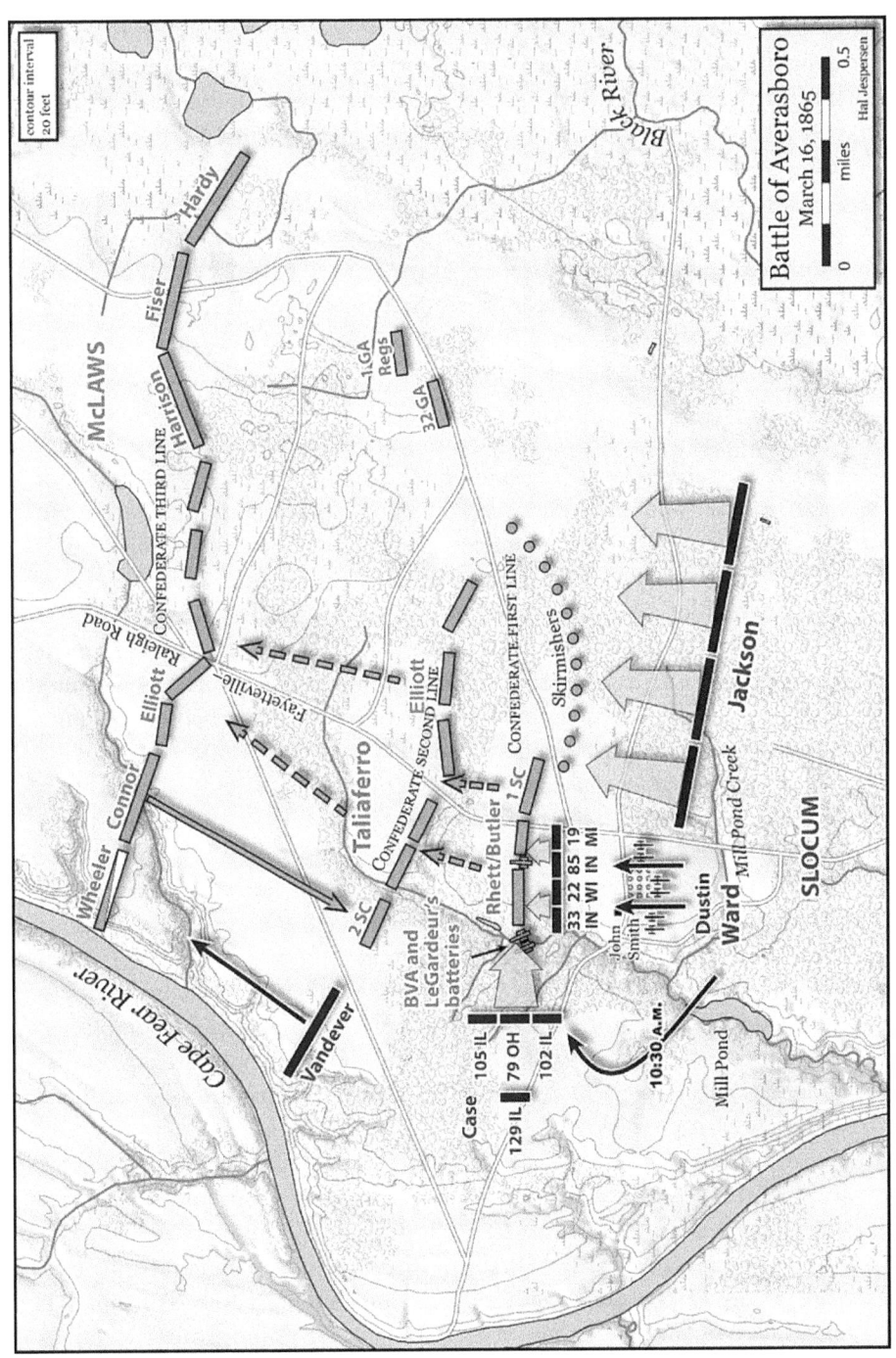

ceived no artillery fire. When they reached the Confederate works, they immediately viewed an appalling scene of carnage that made clear the reason for the stilled artillery. One private later wrote, "It was the terriblist [*sic*] slaughter of men that I ever witnessed." Sergeant Dickinson of the 22nd Wisconsin saw six white horses, "dead and horribly mangled which had evidently ... been hitched to the limber" that had exploded. "The gunners and drivers were laying about, what was left of them, mangled. A wounded Confederate gunner laid in the mud. He had been hit by a cannon ball from one of our guns, which had gone through at least six feet of earth works, it had torn off the whole right side of his body, and he begged of our men to shoot him, to put him out of misery and pain; but he only lived a few minutes."[17]

The remains of Rhett's brigade and the BVA fell back to Join Elliott's brigade anchoring Hardee's second line of defense. By now the full weight of the 20th Corps' infantry divisions and Kilpatrick's cavalry were in line and bearing down on Hardee's second line of defense. It was not long before that line disintegrated as well and fell back on the third line anchored by McLaw's division. Hardee's third and final line of defense was a strong one. With his left flank held by Wheeler's cavalry and protected from a flanking movement by the Cape Fear River, and his right flank similarly protected by a swamp hugging the Black River, his 8,000 troops were well entrenched in as strong a defensive position to be hoped for against Sherman's 20,000 soldiers.

An attempt was made by Vandever's brigade of Slocum's corps to turn Hardee's right flank in the mistaken belief that it was exposed. The attack was soon abandoned when it was clear that the Confederates were dug in all the way to the river. Further attempts to breach the line were hampered by the rains and muddy conditions preventing the full complement of Slocum's corps to reach the battlefield for a final attack.

After darkness, Hardee ordered his outnumbered command to evacuate the field to head north and join Johnston's forces. He had accomplished one part of his goal by delaying the advance of Sherman's 20th Corps, but at a high cost, suffering 500 casualties. Most of these casualties were artillery, including a battered BVA.

The BVA's exhausted men with the rest of Hardee's force marched toward Bentonville thirty miles away. There they would join Johnston's Army of the Tennessee for a final battle with Sherman. Opinions varied on their prospects. Captain Charles Inglesby of Rhett's brigade commented the men were "a sleepy, worn out, hungry and altogether unhappy body of men."[18] On the other hand, Major Burnett Rhett, commander of the artillery battalion in which the BVA was included, buoyed his men announcing to them as he

Thirteen. *"It is now a question of very few days"*

rode down the line that France had recognized the Confederacy and would soon send warships to break the Union blockade.[19]

March 19 was the day of the last major offensive of a Confederate army. Johnston had arrayed his diminishing forces in a wide arc south of Bentonville and west of the Bentonville Road. The line extended about one mile in a southeasterly direction facing Davis's corps of Sherman's army. The far, left end of the line was occupied by Butler's and Elliott's brigades, and the BVA in the artillery battalion of Major Rhett.

The "Last Grand Charge" of the Army of the Tennessee proceeded all along the line of the left wing of Johnston's army. Rhett and Elliot's brigades moved forward with the rest of the brigades of the right wing and would spear head an assault on the center of the Union line. Unaccountably, Rhett's artillery battalion with the BVA was left in reserve and never called upon to actively support Rhett's and Elliott's advance. This was especially curious in that the BVA was one the few veteran artillery battalions at Johnston's disposal.

Though the BVA was not be actively engaged in the final battle, its losses and suffering would continue in a deeply personal way during the surrender and the long journey home. It would be especially tragic for one of its number, Willie Hardee, General Hardee's son.

In 1864, Hardee had left school, desperately wanting to fight for the Confederacy. Assigned to a staff position and most of the time out of the line of fire, he thought an artillery assignment would provide him with better opportunities for action. In February 1865, the sixteen-year-old joined the BVA. He soon became disenchanted with the life of an artilleryman, and on the march from Averasboro to Bentonville, appealed to his father to allow him to join the 8th Texas Cavalry, the legendary Terry's Texas Rangers. He reluctantly assented, but only after the commanding general himself, Joseph Johnston, had agreed to offer Willie a staff position, an opportunity he politely declined.

The young Hardee soon had his horse and was in the midst of the battle. His father was called to the right flank of the Confederate line where a division of Sherman's troops had made a breakthrough. It took several hours for the Confederates to organize a successful counterattack, sending Sherman's troops back in disorder, and Hardee's pleasure at the success was hard to contain.

His buoyant feelings were soon dashed, however, when he saw Willie slumped forward on his horse, being supported by a fellow Ranger. A severe chest wound would prove mortal. He died on March 24. He was given a military funeral attended by his father and his former comrades in the BVA.[20]

Another BVA artilleryman fell at Bentonville. Though the BVA was held in reserve, one of its men, Private George Stoney, decided to fight with another unit. During the battle, while talking with Captain Edward Whaley of the 1st South Carolina Infantry, he was struck by an artillery shell that nearly cut him in two. Despite the severe injury, Stoney remained alive and conscious for a while. BVA corporal James Stuart, now attached to Hardee's staff, described the scene:

> Stuart Simkins, a Beaufort boy came up to me and said, "Jimmie, George Stoney has just been carried off the field mortally wounded".... He was just nineteen years old, a splendid boy developing into a very fine man. He died that night. None of his friends were with him, only a nurse.... The Beaufort Artillery were camped nearby when he died and did not know it until next morning. Here were all of his relatives and friends and schoolmates. The artillery was not in action that day.
>
> They found an old log house on the farm nearly with an earth floor. Here they dug a grave and his cousin Edward Cuthbert read the Episcopal service above him with the roar of battle still going on in the front. I have never heard that his grave was ever disturbed afterwards.[21]

At 10:00 AM the next day, March 21, Johnston's army began its retreat from Bentonville. The artillery including the BVA evacuated first, the infantry following the next day. The heavy, incessant rains continued, making progress slow. Despite the retreat; Johnston considered Bentonville a moral victory for his Army of the Tennessee—an army that had endured harsh criticism for its lackluster performance during the Atlanta campaign. Johnston wrote to Robert E. Lee on March 23, "The moral effect of these operations has been very beneficial. The spirit of the army is greatly improved and is now excellent."

However upbeat his assessment of morale, Johnston knew this was the beginning of the end, informing Lee in the same communication, "Sherman's force cannot be hindered by the small force I have. I can do no more than annoy him."

While Johnston's army marched north, events in Virginia were moving swiftly culminating in Lee's surrender of the remnant of the Army of Northern Virginia at Appomattox on April 9. But "Old Joe" hung on two more weeks, surrendering finally to Sherman on April 26, near Durham, North Carolina.

The BVA's bugler, Daniel Benjamin Rhodes, described later in his reminiscences what transpired during those two final two weeks:

> After this battle [Bentonville] we returned to Smithfield where we waited for two weeks in order that the remainder of the Army of the Tennessee might return and join us. Lieut. Rhodes, who had been off on sick furlough but had been detained at Raleigh by General Beauregard [commander of the Military Division of the West]

Thirteen. "It is now a question of very few days" 145

also joined us at Smithfield. From there we marched to Raleigh, the enemy following us. Between Raleigh and Greensboro, the first armistice took place. We tarried there for two days but no agreement having been arrived at, we started our retreat.

Imagine our feelings if you can. About Greensboro we heard rumors of General Lee's surrender. Our officers went to General Anderson [Brigadier General Robert H. Anderson, Anderson's brigade, Taliaferro's division] to find the truth about it. But he did not know anything. He would go and see. He did go and found it was really so. Then the second armistice was called, and terms were arranged.

We were then ordered to park our battery at Greensboro and turn in our horses to U.S. Agents and receive our paroles. Captain Stuart then turned the company over to Lieut. Rhodes to bring back to South Carolina as Capt. Stuart could rejoin his own family by a shorter route. Lieutenant Rhodes brought us back to Chester and discharged us there, comrades of four years then parting to see our scattered families and friends, finding refuge in every quarter of the State. We divided into squads to keep together as much as possible, some having no homes to return to.[22]

Private James R. Stuart described his journey to find his relatives:

I started for home. On my horse, my boy Flanders on another. We went first to Camden, S.C. where my Uncle Henry was and my sister Sarah. Then on the next day towards Edgefield. Flanders had a fever that night, so I got a farmer to give him a bed, and I slept on my blanket by the horses in the yard. We had to guard our horses with so many disbanded soldiers going home in every direction.

We reached Edgefield where my Aunts Sarah and Emily Barnwell were with their sister Aunt Annie, wife of Reverend Edward Walker, Rector there. There I left Flanders with his father Jack and went over to my mother in Georgia.

The war was ended.[23]

Epilogue
"Everything was going to confusion and ruin"

By the end of the war, most of the planters and their families had abandoned their plantations in St. Helena Island and Beaufort, never to return. Homes of BVA soldiers or their relatives in Beaufort had been confiscated and refitted for use by the occupying Federal forces. Ironically, the Steven Elliott house on Bay Street became the headquarters for the Union army newspaper, *New South*, a vehicle to publicize the efforts of the occupying Northerners on behalf of the newly freed slaves. Next door was the headquarters of the union commanding officer of the occupying forces, General Rufus Saxton. Cannoneer Lewis Reeves Sam's house became a hospital for African American patients and the homes of the Sams, Barnwells and Talbirds were converted to hospitals.

Confiscation of the St. Helena plantations by the United States government was moving slowly but inexorably by foreclosing on the properties for nonpayment of taxes. Many of the great plantations of the Fripps, Coffins and Chaplins were subdivided and sold in parcels of a size and cost that could be afforded by small farmers. The process of resale was hardly smooth or easy, yet by 1865, 347 blacks, most of them former slaves, had purchased land on St. Helena Island.

Only a handful of BVA veterans of the war returned to Beaufort to try to make a go of it, and those that did found a town transformed from the comfortable watering hole of the of the 1850s, to a "Yankee garrison ... [where] there are no white people ... and Negroes are occupying the houses."[1] Or as one former Hilton Head planter sarcastically put it, "The town is not fit for a white Lady to stay in, Yankees and negroes are all the rage."[2]

Captain Hal Stuart and his wife Sarah were one of the few families to return and remain in Beaufort; but by 1866 Sarah was disillusioned and depressed, writing to her aunt "things in Beaufort still seem very trying ... life is horrid there." She complained she had just one servant to cook and wash for her and care for her son.

Though about seventy-five of the original residents had returned, "no one seems to be in their own homes ... our dear old home is desolated and desecrated ... the negroes are now cutting our window sills for fire wood ... as our island homes and property are all given to our former slaves for three years and at the end of that time, our ruin will be complete."[3]

Captain Stuart became one of the most respected and successful men in Beaufort's postwar years. In addition to being elected captain of the reorganized BVA in 1876, he served on the vestry of St. Helena church for more than fifty years and was elected president of Beaufort College.[4]

Stephen Elliott's return to the family plantation in Beaufort was bittersweet and the welcome his former slaves gave him was a sign of the times. "Our negroes are living in great comfort," he confided to Mary Chesnut. "They were delighted to see me and treated me with overflowing affection. They waited on me as before, gave me beautiful breakfasts, splendid dinners etc. etc. But they firmly and respectfully informed me: 'We own this land now. Put it out of your head that it will ever be yours again.'"[5]

He found a small house for his wife Charlotte and three sons at Bay Point on Port Royal sound—a hut really—that he had used before the war for his fishing excursions. Indeed, he was left to fall back on his fishing to eke out a living. He ran for Congress and was defeated but was soon successful in his bid for election to the state legislature. Soon after that he was appointed the superintendent of transportation for the South Carolina Railroad in Aiken.

During the pivotal "Battle of the Crater" at Petersburg, he had been seriously injured, his right arm shattered. These and other injuries he had endured during the war fated him to a to a painful and precipitous decline in health that led to his death on February 21, 1866.

In death Elliott became an icon for many South Carolinians, and a potent symbol of the "lost cause" movement in South Carolina. In July 1873, the South Carolina Monument Association, made up primarily of women with a mission to remember and commemorate the Confederate cause, commissioned a monument to be erected across from the South Carolina capitol building in Columbia. The monument would be a homage to the individual Confederate soldier. It depicted a picket on guard holding his rifle upright with its bayonet fixed. Though it was meant to represent the common soldier, the model for the face of the soldier was that of Stephen Elliott.[6]

Perhaps it was Elliott's stoic resistance as commander of Fort Sumter that prompted this choice. William Trescott—the same Trescott that harangued the BVA at the Fourth of July banquet in 1858—was commissioned to compose the monument's inscription. The result was a model of "lost cause" ideals, its text reproduced on at least a dozen other monuments in the south and extolled by novelist Larry McMurtry as "as one of the noblest pieces of southern prose ever produced in the South."[7]

The inscription memorialized those soldiers who

> IN THE RARE HOURS OF IMPRISONMENT,
> IN THE HOPELESSNESS OF THE HOSPITAL
> IN THE SHORT, SHARP AGONY OF THE FIELD,
> FOUND SUPPORT AND CONSOLATION
> IN THE BELIEF
> THAT AT HOME THEY WOULD NOT BE FORGOTTEN
> RECOGNIZE THAT THESE WERE MEN
> WHOM POWER COULD NOT CORRUPT,
> WHOM DEATH COULD NOT TERRIFY,
> WHOM DEFEAT COULD NOT DISHONOR

Former BVA Ordnance Sergeant James Reeve Stuart described the difficult and disoriented time he experienced in the years immediately after the war:

> I tried to get a country school but failed. I went into Augusta, Georgia, and opened a studio and, queer enough, made about $1,500 in six months. But everything was going to confusion and ruin. My brother was out in charge of a plantation 20 miles away, by an old college mate, Mr. Tom Neely, and we all gathered there—his wife and six children, my mother and two aunts Sarah and Emily and our servants who had been with us all through the war, Jack and his wife, August and others. I managed to get some orders for portraits even here. But at the end of the year, Neely had to give up the place, so we all went to our old place, Beaufort, South Carolina. The old place swarmed with carpetbaggers and negroes. Our own homes stood there, but in the hands of others.[8]

Stuart would eventually move to Wisconsin and open a studio and pursue a successful career as an artist.

Assistant Surgeon Thomas Osborn Barnwell joined the BVA in May 1863 and served with the battery to the end of the war. After the war he settled in Adams Run in Christ Church Parish near modern day Mt. Pleasant, establishing a medical practice and partnering with his brother Edward planting rice.

Nathaniel Barnwell Fuller, "Nat," of the Beaufort District, started as a private with the BVA at the beginning of the war and was promoted to corporal in March 1862. Severely wounded at the second battle of the Pocotaligo, he was promoted to 3rd sergeant in April 1864 and served with the

BVA until the end of the war. After the war he became an Episcopal minister, serving in dioceses in South Carolina, Florida and Texas.

Sergeant Nathaniel Heyward Barnwell participated in every engagement of the BVA and made the crucial shot that sunk the George Washington gunboat. In June 1863, Major Stephen Elliott recommended him for promotion to second lieutenant, writing, "I certify that N. Heyward Barnwell has been in service since the commencement of the war; that he is a high-toned gentleman, and accomplished instructor in tactics and a cool and skillful gunner in battle. At Pocotaligo he served a piece with two men after the others been shot, and on a subsequent occasion ... destroyed a steamer [the USS *George Washington*] with the second shot from his gun." After the war he took up farming in South Carolina and Georgia.[9]

Barnwell's brother Arthur was one of the youngest members of the BVA, joining the battery in 1863 at the age of seventeen. Like many young members of a battery or regiment, he was assigned duty as the battery's guidon bearer. The guidon was a swallow-tailed marker flag used to identify the unit. While the responsibility of carrying the guidon was ostensibly an honor, it was a mixed blessing as well, as it was often the target of enemy guns during battle.

Stephen Barnwell, the son of the Reverend William H. W. Barnwell of Beaufort, may well have had the most colorful service of any members of the BVA outside of Stephen Elliott. Barnwell was the sergeant in charge of one of the cannons. He was assigned by Major Elliott to recover the guns from the sunken Federal gunboat, USS *George Washington*, and was successful in saving one of them.

When Elliott commanded Fort Sumter, he experimented with torpedoes for use against Federal ships blockading Charleston. He sent for Barnwell, George Stoney and James Reeves Stuart to assist him in these experiments.

When Elliott left Sumter for command in Virginia, Barnwell accompanied him as his aide until the end of the War. When Elliott was reassigned to South Carolina and division command in Lieutenant General Joseph Johnston's army in December 1864, Barnwell received a promotion to captain. Wounded at the Battle of Bentonville, he suffered a broken rib due to grape shot and was temporarily hospitalized in Greensboro.

Released from the hospital several weeks later, he reunited with his brothers Edward and Joseph and joined the entourage of Confederate President Jefferson Davis fleeing south to Georgia. When Davis and his escort were cornered in Irwinville, Georgia, Barnwell managed to escape by running through a thicket covered creek and making his way safely to Valdosta.

Forty years later, Mrs. Jefferson Davis inquired after him, asking a mutual friend, "Is little Stephen Barnwell alive? Tell me all you know of that gallant young soldier whom I shall never forget."[10]

Lt. Middleton Stuart Elliott also had a memorable climax to the war. A graduate of the Citadel and brother of Stephen Elliott, he began the war as a private in the BVA, then was detached from the BVA for assignment as an engineer receiving a lieutenancy in the Engineer Corps. He was for a while on the staff of the chief engineer at Savannah until October 1864 when he was transferred and promoted to staff officer with the headquarters of the Army of Northern Virginia at Petersburg. He was with the Army during its final retreat and surrender at Appomattox. After the war he married Ann Stuart Rhett and found a position as deputy collector of customs for Beaufort.

Henry DeSaussure Elliott enlisted in the BVA in July 1863 and served with it as a private for the duration of the War. After the war he attended the college of Charleston then moved to Beaufort where was a truck farmer on Cane Island. He later was appointed master of tugboats for Port Royal Sound.

Another DeSaussure, C. A. DeSaussure, was one of the youngest recruits of the BVA. He enlisted at age sixteen with the 6th South Carolina Infantry where his father served as assistant surgeon. After the six-month enlistment period he again followed his father into the 8th South Carolina Infantry. In November 1863, he transferred to the BVA.

Because of his young age, he ultimately became one of its last survivors. Employed most of his life with the Southern Railway and living in Memphis, Tennessee, he attained the position of commander-in-chief of the United Confederate Veterans at its annual reunion at Montgomery, Alabama in 1931. The UCV was the largest and most influential of the Confederate reunion groups in the United States with a membership in the tens of thousands. During the height of its influence in the 1890s, it promoted and funded the erection of monuments to the Confederate cause.

In a letter dated June 17, 1931, he acknowledged the invitation by the Steven Elliott Chapter of the UDC in Beaufort to attend its "Annual Celebration" of the BVA on June 27. The letter was addressed to Lieutenant Colonel Claud C. Smith, commanding officer of the 263rd Regiment of the United States Coastal Artillery of the South Carolina National Guard, the contemporary iteration of the BVA, and one of the organizers of the event. The significance of the commander of the regiment, as an official of the United States military, recognizing the BVA was not lost on DeSaussure as he wrote, "It has given me unalloyed pleasure to think of the continuance of the organization and its recognition, as of its basic worth, by the government."

In his letter, DeSaussure makes mention of another BVA survivor living in New Orleans, Charles Woodward Hutson. "I would be greatly pleased if C. W. Hutson ... could be there. Though still active, he is 90, and his means are quite limited." Hutson graduated from the South Carolina College (the forerunner of the University of South Carolina) in 1860 and was a private with the BVA throughout the entire war. After the war he joined the faculty of South Carolina College, then moved on to the University of Mississippi at Oxford as a professor of history and completed his academic career at the University of Texas, retiring to New Orleans.

Several BVA veterans found positions in the clergy of the Episcopal Church, including Stephen Elliott Barnwell, sergeant in the BVA, who served as an Episcopal priest in Georgia and Kentucky after the war.

BVA Sergeant Robert Barnwell Fuller, "Barney," was present at the firing on Fort Sumter and in the Battle of Port Royal. In June of 1863 he was detached from the unit to serve Elliott, then returned to the BVA in January 1864 and promoted to second lieutenant. After the war he returned to Beaufort and served as the Beaufort County treasurer.

Little was heard of the unit for a decade after the war during the active years of Reconstruction. While many of the old families with connections to the BVA left Beaufort permanently, some did return. What they found was a Beaufort in the process of transformation, and these changes were ominous to them.

Now many blacks held elective office serving in the state Senate and South Carolina House of Representatives, men like the former slave, John Bascomb, who represented Beaufort in the House of Representatives, and R. H. Gleaves, who served as Lieutenant Governor of South Carolina from 1872 to 1876.[11]

They were shocked to find that many of the occupying Union soldiers were black. Former Beaufort planter Robert Habersham complained that the "Negro meetings were plotting insurrection, murder and conflagration" and were scheming to ignite a war of the races.[12] And indeed, racial tension ran high in Beaufort and the surrounding parishes. The *Charleston Courier* in its October 19, 1865, edition reported "the owners of the lands are regarded as intruders and feel so insecure that they consider it unsafe to return with their families to their homes."

Sections of the mainland of Beaufort County were considered dangerous for blacks and whites. African American soldiers were special targets of white harassment according to Laura Towne, one of the leaders in the Port Royal Experiment on St. Helena Island who taught and provided aid to former slaves.

The black majority began the annual celebration of Emancipation Day on January 1. Hundreds of blacks participated in parades and heard speeches by political and military dignitaries. The National Military Cemetery was dedicated in Beaufort on May 31, 1877. There black soldiers would be interred, and the celebration of Memorial Day was inaugurated.

But the political climate was changing nationally with significant local consequences for Beaufort's African Americans. Soon after his election in 1876, President Rutherford B. Hayes ordered Federal troops withdrawn from the State House of South Carolina, troops mandated with the responsibility to protect black and white Republicans serving in state government. This action marked the beginning of the end for Reconstruction and the advances it had made for African Americans. The federal government would no longer be obligated to protect the Constitutional rights of its black citizens.

During Reconstruction, military units that fought for the Confederacy were banned from state service and discouraged from holding reunions. But with the Hayes order of 1876, the remaining veterans of the BVA in Beaufort felt emboldened to meet, and former Captain Henry Stuart began an effort to reorganize the unit.

Thus, on Tuesday, March 12, 1878, former members of the BVA met on the steps of the Beaufort County Courthouse. The *Beaufort Gazette* reported:

> In response to the call last week the resident members of the famous Beaufort Volunteer Artillery met at the office of the County Auditor Tuesday.... Captain H. M. Stuart, who led the Company through the late war was called to the chair and Mayor F. F. Sams was elected Secretary.... On motion of Mr. M. M. Hutson it was resolved that the Company be reorganized, an election was held resulting in the choice of Dr. H. M. Stuart as Captain; 1st Lieutenant, J. J. Rhodes; 2nd Lieutenant, R. B. Fuller. Captain Stuart was requested to communicate with the Adjutant General and inform him of the action of the Company and ask for instruction.
>
> Twenty-six veterans of the BVA attended the meeting and decided the Arsenal would be the unit's headquarters. By 1879, the unit's personnel numbered forty-eight.[13]

Not everyone was pleased at the resurgence of the BVA. Writing to BVA veteran Nathaniel "Nat" Barnwell, Hal Stuart commented: "No effort was made after the war to reorganize until 1878. Then the negroes (particularly the women) were so threatening in their talk. There were two colored companies in the town and no white organization. I took steps to reorganize the Company and succeeded beyond my expectation."

Over the coming decade the unit requested from the United States Navy the return of two brass cannons captured by the BVA in its ambush of the USS *George Washington*. Thus in 1881, nineteen years after the cannons were confiscated by the Navy, they were returned to Beaufort.

After the war, the BVA veterans commissioned a posthumous portrait of their former captain Stephen Elliott. Painted by his former friend and comrade-in-arms James Reeves Stuart, Elliott is depicted not with the BVA, but posed in front of the battered interior walls of Ft. Sumter which he commanded during the period of constant Union assaults to capture this ultimate symbol of Confederate defiance.

Meanwhile, Beaufort developed a reputation as a Reconstruction success story. The local economy flourished and blacks played a pivotal role in all aspects of its life as political leaders, soldiers and economic drivers. The BVA was one of the few, acceptable remnants of the old Confederacy. Like some other Confederate veteran organizations in the South, it survived and perpetuated its memory by finding a place in the reality of the new south and life in a reunited nation.

Nowhere was this more evident than its participation in the festivities surrounding the visit of former General and United States President Ulysses S. Grant on Emancipation Day in 1880. Grant was making a tour of the South and was greeted with enthusiasm in many southern communities. It was decided he would make a brief stop in Beaufort. A welcoming committee was hastily organized comprised of both former Confederate and African American soldiers, black political leaders and Northern and Southern merchants meant to symbolize the successful cooperation of races in this former bastion of secession and slavery.[14]

When he arrived a parade of elegant carriages accompanied the former president along Bay Street. And, as he approached the bluffs overlooking the river he saw the Beaufort Volunteer Artillery, commanded by Dr. Hal Stuart, welcoming him with a thirteen-gun salute.

* * *

On February 9, 1866, on Morris Island within sight of Charleston and Fort Sumter, the 1st South Carolina Volunteers, redesignated as the 33rd United States Colored Troops, was mustered out of service. Colonel Thomas Wentworth Higginson had long left his duty as its first commander, but his replacement, Lt. Colonel Charles Trowbridge, held a similar place in their esteem. For the occasion Colonel Trowbridge delivered an eloquent and heartfelt farewell to his troops in General Order Number One:

> COMRADES: The hour is at hand when we must separate forever, and nothing can take from us the pride we feel, when we look upon the history of the "First

South Carolina Volunteers," the first black regiment that ever bore arms in defense of freedom on the continent of America.

On the 9th day of May, 1862, at which time there were nearly four millions of your race in bondage, sanctioned by the laws of the land and protected by our flag,—on that day, in the face of the floods of prejudice that well-nigh deluged every avenue to manhood and true liberty, you came forth to do battle for your country and kindred.

For long and weary months, without pay or even the privilege of being recognized as soldiers, you labored on, only to be disbanded and sent to your homes without even a hope of reward, and when our country, necessitated by the deadly struggle with armed traitors, finally granted you the opportunity again to come in defense of the nation's life, the alacrity with which you responded to the call gave abundant evidence of your readiness to strike a manly blow for the liberty of your race. And from that little band of hopeful, trusting, brave men who gathered at Camp Saxton ... amidst the terrible prejudices that surrounded us, has grown an army of a hundred and forty thousand black soldiers, whose valor and heroism has won for your race a name which will live as long as the undying pages of history shall endure.

Soldiers, you have done your duty and acquitted yourselves like men who, actuated by such ennobling motives, could not fail; and as the result of your fidelity and obedience you have won your freedom, and now, how great the reward! It seems fitting to me that the last hours of our existence as a regiment should be passed amidst the unmarked graves of your comrades, at Fort Wagner. Near you rest the bones of Colonel Shaw, buried by an enemy's hand in the same grave with his black soldiers who fell at his side; where in the future your children's children will come on pilgrimages to do homage to the ashes of those who fell in this glorious struggle.

Now that you are to lay aside your arms, I adjure you, by the associations and history of the past, and the love you bear for your liberties ... to seek the paths of honesty, virtue, sobriety, and industry, and ... grow up to the full stature of American Citizens.[15]

In the postwar era, the men of the 1st South Carolina regiment would experience freedom for the first time, if not all of its fruits. Freedom, they would learn, did not necessarily guarantee equality. In the same year as the regiment's mustering out in 1866 the former states of the Confederacy were passing segregationist laws known as the Black Codes, designed to restrict blacks' freedoms and put in place onerous restrictions on wages.

Returning to their home states in Georgia, Florida and South Carolina, they married and raised families, and took up a variety of trades such as carpenters, tradesmen, farmers, preachers, entrepreneurs and politicians. One of the veterans, Thomas Long, served in Florida's state senate and sponsored a bill that established a public school system in the state. Prince Rivers began an ambitious career in South Carolina as a magistrate, a member of the state house of representatives and major general of the state militia.

Susie King Taylor married a soldier of Company E and for a while taught black children and adults in Savannah how to read and write before moving to Boston. There she worked as a servant, and actively organized relief work for the Grand Army of the Republic, a Union Veterans organization.

Charles Trowbridge returned to New York and served four terms as an alderman for the 10th Ward of Brooklyn before moving to Minneapolis in April 1882. On a return trip from a vacation in Florida, his ship docked briefly at Port Royal. Looking over the dockhands loading cotton, he was amazed to see Fred Brown, a sergeant of Company D, the very soldier that had saved Trowbridge's life on one of the Florida expeditions.

Trowbridge quickly ran to shore and threw his arms around Brown, delighted at this chance meeting of his old war comrade. The sight of a white and black man embracing was too much for two Southern "ladies" nearby. As Trowbridge waved farewell to Brown from the ship's upper deck, one of the women yelled out loudly for him and other passengers to hear, "Did you see that old white man kiss that nigger?"[16]

After the war Higginson did not return to the pulpit, but made a comfortable living speaking and writing, devoting himself to literary pursuits, most notably as an editor and friend of Emily Dickinson. A frequent contributor to the *Boston Globe* and *The Nation*, he found time to write more than 500 essays and edited thirty-five books, including a history of the United States, a novel, and, as a devoted supporter of women's rights, a column for the *Woman's Journal*. Living in Cambridge with his second wife, Mary Potter Thacher, he served two terms as a Republican representative to the Massachusetts legislature and made an unsuccessful bid for Congress.

His prewar credentials as a reformer and Renaissance man remained impeccable, with involvements in such diverse organizations as the Society of American Friends of Russian Freedom, the American Antiquarian Society, and the Intercollegiate Socialist Society. An advocate for the poor and the homeless, he was outspoken in his opposition to anti–semitism and anti–Catholicism.

In June 1867, the *Atlantic Monthly* published his article, "Negro Spirituals," where he described the Gullah-inspired spirituals he heard sung by the men of the 33rd during the war:

> Often in the starlit evening ... entering the camp, I have silently approached some glimmering fire, round which the dusky figures moved in the rhythmical ... dance the negroes call a "shout," chanting, often harshly, but always in the most perfect time, some monotonous refrain. Writing down in the darkness, as I best could,—

perhaps with my hand in the safe covert of my pocket,—the words of the song, I have afterwards carried it to my tent, like some captured bird or insect, and then, after examination, put it by. Or, summoning one of the men at some period of leisure,—Corporal Robert Sutton, for instance, whose iron memory held all the details of a song as if it were a ford or a forest,—I have completed the new specimen by supplying the absent parts.[17]

Characteristically, he gave credit to one of his men—Robert Sutton—as a collaborator. He was especially generous in his praise of one of the spirituals titled "I Know Moon Rise," commenting, "Never, it seems to me, since man first lived and suffered, was his infinite longing for peace uttered more plaintively."

Higginson died on May 9, 1911, at Cambridge. He received a military funeral, an honor guard of black soldiers, his casket draped in the worn, original flag of the First South Carolina Volunteers. We do not know the details of his burial, but perhaps we can imagine a black chorus singing in tribute to him the spiritual "I Know Moon Rise."

> I know moon-rise, I know star-rise
> Lay dis body down.
> I walk in de moonlight, I walk in de starlight,
> To lay dis body down.
> I'll walk in de graveyard, I'll walk through de graveyard,
> To lay dis body down.
> I'll lie in de grave and stretch out my arms;
> Lay dis body down.
> I go to de judgment in de evenin' of de day,
> When I lay dis body down;
> And my soul and your soul will meet in de day
> When I lay dis body down.

Appendix I: Rosters

Muster Roll, March 14, 1862, Beaufort Volunteer Artillery

Captain: Stephen Elliott
1st Lieutenant: Hal M. Stuart
Junior 1st Lieutenant: John J. Rhodes
Senior 2nd Lieutenant: J. A. Hamilton
Junior 2nd Lieutenant: John T. Baker
1st Sergeant Robert M. Fuller; 1st Sergeant C. H. Willcox; Quartermaster Sergeant C. H. Willcox; 1st Sergeant Benjamin Sloman; 2nd Sergeant R. B. Fuller; 3rd Sergeant John F. Chaplin; 4th Sergeant William Thompson; 5th Sergeant R. T. Sams; 6th Sergeant H. M. Fuller.

1st Corporal S. E. Barnwell; 2nd Corporal M. W. Fripp; 3rd Corporal James Reeves Stuart; 4th Corporal D. L. Thompson; 5th Corporal R. H. Barnwell; 6th Corporal B. E. Fuller; 7th Corporal J. V. Fickling; 8th Corporal John H. Fripp; 9th Corporal John F. Porteous; 10th Corporal J. S. Gibbs; 11th Corporal D. E. Durban; 12th Corporal Julius B. Bell. Artificer: John E. Talbird.

Privates

Benjamin C. Adams; J. S. Anderson; D. B. Baker; S. T. Baker; N. H. Barnwell; S. E. Barnwell; John Bell; S. E. Blount; S. E. Blount; H. E. Bold; Joseph W. Bold; P. B. Catherwood; A. V. Chaplin; C. W. Chaplin; J. E. Chaplin; M. P. Chaplin; W. A. Chaplin; Robert Oswald Choven; P. F. Cole; T. F. Cuthbert; William C. Danner; W. C. Davis; Thomas B. Ellis; Benjamin E. Farris; J. E. Fripp; M. J. Fripp; R. F. Fripp; P. D. Givens; L. H. Glover; Wilson E. Hall; John Jenkins; E. W. Joyce; J. W. Keyser; Asa Lawton; Judson Lawton; M. M. Leverett; A. Miller; P. D. Morcock; H. C. Morgan; H. Morris; E. N. Murdaugh; Charles A. Myers; S. E. McGrath; R. W. Norton; John Oswald; J. W. Patterson; W. H. Perryclear; T. S. Rhett; Albert Rhett; D. B. Rhodes; H. W. Rice; J. D. Richardson; Lewis Same; S. A. Sams; J. G. Sams; J. V. Sams; L. R. Sams; T. F.

Sams; George M. Stoney; W. E. Townsend; S. B. Trescott; H. F. Veitch; E. F. Walsh; R. Walther; John H. Webb; P. G. Webb; W. P. Willcox; H. Zealy.

Muster Roll, April 1865, Beaufort Volunteer Artillery

Captain: H. M. Stuart
Senior 1st Lieutenant: J. J. Rhodes
Junior 1st Lieutenant: J. T. Baker
Senior 2nd Lieutenant: R. M. Fuller
Junior 2nd Lieutenant: R. B. Fuller
Assistant Surgeon: T. O. Barnwell
Sergeant Major: J. Richardson
Quartermaster Sergeant: C. H. Willcox
1st Sergeant: B. W. Sloman
2nd Sergeant: N. H. Barnwell
3rd Sergeant: N. B. Fuller
4th Sergeant: H. M. Zealy
1st Corporal: M. W. Fripp
2nd Corporal: J. B. Bell
3rd Corporal: J. H. Fripp
4th Corporal: K. P. Lanneau
5th Corporal: W. H. Perryclear
6th Corporal: S. R. Stoney
7th Corporal: T. B. Ellis
8th Corporal: D. Hemphill
Bugler: D. B. Rhodes
Guidon: J. M. Brawley
Artificers: J. E. Talbird; A. Miller; B. E. Farris.

Privates

J. C. Adams; M. S. Adams; J. G. Allen; J. S. Anderson; S. T. Baker; J. S. Barker; A. Barnwell; M. S. Barnwell; E. A. Bell; John Bell; S. E. Blount; T. M. Blount; A. J. Boineau; S. Boineau; H. E. Bold; J. W. Bold; W. A. Branch; G. Brunson; A. Budden; J. Burnett; E. A. Carmichael; T. B. Catherwood; A. V. Chaplin; B. T. B. Chaplin; C. E. Chaplin; C. W. Chaplin; J. E. Chaplin; J. F. Chaplin; J. J. Chaplin; J. P. Chaplin; M. T. Chaplin; W. A. Chaplin; W. H. Chaplin; A. R. Chisolm; J. W. Colcock; T. T. Cole; H. Cunningham; P. D. Givens; W. M. Graham; R. H. Hagood; W. E. Hall; J. A. Hamilton; B. Hardee; J. F. Hardee; W. P. Hardee; F. S. Harley; P. T. Hayne; H. P. Holcombe; A. G. Holmes; C. W. Hutson; M. M. Hutson; W. M. Hutson; O. P.

Jackson; J. D. Jamison; D. Jenkins; M. Jenkins; T. F. Curtis; E. B. Cuthbert; E. P. Cuthbert; J. A. Cuthbert; R. Cuthbert; T. F. Cuthbert; W. C. Davis; C. A. DeSaussure; J. A. DeTreville; T. C. Dow; H. D. Elliott; J. V. Fickling; D. A. Fripp; M. J. Fripp; H. M. Fuller; R. M. Fuller Sr.; J. S. Gibbes; R. M. Gibbes; W. O. Jenkins; J. Jerald Jervey; A. W. Johnson; J. F. Johnson; C. W. Jones; E. A. Jones; G. Killian; G. D. Ladd; A. Lanneau; E. B. Lesesne; J. Mackey; S. E. McGrath; H. Mew; J. R. Mew; D. A. Miller; E. Mitchell; E. P. Moore; P. D. Morcock; C. H. Morgan; George Munro; F. W. Murdaugh; C. A. Myers; H. M. Myers; J. J. Neil; J. J. Patterson; J. W. Patterson; A. Rhett; J. R. Rhodes; D. P. Sams; F. F. Sams; J. G. Sams; J. V. Sams; L. R. Sams; S. A. Sams; T. F. Sams; E. B. Stoney; James Reeves Stuart; D. L. Thomson; William Thomson; W. H. Thomson; W. H. Townsend; H. F. Veitch; W. Verree; E. F. Walsh; W. P. Willcox; J. B. Willkie; W. B. Wilson.

First South Carolina Regiment Roster

Colonel

Thomas Wentworth Higginson

Major

James Strong

Captains

George Dolly, Robert Hamilton, William James, Levi Metcalf, William Randolph, James Rogers, James Tonking, Charles Trowbridge, Henry Whitney.

Adjutant

George Dewhurst

First Lieutenants

George Chamberlain, Charles Davis, George Dewhurst, William Donilson, Albert Ferrell, Jesse Fisher, Mathew Hall, James O'Neill, James Pomeroy, Enoch Robbins, William Stockdale, Albert Terrell, Joseph Thibadeau, Albert Tirrell, Chauncey Webster, Ephraim White.

Second Lieutenants

Aaron Brown, Asa Childs, Robert Davis, James Furman, Robert Gaston, Frederick Goodrich, Frank Gould, Charles Hooper, William Hyde,

Benjamin Manning, Eli Merriam, Charles Parker, Niles Parker, Wallace Sampson, Mirand Saxton, John Searles, John Selvage, John Thompson, John Trowbridge, Harry West, James West, Nelson White, Earl Wilber, Henry Wood.

Sergeants

Abram Baker, Fortune Baker, Henry Beach, Robert Bolin, Frederick Brown, Isaiah Brown, Ned Burk, Lazarus Fields, Thomas Fields, Edward Hyde, Abraham Jackson, Clarence Kennon, James Lang, William McCrae, Henry McIntire, Isaac Middleton, Adam Miller, John Mills, George Mitchell, Samuel Morse, Barcus Phoenix, Prince Rivers, Julius Shemeltella, Leonard Small, Daniel Spaulding, William Tompkins, Robert Vondross, Cuffee Washington, Paul White, Harry Williams, Jacob Wilson, Cato Wright.

Corporals

Henry Adams, Caesar Allston, John Bennett, Eli Billinger, Andrew Bryant, Dick Camble, Samuel Coen, Simon Cryer, Nero Cuthbert, Jupiter Eastling, Redick Evans, William Felder, Stephen Forester, Edward Frazier, Aaron Fuller, William Grant, Henry Gray, Frank Grayson, Edward Green, May Green, Richard Green, Henry Grey, David Hall, Joseph Holder, Major Howard, William Jackson, Isaac Jenkins, July Jenkins, Prince Lampkins, Abraham Lancaster, William Lang, William Latsin, Thomas Long, William Long, Benjamin Martin, John Martin, William Middleton, Peter Miller, Chance Mitchell, George Moses, Andrew Murray, Edward Peam, Fred Peterson, Robert Powell, Moses Rhoads, Moses Rhodes, John Rivers, Hamilton Robison, Jonas Simmons, Loudon Simmons, Ishmael Small, Benjamin Smith, Joshua Stewart, Solomon Stuart, Robert Sutton, Charles Talbot, Jack Tumor, Henry Vaught, James Walker, Samuel Washington, Charles Wiley, William Williams, April Wise.

Privates

Randolph Abbott, John Abrams, August Acorn, Braddock Adams, David Adams, Henry Adams, James Adams, John Adams, Philip Adams, Richard Adams, Scipio Adams, William Adams, Braddock Adnes, Cato Aids, Joseph Aiken, August Aikens, Jonas Aikins, Lazarus Aikins, August Akens, Fred Albert, Prince Albert, Frank Albertee, Scipio Albright, Charles Alexander, William Alfred, Doctor Allen, John Allman, Caesar Allston, Charles Allston, Daniel Allston, Scipio Allston, William Allston, Andrew Anderson, Barrick Anderson, Charles Anderson, Clifford Anderson, James Anderson, Jeremiah Anderson, Paul Anderson, Robert Anderson, Samuel Anderson,

Thomas Anderson, John Andrews, Charles Armstrong, Edward Atkins, Amos Atkinson, Frank Aukram, Scipio Austin, Henry Baker, Irvin Baker, Sandy Baker, Thomas Baker, William Baker, John Balony, Eric Bandridge, Grantville Barber, Anthony Barnwell, Febb Barnwell, Paul Barnwell, Sam Baro, Primas Bawack, James Bayley, London Bayley, Samuel Beasley, Henry Belfast, Allen Bell, Nicholas Benjamin, Paris Benjamin, William Benjamin, Josiah Bennett, Paul Billy, Charles Binyard, Luke Bird, Taffy Bird, Joseph Black, Abram Blake, John Blake, George Bland, Joseph Blocker, Nicholas Boen, Middleton Bolton, John Bonketon, John Boston, Prince Boyde, David Bram, Ham Bran, Jeff Brane, Adam Brewin, Moses Brewin, Nat Brewin, Anthony Bright, Jack Brisbane, Isaac Brisburn, Campbell Bristen, Cato Brooks, Quabner Brooks, Abel Brown, Abram Brown, Alfred Brown, August Brown, Barnwell Brown, Cato Brown, Chester Brown, Dick Brown, Edmund Brown, George Brown, Harry Brown, Henry Brown, Jacob Brown, James Brown, James Brown, James Brown, John Brown, John Brown, Josiah Brown, Peter Brown, Philip Brown, Phillip Brown, Richard Brown, Samuel Brown, Sandy Brown, Somers Brown, Thomas Brown, William Brown, York Brown, John Brownson, Henry Brush, Hamilton Bruton, David Bryan, Frank Bryan, Abraham Bryant, Andrew Bryant, Charles Bryant, Samson Bryant, Tom Bryant, Isaac Buckster, John Bunch, August Burke, Jack Burns, Primus Burns, Samson Burton, Bill Butler, Thomas Butler, Thomas Butler, Joseph Calhoun, Aaron Callum, Fortman Camble, Parson Camble, Toney Camble, York Camble, Augustus Campbell, Bristow Campbell, Frank Campbell, Hampus Canada, Mike Capers, March Carrison, Scipio Carroll, Cain Carter, James Cashman, Joseph Caswell, Abram Chaplin, Baltimore Chaplin, Chance Chaplin, James Chaplin, July Chaplin, June Chaplin, March Chaplin, Toney Chaplin, Ansel Chatman, James Childs, Benjamin Chisholm, Chester Chisholm, Kitt Chisholm, Stuart Chisholm, Paul Chism, Peter Chism, Peter Chism, Peter Chisom, Aaron Christopher, Mark Clark, Philip Clemment, Edmund Cloud, James Coalman, April Coen, Elie Coen, Israel Coen, Antony Coffin, Thomas Colcock, Bill Coleman, Joshua Collins, Edward Colvin, Doctor Cook, Moses Cook, Butter Cookson, Denis Cooper, Kane Cooper, Robert Cooper, Freeman Copeland, Thomas Cornelius, Ellis Cousins, Green Cousins, Manuel Cox, James Coyle, Abner Crawford, Samuel Crawford, August Crayton, Smart Crumbie, Joseph Cryer, William Cummings, Benissett Cupper, Samson Cuthbert, Charles Cyrus, Abraham Dallagall, George Daniel, Peter Danno, Jack Darner, Augustus Dorsey, Gilbert Davenport, Henry Davenport, Cippio Davis, Edward Davis, James Davis, Samuel Davis, Silliam Davison, Augustus Dawsey, James Dawson, Cuffee Day, Richard Days, Henry Dean, John Deas, Robert Defoe, Barilt Delancy, Abraham Delegall, John Delifers, Horace Delong, Moses Demmick,

Washington Demry, John Dens, Joseph Derry, William Devines, Henry Dial, John Dierce, Robert Dingle, Robert Dingley, Martin Dixon, Joseph Doe, Jake Dorrester, Charles Dorsey, Benjamin Drayton, Kit Duke, Caesar Dunham, Charles Dunham, Manson Dunham, Andrew Dusane, Henry Dyall, Billy Eddy, Paris Eddy, James Edwards, Middleton Edwards, Olin Edwards, Robert Edwards, Adam Elbert, January Elliott, Richard Ellis, Toby Ellis, Thomas Elmone, Frank Emberson, William English, Samuel Enlius, Gabriel Eugee, Samuel Eulins, John Evans, Ishmael Everett, Samuel Ewlins, William Farmer, Stephany Feelins, Mingo Felton, Edward Ferguson, Hamilton Ferguson, Lewis Field, Paul Field, Adam Fields, Daniel Fields, Lazarus Fields, Robert Fields, Adam Filer, Richard Finick, Henry Fisher, Moses Fisher, Davis Fleming, Prince Fleming, Walter Flowers, Adam Floyd, Caesar Floyd, Charles Floyd, Jack Floyd, Jerry Floyd, Benjamin Forester, Jacob Forester, Charles Fowler, Robert Frampton, Benjamin Francis, Claret Francis, Cato Frazier, George Frazier, Jeffrey Frazier, Joshua Frazier, Noah Frazier, Samuel Frazier, Shadroc Frazor, Robert Freeman, Frederick Fripp, Ishmael Fripp, Jonas Fripp, Quash Fripp, Renta Fripp, Simon Fripp, Thomas Fripp, Friday Frost, Abram Fuller, Cuffey Fuller, Gilbert Fuller, Ishmael Fuller, James Fuller, Richard Fuller, Hamilton Furguson, Bony Gadsden, William Gadsden, Simon Gadson, William Gaines, Benjamin Gardner, Frank Gardner, Paris Gardner, Henry Garnet, Alfred Garrett, John Garret, Ishmael Gaut, Will Gaylor, Steppeny Geddes, Andrew General, Ajax George, August Getters, Emanuel Getters, Ruben Gibbens, Samuel Gibbons, Norris Gibson, Richard Gibson, John Giddings, Benjamin Giger, Can Ginlark, Judge Goff, Edward Gold, Peter Gold, Charles Gomes, Robert Goodwin, Green Gordon, Handy Gould, Edward Gould, Peter Gould, Handy Gowd, Ansel Graham, William Graham, James Grand, Abram Grant, Charles Grant, Daniel Grant, James Grant, Joseph Grant, Lester Grant, Prince Grant, Simon Grant, William Grant, William Grant, Daniel Grason, Henry Gray, Frank Grayson, James Grayson, Witlow Grayson, Amos Green, Benjamin Green, Bozan Green, Cato Green, David Green, Edward Green, George Green, Hilliard Green, Jack Green, Jackson Green, Jackson Green, John Green, Joseph Green, Joseph Green, July Green, Luck Green, Quaker Green, Richard Green, Samuel Green, Samuel Green, James Gregg, Nathan Grier, Robert Griffin, Caesar Grocen, Simon Grove, Henry Groves, Lancaster Habishen, Francis Hagee, Frank Hagen, Ansel Haggard, Carolina Haines, Joseph Haines, Nathan Haines, James Hains, Alexander Hall, Ambrose Hall, Essex Hall, Robert Halsey, Edward Hamblin, Abram Hamilton, Carolina Hamilton, Frederick Hamilton, Robert Hamilton, Sandy Hamilton, David Hammon, Joseph Hammon, Robert Hampton, Wade Hampton, Thomas Hanandos, William Happy, Luke Haris,

Henry Harker, Richard Harner, Arthur Harris, Edmund Harris, George Harris, George Harris, George Harris, Isaac Harris, William Harris, Henry Harrison, John Harrison, Philip Hartley, Ned Hartson, Richard Harver, Cyrus Hawkins, Frank Haynes, Henry Haynes, James Haynes, Robert Haynes, Scipio Hayward, Abraham Haywood, Adam Haywood, Edward Haywood, James Haywood, Jerry Haywood, Mike Haywood, Paul Haywood, Richard Haywood, Scipio Haywood, Simon Haywood, Jacob Hazard, Ansel Hazzard, Benjamin Hazzard, Joel Henderson, John Henry, William Herb, Charles Herron, Abel Hewitt, William Hewlin, Cupid Heywood, Mike Heywood, Richard Hicks, Jefferson Hill, John Hill, Samuel Hill, James Hills, Jeremiah Hines, Lancaster Hobisher, Henry Hodge, John Hodge, George Hodges, John Hodges, Thomas Hodges, Joseph Holder, Charles Holmes, Richard Holmes, Adam Hooper, Cornelius Hopkins, William Hopkins, Peter Hosendove, David Houston, Jeff Houston, Samuel Houston, Charles Howard, Major Howard, Richard Howard, Richard Howard, Scipio Howard, Turner Ho, Aaron Hudson, Shadrick Hudson, Francis Hugee, Joseph Hughes, Ambrose Hull, Arch Hull, Edward Humphreys, Archie Hunter, Joseph Hunter, Robert Hunter, Wallace Hunter, William Hurb, Ambrose Hurl, Ned Hurtson, Abraham Jackson, Abram Jackson, Anthony Jackson, Caesar Jackson, Cuffee Jackson, Edward Jackson, Ephraim Jackson, Jake Jackson, Nathaniel Jackson, Robert Jackson, Samuel Jackson, William Jackson, Cain Jenkins, Chancy Jenkins, Henry Jenkins, Isaac Jenkins, Isaac Jenkins, Isaac Jenkins, James Jenkins, John Jenkins, Lewis Jenkins, Peter Jenkins, Sanco Jenkins, Sharper Jenkins, Thomas Jenkins, Tony Jenkins, Joseph Jennings, Abraham Jewell, Damond Johns, Richard Johns, Abram Johnson, Ceazer Johnson, Isaac Johnson, Josiah Johnson, Moses Johnson, Ned Johnson, Peter Johnson, Samuel Johnson, Titus Johnson, William Johnson, William Johnson, Peter Joiner, Thomas Joiner, Cambric Jones, Cato Jones, Davis Jones, Frederick Jones, Hasley Jones, Henry Jones, Jupiter Jones, Killis Jones, Marcus Jones, Ned Jones, Paul Jones, Warren Jones, Moses Joy, John Judge, Caesar Keat, Samuel Kella, Aaron Kellum, Esau Kelson, Esau Kilson, Andrew King, Benjamin King, George King, Harry King, Henry King, James King, James King, Lankaster King, Ned King, Paul King, Minus Kirk, William Knight, James Knowlin, Edward Lamkins, Backus Lance, Benjamin Lane, Louden Langley, Jacob Larnes, Jack Latsin, Stephson Latson, Adam Laud, Harry Lawns, Albert Lawrence, Jacob Lawrence, John Layem, Alexander Layen, Henry Lee, John Lee, Peter Lee, Wesley Lee, William Lee, James Lemon, James Lencey, Smart Lewis, Stephen Likeness, James Lincey, Abraham Lincoln, Dublin Little, Lew Little, Prince Lloyd, Peter Lock, Jackson Long, Rodrick Long, Bounty Lorraine, Elias Lottery, Adam Loud, Bounty Louine, Robert Loundes, Spark

Loundes, Benjamin Low, Robert Lowndes, Spark Lowndes, Harry Lowns, Felix Loyd, James Lurcey, John Lycurgus, Edmon Mack, Samuel Mack, William Mack, Daniel Mackintosh, Pompey McCloe, Charles Madison, Charles Madison, Zachariah Magill, Solomon Major, Benjamin Managault, Benjamin Manego, Mingo Manigo, Peter Manigo, Morris Manning, Albert Manuel, Jack Manuel, John Mapson, John Mapson, Isaack Mark, Robert Mark, Samuel Mark, Ward Markham, Henrick Markteer, Abram Martin, Abram Martin, Marianna Martin, Samuel Martin, Samuel Martis, Benjamin Mason, Cesar Mason, Henry Mason, Alix Maxwell, Benjamin Maxwell, Benjamin Maxwell, Edward Maxwell, James Maxwell, Peer Maxwell, William McArthur, William McCarter, Wiley McClelland, Pompey McCloe, Joshua McCormick, Cruel McCrae, Joseph McCrea, Charles McCree, Tecumseh McDonald, Hope McEntryre, Zachariah McGill, August McIntosh, Daniel McIntosh, Robert McIntosh, Simon McIntosh, William McKenna, Richard McKinney, July McKnight, Paul McKnight, Toby McKnight, Henry McMillen, Henry McMiller, Poke McPherson, Ishmael McPherson, Levi McQuane, William McQuane, Charles McQueen, Cowell McRae, Gilbert McRae, Joseph McRae, Crowell McRay, Gilbert McRay, Gabriel Means, Gabriel Meens, June Mengen, Simon Mention, Jeffery Merriam, Levi Metcalf, Paul Midas, Daniel Middleton, George Middleton, Gordon Middleton, Isaac Middleton, Jack Middleton, Lemas Middleton, Sam Middleton, Scipio Middleton, Albert Miers, Aaron Mike, Charles Mike, Moses Mike, Henry Milledge, George Miller, Joseph Miller, Lewis Miller, Paul Miller, Scipio Miller, Thomas Miller, Gloster Mills, John Mills, William Mills, William Minton, Albert Mirs, Calvin Mires, Joseph Mitchel, Chance Mitchell, George Mitchell, Jerry Mitchell, Scipio Mitchell, Henry Mixen, James Monroe, Isaac Moody, Whitman Moore, James Mootra, William Moran, Samuel Morant, William Morant, Alexander Morran, Stephen Morrill, Cato Morris, Gibson Morris, John Morris, Primus Morris, William Morris, Ben Moultrie, Henry Mungen, Mosses Mungen, June Mungeon, Henry Munger, Henry Mungin, Shedrick Mungin, James Munroe, Andrew Murray, Charles Murray, Albert Myers, Benjamin Myers, Charles Myers, James Myers, Joseph Myers, Toney Myers, William Myers, Lewis Napoleon, Martin Nateel, Sabe Nateel, Josiah Navels, Isaac Neel, Isaac Neil, Jeffery Nerriani, John Nesbit, Sharper Nesbit, Abner Nichols, William Night, Syke Nightingale, George Noble, William Noble, William Nugent, Samuel O'Neil, Samuel Osburn, Samuel Osburn, Jr., Thomas Oswald, Charles Panary, Benjamin Papina, William Papina, Ben Parker, Jack Parker, Peter Parker, Davis Parkman, Hope Parkman, Moses Parkman, Thomas Parkman, Charles Parrary, Peter Parson, William Parson, Stephen Pascall, Stephen Paterson, Alexander Patterson, Henry Patterson, Pomfrey Patterson,

Billy Paul, Samuel Payton, Charles Penary, Samuel Pulling, John Quincy, Joseph Ravenel, Jacob Raws, Albert Rayford, Charles Raymond, Benjamin Read, Daniel Reddin, Taylor Redick, Edmond Reding, Benjamin Reed, Kuggo Reed, Stepney Reynolds, Jacob Richards, Aleck Richardson, George Richardson, Joseph Richardson, Richard Richardson, Thomas Richardson, Daniel Riley, Toby Riggs, Agrippa Riley, Jacob Riley, George Rivers, Jack Rivers, John Rivers, Glasgon Roberts, John Roberts, Samuel Roberts, Samuel Roberts, Moses Robertson, Abram Robinson, Abram Robinson, Cato Robinson, Hamilton Robinson, Hamilton Robinson, Isaac Robinson, James Robinson, Jeffrey Robinson, John Robinson, Joseph Robinson, Moses Robinson, Peter Robinson, Prince Robinson, Richard Robinson, Statia Robinson, William Robinson, John Robison, Edward Rockingbough, Benjamin Rodan, Bartese Rodney, William Rogers, Wiley Roon, Fortune Ross, Jacob Rowels, Sambo Rulidge, Jeff Rump, Jackson Ryals, John Ryals, Albert Sammis, Bryant Sampson, James Sanches, Simon Sanches, James Sannus, Manuel Sansas, James Sansus, Toby Sargent, Jerry Savage, Ishmael Scott, James Scott, Richard Scott, Rodwell Scott, Guy Scribbius, Robert Scribbius, Frank Seabrook, Joseph Seabrook, Lawrence Seabrook, Porter Seabrook, Mingo Seigler, Andrew Sellers, Alexander Seymour, Charles Seymour, Mustaffy Shaw, Pintard Shepard, Albert Sherftall, Wallace Shingleton, Albert Shuftall, Aaron Simmons, Benjamin Simmons, Bryce Simmons, Dick Simmons, Edward Simmons, Fortune Simmons, Frank Simmons, Isaac Simmons, Ishmael Simmons, Jack Simmons, Jacob Simmons, Jeffrie Simmons, Jerry Simons, Mingo Simmons, Richard Simmons, Robert Simmons, Samuel Simmons, Thomas Simmons, William Simmons, William Simmons, Benjamin Singleton, Billy Singleton, Cyrus Singleton, January Singleton, Mingo Singleton, Tony Singleton, George Sinkle, Henry Sloan, Syrus Small, Ishmael Small, Miles Small, Mundy Small, Ned Small, Peter Small, Sharper Small, Anthony Smith, Benjamin Smith, Frank Smith, John Smith, John Smith, Joseph Smith, Luke Smith, Philip Smith, Sampson Smith, Thomas Smith, Benjamin Snooks, Israel Snow, Israel Snow, James Spaulding, Leonard Spaulding, March Spaulding, King Sterritt, Jesse Stevens, John Stevens, May Stevens, Mingo Stevens, Samuel Stevens, James Steward, Wesley Steward, Benjamin Stewart, Isaac Stewart, Israel Stewart, Jessie Stiles, Henry Stone, Morgan Strickland, Josiah Stripling, Bram Strobert, Edward Stuart, Israel Stuart, Isaac Sweet, John Swinton, Samuel Tambull, Ansil Tatnall, Ansel Tatnum, Douglass Taylor, Edward Taylor, Edward Taylor, Glasco Taylor, Glasgow Taylor, Green Taylor, Redick Taylor, Reuben Taylor, William Taylor, William Taylor, Edward Team, Cornelius Thomas, Cudjo Thomas, James Thomas, Joseph Thomas, Louis Thomas, Nathan Thomas, Quamley Thomas, Robert Thomas, Russell Thomas, Jack

Thomas, William Thomas, Quamley Thomson, Henry Tillman, Richard Tillman, Abraham Timmons, Shadrack Timmons, William Tonsel, Robert Tornel, Robert Trael, Jonas Trewel, Quash Tripp, Jonas Truell, Robert Truell, Henry Truesdell, Daniel Tucker, Shadrach Tumult, Samuel Turnbull, Benjamin Turner, Howe Turner, Jack Turner, David Twine, Lerous Upright, James Vamose, Robert Vandross, William Vandyke, Joseph Vanhorn, July Vanhorn, Thomas Vanilla, Charles Vanness, George Vanness, James Vanross, Charles Varness, George Varness, George S. Varness, William Verdier, Charles Verness, Peter Vigul, Benjamin Walker, Thomas Walker, Benjamin Wallace, Thomas Wallace, David Wanton, John Wanton, Joseph Wanton, Pete Ward, William Ward, Cate Waring, Ackless Washington, Bristol Washington, Cato Washington, Cuffee Washington, Edmund Washington, George Washington, George Washington, George Washington, George Washington, Jackson Washington, James Washington, Joseph Washington, Manuel Washington, Moses Washington, Moses Washington, Robert Washington, William Washington, Leon Watkins, Aaron Watson, Berry Watson, Edward Watson, Jacob Watson, William Watson, Jeffer Way, Prince Weathers, Bird Weaver, Daniel Weaver, Samuel Webb, Sampson Weely, Bony Weston, Joseph Weston, Perry Weston, Putnam Weston, Yorick Weston, Prince Wethers, Luke Whight, Abraham White, Abram White, Daniel White, Gaubner White, James White, James White, Prime White, William White, Charles Whiters, George Wick, Edward Wiggins, William Wight, Isaac Wilkins, Charles Williams, Daniel Williams, George Williams, Harry Williams, Higgins Williams, James Williams, James Williams, James Williams, James Williams, James Williams, Joseph Williams, Lazarus Williams, Manuel Williams, Merritt Williams, Morris Williams, Nelson Williams, Ogoff Williams, Robert Williams, Sinclair Williams, Sylvester Williams, William Williams, Willis Williams, Yorick Williams, Robert Wilson, Price Wilson, Robert Wilson, William Wilson, William Wilson, Alexander Wing, Charles Winkeson, Morris Winley, John Winslow, Ned Wood, Thomas Woodruff, Hammond Woods, William Woods, Benjamin Wright, Evans Wright, Henry Wright, John Wright, Joseph Wright, Luke Wright, Prince Wright, Sandy Wright, Winsor Wright, Cain Wynn, Janes Yore, Rogers Young, Tecomcy Young, Thomas Young, Thursday Young, Wilson Young.

Musicians

John Abrams, Peter Benkiser, Harrison Carrison, Smart Chisholm, Charles Daniel, Jerry Ensim, Jerry Eusim, Edward Haywood, Edward Herns, Edward MacIntosh, Thomas Ponshot, Camus Powell, Henry White, Edward Wiggins, John Williams, Joseph Williams, Paul Wilson, David Wright.

Chaplain

James Fowler

Wagoners

Daniel Bird, Simon Fripp

Medical Staff

Surgeons: Seth Rogers, William Crandall
Assistant Surgeons: James Hawks, Thomas Minor, Edward Stuard
Hospital Steward: Edward Hill

Appendix II: Two Addresses

William Henry Trescott, Address to the Beaufort Volunteer Artillery

July 4, 1850

Three-quarters of a century have verified the fears of the founders of the Union, and each year has deepened the lines of sectional division—roused into fiercer anger, sectional sentiment, and forced into more fatal conflict sectional issues—until now, when we see the reckless strife of selfish interest—the quick jealousy—the strong antipathies that divide section from section and class from class; the most hopeful believer in the stability of the country must acknowledge that while our forefathers framed a government they failed to create a nation. For what has been the great political triumph of our domestic legislation, since the adoption of the Federal Constitution? Why the passage of the Missouri compromise? It was carried after a struggle of unparalleled excitement and was accepted by a grateful constituency as the joint victory of wise statesmen and a conservative people. Now, what is the Missouri compromise but a broad declaration, that in the American Union there are two people, differing in institutions, feelings, and in the basis of their political faith—that the government could not legislate for both on the same principles and on the same subject, and therefore that as to certain matters of great political interest, they must, by an imaginary line, be separated. Since that line has been drawn, the practical separation has grown wider and wider, and circumstances have again forced upon us the question—shall it continue?

Is there a mode by which it may be obliterated, and the two people be made one? Or shall this imaginary line become a real boundary, and the two people, bidding each other a friendly but firm farewell, enter upon their future paths as separate and independent nations?

Republican party reversed the experiment and sought the same end by striving to identify the constitution with the popular will, and we are in the midst of that disastrous experiment. It has resulted in the developing of two popular wills—a Northern and a Southern—and in spite of the party zeal, against the vehement protests ... these two wills have concentrated upon their fundamental principle, and stand opposed in undisguised and inextinguishable hostility.

Fellow-citizens, national sentiment is never slightly stirred. The same Providence who piled up the mountains and poured out the rivers, in order to divide men into separate nations, has given to each nation its peculiar institutions, its special character. He knows when and how to harmonize them for his wise purposes; it is our duty to preserve those national distinctions in their vigour and purity. When, then, in any country you find two populations characterized by different institutions ... so resolutely opposed that a surrender of the one to the other is necessary to national unanimity.

The tendency and scope to what I have now briefly and imperfectly said, may be summed up thus: While it is impossible for us to foresee the future of our national history, we can yet see enough to warrant us in believing that if the alternative placed before us be the abandonment of the institution of slavery or the dissolution of the Union, that then the past history of the whole world—the great natural divisions of the continent, and the consenting testimony of the national sentiment, all indicate that the dissolution of the Union is the next step in the path of our history. And when I say the abandonment of the institution, I do not mean the extreme necessity of emancipating our slaves, deserting our fields, and diverting our decimated capital into strange and unnatural channels, but I mean the necessity of existing in toleration in the commonwealth, of yielding one hairbreadth of our full political equality, as necessary, efficient, honourable constituents of the great American Empire. We know our value. The history of past civilization is open for our study, and we see that every nation that has impressed its spirit and its institutions in beneficial influence upon the times—the Arab, the Roman, the Norman—have all been slaveholders. We see that all the great achievements of the world's art—the Greek Drama, the Roman Law, the untold wealth of modern manufactures—have sprung from and been sustained by slaveholding people. We know our value. The history of our own country is before us; we know from which section sprang the great minds of the revolution; we know whose blood has illustrated the history of three great national wars; we know what great staple feeds the world's traffic, and we know that without slavery the pride of Northern prosperity would be broken, the power of British commerce sapped, and millions of so-called freemen would perish in their destitution.

We know our value. We know that we are the great conservative element of this colossal commonwealth. For all that we are, and all that our Northern brethren are, through us, we believe ourselves, under God, indebted to the institution of slavery; for a national existence, a well ordered liberty, a prosperous agriculture, an exulting commerce, a free people and a firm government; and we believe that without slavery, the Union could guarantee us none of these things. That the result of this struggle will be its dissolution, no man ventures to prophesy—no man dares to hope. The vast, unbounded future lies before us, but shadows, clouds, and darkness rest upon it.

William H. Trescott, Address Delivered in the House of Representatives of South Carolina in Honor of Stephen Elliott Jr.

Friday, September 7, 1866.

General Elliott was no ordinary man. Beside his individual virtues, he was the representative of much in Carolina life that has passed away forever; and the circumstances under which we are met today to do honour to his memory, may well fill all our minds with sad and serious thought. Since I have been a Member of this House, it has been my painful privilege to join more than once in the expression of our sorrow for the loss of colleagues, honoured in their lives and mourned in their deaths. Then, however, our sorrow was not without hope. Our grief was tempered with patriotic pride; we believed that they were martyrs in a holy cause. We felt as we laid them gently and reverently upon the bosom of the State they loved, that the time was not far distant when that State, free, strong, radiant in the glory of their fame, would gather her living children around the graves of her dead, and consecrate their memories to immortal gratitude. And they themselves went out to meet death with joy, in the assurance of victory....

We know now, that for our lost cause such a life as Stephen Elliott's was a great and useless sacrifice; but for that very reason ought it to hold a dearer place in our affections. Indeed, I use no exaggerated language when I say that such lives are doubly precious to us now, for they are our only vindication to posterity. We have but a sorrowful history to teach our children. We must tell them that, in the pride of a strength and wisdom which we did not possess, we inaugurated a revolution which we could not achieve—that, in the unequal strife, our past power and our future hopes were alike broken in blood. Our vindication with them and in history must be that we ventured on this terrible issue in an honest, earnest, unquestioning conviction of the truth, under the solemn obligation of our duty to maintain inviolate those principles of constitutional liberty which we had inherited.

These brave men hid in their wounds and carried to the safe and sacred custody of the grave, the honour of the cause they served. And the example of a man like General Elliott is only the more valuable because he was not one of the great names of history. He commanded no large armies; he won no famous battles. He simply did his duty where his country put him.

The late general Stephen Elliott having built a church upon his own plantation, preached regularly and most efficiently to the slaves of the neighborhood. They were both members of a family long and honourably known in the history of the State. Among the earliest settlers of the colony, they were established in name and fortune at the Revolution. Without attempting to achieve that sort of reputation which attaches to eminent public life, they possessed, and through many generations maintained, a large and useful local influence, representing their parishes in the House and the Senate of the State Legislature; cultivating with success their extensive estates, exercising a graceful and genial hospitality, and discharging, with conscientious responsibility, their duties as citizens.

From godly Boston and pious Providence came the crowded slave-ships, and the white man's brain and the black man's strength worked together to send cargo after cargo of rice and indigo to the mother-country.... Every year broader fields grew white with the great staple of their agriculture.... Wealth brought elegance to their homes, and culture gave finish to the natural refinement of their manners.... They were kind masters, good neighbours, true friends, active and intelligent planters.

In politics they were believers in a very simple creed: It could be summed up in one commandment—"Love South Carolina." I will not vindicate its wisdom. All very strong feeling is apt to run into error by its exaggeration. A statesman would call it narrow; a philosopher would call it weak; but it was broad enough to cover their lives, it was strong enough to support them in death. If I have dwelt too long upon the character of this community, the House will forgive me. For many years I lived among them. I speak of men I loved, of homes in which I was welcome. I cannot forget that of those I knew, many a proud head is humbled, many a brave heart is still, many a sweet and gentle face is shadowed with an everlasting grief. The fire on their hearths is gone out for ever; Ribaldry and ruffianism have run riot in homes where dwelt domestic love and household honour. And, by an act of cruel, lawless, and iniquitous spoliation, a whole society, which, in its traditions, its industry, its courage, its refinement, and its virtues, represented for many generations the best traits of Carolina character, has utterly perished.

General Beauregard selected Major Elliott to take command of the fort [Sumter]. He accepted this duty as he did all others, modestly and resolutely, and on the night of the 4th of September 1863, he crossed the harbour and entered upon his command. To undertake this duty required something higher than ordinary courage. There were brave men who considered it hopeless. Few believed that those ruins could resist the force which had so far destroyed them. The soldiers who entered these broken walls and shattered casemates, went there to die, because the honour of their State required it. To perform this required the facility of imposing his own resolution upon every man of his command, and centering into himself the unwavering confidence of those whom he directed. It required calmness, self-possession, and that indomitable will which, by some strange influence, seems to impart to the very dead material, the stone and brick and wood with which brave men work, a power of living resistance. This duty he undertook, and this duty he performed.

Admiral Dahlgren determined to test the assertion that Sumter was "a harmless mass of ruins," summoned the fort to surrender.... Major Elliott [replied to Dahlgren that he could have Fort Sumter when he took it and held it. You all know how on the night of the 9th September, thirty launches, supported by a portion of the naval force, attacked the fort and were signally repulsed, leaving one hundred and thirteen in the hands of the garrison. You all know how the fort was held until the enemy, in sullen confession of their inability to take it, confined their hostile demonstrations to distant and ineffectual bombardment....

Mr. Speaker, history may write another judgment than ours upon the justice of the cause in which we fought: The firing of the first gun upon Fort Sumter may be remembered in after days as the first rash act of a wild and fatal delusion: but when, in the early summer of 1864, Major Elliott left those ruined walls to join the army in Virginia, he had carved upon their massive fragments a story of Carolina chivalry so simple, so noble, so true, that it will forever kindle the sympathy of brave men for the State he loved, and temper the censure of just men on the State he served.

For his services in Fort Sumter Major Elliott was rapidly promoted; and in 1865, as Brigadier-General, he joined the army of Virginia. He was placed upon the lines near Petersburg. Soon after his arrival the famous mine was sprung, and a portion of his brigade was destroyed by the explosion. While rallying his men to the brilliant and bloody repulse which followed he was shot in the shoulder,—a painful and dangerous wound, which paralyzed entirely his arm. After long confinement to the hospital, he was enabled to resume his duties, although with great difficulty, and was sent back to Carolina ... and placed in command at James' Island. Here he remained until the evacuation of Charleston, from which place he moved with General Johnston in his effort to affect a junction with General Lee. He was severely injured at Bentonville, and this, with the consequence of his wound, compelled him to obtain a furlough and return to the State, which he reached just before the final surrender of the armies of the Confederacy. The cause for which he had bravely fought was lost; The army in which he had served was disbanded; His home was in the possession of the United States armies; His once rich and powerful kinsmen were in exile and in poverty.

He removed his family to a hut on the seashore, which, in former days, had been a rough shelter in his fishing expeditions; and there, day after day, in sight of his own house, within sound of the labour on his own plantation, amid the scenes which recalled the bright hours of his boyhood, his pleasant and prosperous manhood, he fished, and, crossing to the neighbouring village of Hilton Head, carried himself the fish which he had caught, to sell for his subsistence. The sight of this simple, quiet, brave man won respect from all. General Gilmore, who had commanded the United States forces while General Elliott was at Sumter, and whose headquarters were then at Hilton Head, in a spirit worthy of his reputation as a soldier, asked of the Executive his pardon as a special personal favor, and it was granted.

He believed that the issues we had made were irrevocably decided against us; that the interest and honour of the State required that she should lay broadly the foundations of the new life she purposed to lead; that the sooner her legislation was conformed to the constitutional requirements of the Government, the better for all her people, white or black. In this sense he spoke ... and voted. Just as he had done his duty before, so, under the new system which he had accepted, was he prepared to do his duty again. And to-day his strong common-sense view of the duty which lay before him, his freedom from all passion in the perplexing questions which surround us, his undisturbed consciousness of his own purity and honesty of purpose, and the consideration which his eminent services had won, would have made him an invaluable counsellor. But soon after the last regular session he sickened: His constitution had been exhausted by the exposure of camp, the confinement of beleaguered garrisons, the suffering of wounds—and he died.

His last request was that he should be buried by the side of his mother. He was faithful to us in his life—let us be true to his memory. The cause in which he fought has perished. The flag under which he served is furled and put away forever, and over his dust in proud triumph floats the "Star-Spangled Banner." But if we are ever to look again upon that banner as the symbol of a common and a reunited country, its stars must shine kindly upon our dead, and "its ample folds, as they float over the sea and over the land," must cast no shadow of shame on the graves of men like him.

Chapter Notes

Prologue

1. Stuart, *Autobiography*, 18.
2. *Ibid.*, 10.
3. Barnwell, *The Story of an American Family*, 87.
4. Stuart, *Autobiography*, 5.
5. *Ibid.*, 15.
6. Barnwell, *The Story of an American Family*, 62.
7. Rowland et al., *The History of Beaufort*, 382.
8. *Ibid.*, 368–369.
9. Helsey, *Beaufort*, 95.
10. Elliott and Gonzales Family Papers.
11. Helsey, *Beaufort*, 91.
12. Stuart, *Autobiography*, 7.
13. Channing, *Crisis of Fear*, 20.
14. *Ibid.*, 30.

Chapter One

1. Rowland et al., *The History of Beaufort*, 370–371
2. *Ibid.*, 293.
3. Johnson, *Social History of the Sea Islands*, 120–121.
4. *Ibid.*, 118–119.
5. Rosengarten, *Tombee*, 135–136.
6. Johnson, *Social History of the Sea Islands*, 52–55.

Chapter Two

1. Mitchell, *Born in Slavery*. Some readers may find the black dialect that appears periodically throughout the book objectionable. It is an inescapable fact of American history that the vast majority of nineteenth-century Southern blacks were illiterate and attempts to render black quotes or document black conversations (like the WPA oral history project interviewing former slaves) were hampered by not having a standard guide to rendering the unique pronunciation, syntax and diction of blacks. Thus, we are left with a hodgepodge of versions that vary widely.
2. Rowland et al., *History of Beaufort County*, 351
3. Hurmence, *Before Freedom*, 78.
4. *Ibid.*
5. Johnson, *Social History of the Sea Islands*, 141.
6. Rowland et al., *History of Beaufort County*, 363.
7. Johnson, *Social History of the Sea Islands*, 132–33.
8. Rosengarten, *Tombee*, 154.
9. *Ibid.*, 156.
10. Johnson, *Social History of the Sea Islands*, 92.
11. *Ibid.*, 96–97.
12. *Ibid.*, 148.
13. *Ibid.*, 149–50.
14. Rosengarten, *Tombee*, 671–73.
15. Johnson, *Social History of the Sea Islands*, 125.
16. Rosengarten, *Tombee*, 456–458.
17. Olmsted, *Cotton Kingdom*, 510–511.
18. Rosengarten, *Tombee*, 162–163.
19. Johnson, *Social History of the Sea Islands*, 129.
20. *Ibid.*, 190.

Chapter Three

1. Channing, *Crisis of Fear*, 265–266.
2. *Ibid.*, 22.

3. *Ibid.*, 59.
4. Aiken, correspondence.
5. Channing, *Crisis of Fear*, 46.
6. Wood, *Black Majority*, 279.
7. *Ibid.*, 220–221.
8. Hoffer, *Cry Liberty*, 107–118.
9. Holland, *A Refutation*, 75.
10. Gordon, Asa. *Sketches of Negro Life*, 42–44.
11. Lofton, *Revolt*, 62.
12. *Ibid.*, 70.
13. *Ibid.*, 67.

Chapter Four

1. Howe, *What Hath God Wrought*, 395–401.
2. *Ibid.*, 404–406.
3. Davis, *Rhett*, 199–200.
4. *Ibid.*, 201.
5. Rowland et al., *The History of Beaufort*, 429.
6. Edgar, *South Carolina Encyclopedia*, 226.
7. Rowland et al., *The History of Beaufort*, 430.
8. Channing, *Crisis of Fear*, 141.
9. *Ibid.*, 161.
10. *Ibid.*, 165.

Chapter Five

1. Stuart, correspondence, 1911.
2. Trescott, *Oration*, 7.
3. *Ibid.*, 12.
4. *Ibid.*, 13.
5. Provincial Congress of South Carolina, *American Archives*, 578.
6. Wynn, *History of Troop B*, 2–3.
7. *Ibid.*, 3–4.
8. *Ibid.*, 5.
9. Walker, *What Hath God Wrought*, 250.
10. Rowland et al., *The History of Beaufort*, 369.
11. *Ibid.*, 369,372.
12. *Reports and Resolutions*, 1857.
13. *Charleston Mercury*, March 4, 1858.

Chapter Six

1. Rowland et al., *The History of Beaufort*, 444.
2. Coker, *Battle of Port Royal*, 14–15.
3. Rowland et al., *The History of Beaufort*, 446.
4. *Ibid.*, 447.
5. Kauffman, correspondence.
6. Barnwell, *The Story of an American Family*, 190.
7. *Ibid.*, 190–191.
8. Taylor et al., *Leverett Letters*, 92, 95.
9. Barnwell, *The Story of an American Family*, 191.
10. Coker, *Battle of Port Royal*, 60.
11. Barnwell, *The Story of an American Family*, 191.
12. *O.R.*, 6:24, 11.
13. Barnwell, *The Story of an American Family*, 192.
14. *O.R.*, 6:27–29.
15. Coker, *The Battle of Port Royal*, 88.
16. Rowland et al., *The History of Beaufort*, 455.
17. *O.R.*, 6:25.
18. Stone et al., *Battles and Leaders*, 687.
19. McPherson, *The Negro's Civil War*, 58–59.
20. *Ibid.*, 60.

Chapter Seven

1. Wise et al., *Rebellion, Reconstruction*, 6–7.
2. Faust, *Hammond*, 13.
3. Rowland et al., *The History of Beaufort*, 398.
4. Evans, *Confederate Military History*, 390.
5. Wise et al., *Rebellion, Reconstruction*, 7–8.
6. Hutson, letter, 2.
7. Wise et al., *Rebellion, Reconstruction*, 128.
8. Wise et al., *Rebellion, Reconstruction*, 130.
9. U.S. Fish and Wildlife Service, "Pinckney Island."
10. *O.R.*, 14:116.
11. *Ibid.*, 14:118.
12. *Ibid.*, 14:117.
13. *Ibid.*, 14:118.
14. Taylor et al., *The Leverett Letters*, 166–167.
15. Eldridge, *The Third New Hampshire*, 203, 206.
16. Hutson, letter.

17. *Ibid.*
18. *O.R.*, 14:282–284.
19. *Ibid.*, 14:283.
20. Hemphill, letter.

Chapter Eight

1. Wise et al., *Rebellion, Reconstruction*, 106–107.
2. Stone, *Vital Rails*, 75.
3. Taylor et al., *The Leverett Letters*, 101–103.
4. Wise et al., *Rebellion, Reconstruction*, 20–21.
5. *Ibid.*, 95.
6. *O.R.*, 26:25.
7. Taylor et al., *The Leverett Letters*, 137.
8. Wise et al., *Rebellion, Reconstruction*, 132.
9. *O.R.*, 26:181.
10. *Ibid.*, 26:161.
11. *Ibid.*
12. Wise et al., *Rebellion, Reconstruction*, 139.
13. Schmidt, *The Battle of Pocotaligo*, 121.
14. Wise et al., *Rebellion, Reconstruction*, 145.
15. Schmidt, *The Battle of Pocotaligo*, 145, 149.
16. Stone, *Vital Rails*, 116.
17. *O.R.*, 26:185.
18. Stone, *Vital Rails*, 117; *O.R.*, 26:176.

Chapter Nine

1. Stampp, *Causes of the Civil War*, 176–178.
2. Katcher, *Confederate Artilleryman*, 5.
3. Taylor et al., *The Leverett Letters*, 92, 93.
4. *Ibid.*, 122.
5. *Ibid.*, 92.
6. *Ibid.*, 250.
7. Hemphill, letter.
8. Taylor et al., *The Leverett Letters*, 115.
9. *Ibid.*, 128, 139, 160.
10. Hemphill, letter.
11. Katcher, *Confederate Artilleryman*, 20.
12. Taylor et al., *The Leverett Letters*, 297.
13. Katcher, *American Civil War Field Artillery*, 18.
14. *Ibid.*, 20.
15. Beaufort Volunteer Artillery, Memorandum Book.
16. Katcher, *American Civil War Field Artillery*, 13–14.

Chapter Ten

1. Fulghum, *Burning of Bluffton*, 94.
2. *Ibid.*, 91.
3. Wise et al., *Rebellion, Reconstruction*, 218.
4. Fulghum, *Burning of Bluffton*, 142.

Chapter Eleven

1. Ash, *Firebrand of Liberty*, 28.
2. *Ibid.*, 9.
3. *Ibid.*, 17.
4. *Ibid.*, 33.
5. *Ibid.*, 35.
6. Taylor, *A Black Woman's Memoirs*, 42.
7. Rogers, *Wartime Letters*, February 16, 1863.
8. *Ibid.*
9. Ash, *Firebrand of Liberty*, 37–38.
10. *Ibid.*, 48.
11. Dobak, *Freedom by the Sword*, 9.
12. *Ibid.*, 33.
13. *Ibid.*, 39.
14. Ash, *Firebrand of Liberty*, 41.
15. *Ibid.*, 55–56.
16. Rogers, *Wartime Letters*, January 17, 1863.
17. *Ibid.*
18. Ash, *Firebrand of Liberty*, 60.
19. *Ibid.*, 61.
20. *Ibid.*, 64.
21. Ash, *Firebrand of Liberty*, 97.
22. Dobak, *Freedom by the Sword*, 41.
23. Taylor, *A Black Woman's Memoirs*, 55–56.
24. Dobak, *Freedom by the Sword*, 42.
25. *Ibid.*
26. Dobak, *Freedom by the Sword*, 48.
27. Ash, *Firebrand of Liberty*, 192–193.
28. Miller, *Lincoln's Abolitionist General*, 50–52, 102–3.
29. Foner, *Forever Free*, 52.
30. Looby, *Letters of Thomas Wentworth Higginson*, 209–210.

Chapter Twelve

1. Walker, letter, February 13, 1864, South Carolina Historical Society.
2. Taylor et al., *The Leverett Letters*, 206.
3. Wise et al., *Rebellion, Reconstruction*, 359–361.
4. Stone, *Vital Rails*, 214.
5. Wise et al., *Rebellion, Reconstruction*, 291.
6. *O.R.*, 26:422.
7. McNair, *Battle of Honey Hill*, 15.
8. Wise et al., *Rebellion, Reconstruction*, 315.
9. *O.R.*, 26:414.
10. Stone, *Vital Rails*, 218.
11. Wise et al., *Rebellion, Reconstruction*, 325.
12. Scaife, *Joe Brown's Pets*, 125–127.
13. McNair, *Battle of Honey Hill*, 36.
14. Stone, *Vital Rails*, 219–220.
15. McNair, *Battle of Honey Hill*, 38.
16. *O.R.*, 26:432
17. Emilio, *A Brave Black Regiment*, 244.
18. *O.R.*, 26:416
19. Wise et al., *Rebellion, Reconstruction*, 338.
20. Nowlin, J. W. letter to Samuel M. Stone, January 20, 1865, State Historical Society of Wisconsin.
21. McNair, *Battle of Honey Hill*, 58.
22. Wise et al., *Rebellion, Reconstruction*, 338–339.

Chapter 13

1. Davis, *Calamity in Carolina*, 22, 23.
2. Gonzales papers, November 11, 1864.
3. *Ibid.*
4. Gonzalez papers, letter from Colonel Ambrosio Gonzalez to Mrs. A.H. Elliott, January 18, 1865.
5. Gonzalez papers, letter from Harriet Elliott to Emily Elliott, February 18, 1865.
6. Heidt papers, letter from Eliza Agnes Villard to John W. Heidt, December 16, 1863, South Caroliniana Library, University of South Carolina.
7. Bradley, *Last Stand in the Carolinas*, 106.
8. *Ibid.*, 107.
9. Davis, *Calamity in Carolina*, 29.
10. Bradley, *Last Stand in the Carolinas*, 114.
11. *Ibid.*, 115.
12. *Ibid.*, 116.
13. *Ibid.*, 115,116.
14. *Ibid.*, 121.
15. *Ibid.*, 123.
16. *Ibid.*, 123.
17. Dickinson papers, letter from Charles Dickinson to Charles Stone, January 20, 1865.
18. Bradley, *Last Stand in the Carolinas*, 192.
19. *Ibid.*, 199
20. *Ibid.*, 383.
21. Barnwell, *The Story of an American Family*, 196–197.
22. Rhodes, Daniel Benjamin, Reminiscences, Private collection of Rev. Dr. Robert K. Peeples.
23. Barnwell, *The Story of an American Family*, 196–197.

Epilogue

1. Wise et al., *Rebellion, Reconstruction*, 462.
2. Rose, *Rehearsal for Reconstruction*, 347.
3. Wise et al., *Rebellion, Reconstruction*, 462.
4. Barnwell, *The Story of an American Family*, 239.
5. Woodward, *Mary Chesnut's Civil War*, 827.
6. Brown, *Civil War Canon*, 96.
7. *Ibid.*, 97.
8. Stuart, *Autobiography*, 24–25.
9. Barnwell, *The Story of an American Family*, 208.
10. *Ibid.*, 217.
11. Helsley, *Beaufort: A History*, 123–125.
12. Wise et al., *Rebellion, Reconstruction*, 449.
13. *Ibid.*, 490–491.
14. *Ibid.*, 490–491.
15. Taylor, *A Black Woman's Civil War*, 115–118.
16. Trowbridge, *Reminiscences*, 15–17; 30–31.
17. Higginson, *Negroe Spirituals*, June 1867.

Bibliography

Books

Ash, Stephen V. *Firebrand of Liberty: The Story of Two Black Regiments That Changed the Course of the Civil War.* New York: W. W. Norton, 2008.

Barnwell, Stephen B. *The Story of an American Family.* Marquette, 1969.

Berlin, Ira. *Generations of Captivity. A History of African American Slaves.* Cambridge: The Belknap Press of Harvard University, 2003.

Bostick, Douglas W. *Charleston Under Siege: The Impregnable City.* Charleston: The History Press, 2010.

Bradley, Mark L. *Last Stand in the Carolinas: The Battle of Bentonville.* Campbell, CA: Savas Woodbury, 1996.

Brown, Thomas J. *Civil War Canon: Sites of Confederate Memory and South Carolina.* Chapel Hill: University of North Carolina Press, 2015.

Burlingame, Michael. *Abraham Lincoln—A Life. Vol. 2.* Baltimore: Johns Hopkins University Press, 2013.

Cauthen, Charles Edward. *South Carolina Goes to War, 1860–1865.* Columbia: University of South Carolina Press, 2005.

Coggins, Jack. *Arms and Equipment of the Civil War.* New York: Fairfax Press, 1983.

Coker, Michael D. *The Battle of Port Royal.* Charleston: The History Press, 2009.

Crooks, Daniel J. *Lee in the Lowcountry: Defending Charleston and Savannah, 1861–1862.* Charleston: The History Press, 2008.

Davis, Burke. *Sherman's March.* New York: Vintage Books, 1988.

Davis, Daniel T., and Phillip S. Greenwalt. *Calamity in Carolina: The Battles of Aversboro and Bentonville, March 1865.* Eldorado Hills, CA: Savas Beatie, 2015.

Doback, William. *Freedom by the Sword. The U.S. Colored Troops—1862–1867.* Washington, D.C.: United States Army Center of Military History, 2011.

Edgar, Walter. *South Carolina: A History.* Columbia: University of South Carolina Press, 1998.

Eldridge, Daniel. *The Third New Hampshire and All About It.* Boston: Press of E. B. Stillings and Company, 1892.

Emilio, Lewis F. *A Brave Black Regiment: The History of the 54th Massachusetts, 1863–1865.* New York: Da Capo Press, 1995.

Evans, Clement Anselm. *Confederate Military History, Volume V.* Atlanta: Confederate Publishing Company, 1899.

Faust, Drew Gilpin. *James Henry Hammond and the Old South—A Design for Mastery.* Baton Rouge: Louisiana State University Press, 1982.

———. *This Republic of Suffering: Death and the American Civil War.* New York: Vintage Books, 2008.

Foner, Eric. *Forever Free: The Story of Emancipation and Reconstruction.* New York: Vintage Books, 2005.

Glatthaar, Joseph. *The March to the Sea and Beyond: Sherman's Troops in the Savannah and Carolina's Campaigns.* New York: New York University Press, 1985.

Helsley, Alexia. *Beaufort South Carolina: A History.* Charleston: The History Press, 2005.

Howe, Daniel Walker. *What Hath God Wrought: The Transformation of America, 1815–1848.* New York: Oxford University Press, 2007.

Hurmence, Belinda, ed. *Before Freedom,*

When I Just Can Remember: Twenty-seven Oral Histories of Former South Carolina Slaves. Winston Salem, NC: John F. Blair, 1989).

Katcher, Philip. *American Civil War Artillery, 1861–1865*. Oxford: Osprey, 2001.

———. *Confederate Artilleryman: 1861–1865*. Oxford: Osprey, 2001.

Lineberry, Cate. *Be Free or Die. The Amazing Story of Robert Smalls' Escape from Slavery to Union Hero*. New York: St. Martin's Press, 2017.

Lofton, John. *Denmark Vesey's Revolt: The Slave Plot That Lit a Fuse to Fort Sumter*. Kent: Kent State University Press, 1983.

McNair, Robert. *The Battle of Honey Hill South Carolina November 30, 1864*. Cullowhee: Western Carolina Historical Research, Western Carolina University, 2010.

McPherson, James M. *Battle Cry of Freedom: The Civil War Era*. New York: Ballantine Books, 1988.

———. *The Negro's Civil War: How American Blacks Felt and Acted During the War for the Union*. New York: Vintage Civil War Library, 1993.

Morris, J. Brent, ed. *Yes Lord, I Know the Road: A Documentary History of African Americans in South Carolina, 1526–2008*. Columbia: University of South Carolina Press, 2017.

Olmsted, Frederick Law. *The Cotton Kingdom*. Edited by Arthur M. Schlesinger, Sr. New York: Random House, 1984.

Rose, Willie Lee. *Rehearsal for Reconstruction: The Port Royal Experiment*. Athens: University of Georgia Press, 1999.

Rosengarten, Theodore. *Tombee: Portrait of a Cotton Planter*. New York: William Morrow, 1986.

Rowland, Lawrence S., Alexander Moore, and George C. Rogers, Jr. *The History of Beaufort County, South Carolina: Volume 1, 1514–1861*. Columbia: University of South Carolina Press, 1996.

Scaife, William R., and William Harris. *Joe Brown's Pets—The Georgia Militias: 1861–1865*. Macon: Mercer University Press, 2004.

Seigler, Robert S. *South Carolina's Military Organizations During the War Between the States*. Charleston: The History Press, 2008.

Spieler, Gerhard. *Beaufort South Carolina: Pages from the Past*. Charleston: The History Press, 2008.

Taylor, Frances Wallace, Catherine Taylor Mathews, and J. Tracy Taylor. *The Leverett Letters: Correspondence of a South Carolina Family, 1851–1868*. Columbia: University of South Carolina Press, 2000.

Taylor, Susie King, Patricia Romero, and Willie Lee Rose, eds. *A Black Woman's Civil War Memoirs*. Princeton: Markus Wiener, 1988.

Trescott, William Henry. *Oration Delivered Before the Beaufort Volunteer Artillery on July 4th, 1850*. Charleston: Steam-Powered Press of Walker & James, 1850.

Wise, Stephen R., and Lawrence S. Rowland, with Gerhard Spieler. *Rebellion, Reconstruction, and Redemption, 1861–1893: The History of Beaufort County Volume Two*. Columbia: University of South Carolina Press, 2015.

Wilson, Edmund. *Patriotic Gore: Studies in the Literature of the American Civil War*. Boston: Northeastern University Press, 1962.

Wood, Peter H. *Black Majority: Negroes in Colonial South Carolina from 1670 through the Stono Rebellion*. New York: W. W. Norton, 1974.

Woodward, C. Vann. *The Burden of Southern History*. Baton Rouge: Louisiana State University Press, 1960.

Woodward, C. Vann. *Mary Chesnut's Civil War*. New Haven: Yale University Press, 1981.

Primary Sources

Allen, William Francis. William Allen Francis diary. November 5, 1863—July 10, 1865. Letter. November 5, 1863. South Caroliniana Library, University of South Carolina.

Barnwell, Nathaniel B. Letter to H. M. Stuart, 1911. SCHS #557. Box 2. Davis, Nora Marshall. Records relating to the Beaufort Volunteer Artillery. 1864–1934. South Carolina Historical Society.

Beardley, Harrison M. Harrison M. Beardsley papers, 1861–1865. South Caroliniana Library, University of South Carolina.

Bibliography

Blake, George H. Letter, April 9, 1862. South Caroliniana Library, University of South Carolina.

Button, Warner. Letter, June 8, 1862. South Caroliniana Library, University of South Carolina.

Cole, Emmett. Letter, January 28, 1861. SCHS #557. Box 2. Davis, Nora Marshall. Records relating to the Beaufort Volunteer Artillery, 1864–1934. South Carolina Historical Society.

Dickinson Papers. State Historical Society of Wisconsin, University of Wisconsin.

Drake, James B. Letter, March 5, 1862. South Caroliniana Library, University of South Carolina.

Elliott and Gonzalez family papers. Personal Correspondence, 1861–1865. South Caroliniana Library, University of South Carolina.

Elliott, Stephen, Jr. Correspondence, 1858–1866. South Carolinian Collection, University of South Carolina.

Eustis, Patience Izard. Letter, July 20, 1852. South Caroliniana Library, University of South Carolina.

Fletcher (Union soldier) Letter, November 15, 1861. South Caroliniana Library, University of South Carolina.

Fripp family papers. 1838–1918. Letters to Julia Fripp, 1863–1866. South Caroliniana Library, University of South Carolina.

Hatch, Alfred. Letter, October 23, 1863. South Caroliniana Library, University of South Carolina.

Heidt, Eliza Agnes Villard papers. Letter, December 16, 1863. South Caroliniana Library, University of South Carolina.

Hemphill family papers, 1765–1975. Letters, December 14, 1863, April 21, 1864. South Caroliniana Library, University of South Carolina.

Hutson, Charles W. Letter, June 27, 1928. SCHS #557. Box 1. Davis, Nora Marshall. Records relating to the Beaufort Volunteer Artillery, 1864–1934. South Carolina Historical Society.

Jackson, Frederick. Frederick Jackson Papers, April 13-July 10, 1865. South Caroliniana Library, University of South Carolina.

Johnson, John H. John H. Jackson papers, December 2, 1861—February 18, 1864. South Caroliniana Library, University of South Carolina.

Kauffman, Harry. Letter, December 18, 1861. South Caroliniana Library, University of South Carolina.

Lawton, Reynolds and Sams Papers, 1830–1855. South Caroliniana Library, University of South Carolina.

Martin, J. Vinton. Letter, May 18, 1863. South Caroliniana Library, University of South Carolina.

Memorandum Book, Beaufort Volunteer Artillery, 1863–1867. South Caroliniana Library, University of South Carolina.

Nowlin J. W. Letter to Samuel M. Stone, January 20, 1865. State Historical Society of Wisconsin.

Rhodes, Daniel Benjamin. Reminiscences. Private collection of Reverend Robert K. Peeples.

Rogers, Seth. "War-Time Letters from Seth Rogers, M.D. Surgeon of the First South Carolina Afterwards the Thirty-third U.S.C.T. 1862–1863." Florida History Online.

Schmidt, L. G., *The Battle of Pocotaligo*. Self-published, 1993. Beaufort District Collection, Beaufort County Library.

Shedd, Calvin. Calvin Shedd papers, 1862–1864. Letters, June 20, July 29, 1862. South Caroliniana Library, University of South Carolina.

Stuart, James Reeves. Autobiography, 1907. Beaufort District Collection, Beaufort County Library.

United States War Department. *The War of the Rebellion: A Compilation of the Official Records of the Union and Confederate Armies.* 128 Volumes. Washington DC: U.S. Government Printing Office, 1880–1901.

Walbridge, Charles E. Charles Eliphalet Walbridge papers, 1861–1865. Letter, March 16, 1863. South Caroliniana Library, University of South Carolina.

Walker, General W. S. Letter to troops of 3rd Military District, February 13, 1864. SCHS #557. Box 1. Davis, Nora Marshall. Records relating to the Beaufort Volunteer Artillery, 1864–1934. South Carolina Historical Society.

Warren, John D. Papers, 1856–1885. South Caroliniana Library, University of South Carolina.

Wynn, Gerald. 1997, History of Troop B, 202nd Cavalry SCANG. SCHS 557. Box

2. Davis, Nora Marshall. Records relating to the Beaufort Volunteer Artillery, 1864–1934. The South Carolina Historical Society.

Governmental Proceedings

Provincial Congress of South Carolina, *American Archives*, Volume Five, Fourth Series.

Reports and Resolutions of the South Carolina Legislature, 1857.

Internet

Accessible Archives. *Frank Leslie's Weekly*. Part III: 1862–1866. http://www.accessible-archives.com/collections/frank-leslies-weekly/

Blackpast.org. "Denmark Vesey Conspiracy of 1822." http://www.blackpast.org/aah/denmark-vesey-conspiracy-1822

Latin American Studies. "General Ambrosio José Gonzales." http://www.latinamericanstudies.org/gonzales.htm.

J. Mitchell, *Born in Slavery: Slave Narratives from the Federal Writers' Project, 1936 to 1938*, Library of Congress. Digital Collections. https://loc.gov/collections/

National Archives. Civil War. https://www.archives.gov/research/military/civil-war

The Online Books Page *Harper's Weekly*. Volumes 5–9. http://onlinebooks.library.upenn.edu/webbin/serial?id=harpersweekly.

U.S. Fish and Wildlife Service. "Pinckney Island National Wildlife Refuge." https://www.fws.gov/refuge/Pinckney_Island/about.html

Index

American Anti-slavery Society 43
American Revolution 35, 49
Army of the Tennessee 138, 142–4
Augusta Reserve Battalion 129
Averasboro, Battle of 137–42

Barnwell, Nathaniel Heyward 149–50, 153
Barnwell, Robert W. 5, 8–9
Barnwell, Stephen 150–1
Barton, William 84–5, 98
Bay Point 53, 56–7
Beard, Oliver 110
Beaufort College 9, 40, 64, 148
Beaufort District 40–1, 44–6
Beaufort Gazette 40, 153
Beaufort Southern Rights Association 45
Beaufort Volunteer Artillery 9, 17, 43, 47, 63, 66; artillery 92–96; Battle of Averasboro 137–142; Battle of Honey Hill 123–132; Battle of Pocotaligo (first) 75; Battle of Pocotaligo (second) 78–86; in Battle of Port Royal 56–62; camp life 87–91; history 49–52; last days 143–5; post war 148–154
Beaufort, South Carolina 43, 44, 48, 53, 55–56, 61, 63, 65–7, 97, 103, 111–2, 115, 117, 119, 147; Arsenal 9; history 3–9, 13–18; Lafayette's visit 13–4
Beauregard, Pierre G.T. 76, 78, 101, 116, 124, 135, 144, 174
Beecher, James 129
Bees Creek Hill 85
Benton, Thomas Hart 42
Bentonville, Battle of 142–4
Black Republican 46
Bluffton, SC 43; burning of 97–101
Bluffton Boys 43
Bluffton Movement 43

Boyd's Landing 68, 126, 131
Brannan, John 77–8, 80, 84
Broad River 3, 7, 67, 70–1, 125
Brown, John 10–1
Butler, Benjamin 104

Calhoun, John C. 41, 45
Camden, SC 35–6
Camp Hardee 72
Camp Saxton 103, 105, 111
Case, Henry 140
Chaplin, Benjamin, Sr. 13, 51
Chaplin, John 19–20
Charleston, SC 3, 10, 15, 29, 24, 25, 27, 32–3, 35–7, 39–40, 43, 44, 48–50, 54, 63, 72, 76–7, 83–5, 96, 98, 117, 119–20, 124, 126–7, 130, 133–6, 150–1, 154, 175
Charleston and Savannah Railroad 63, 68, 72–3, 76–7, 84, 120, 133–4
Charleston Armory 2, 93
Charleston Light Dragoons 83
Charleston Mercury 11, 45, 51, 91, 123–5
Chesnut, Col. James 36
Christ, Benjamin 74–5
Clay, Henry 42
Coffin, Thomas A. 13
Coffins Point 22–3
Colcock, Charles 84, 126–7, 131
Colcock, John 78
Combahee River 63–9
Contrabands 104, 105, 108
Cooperationists 45–6
Coosaw River 64, 66
Coosawatchie River 76–8, 84–5, 125–6

USS *Darlington* 110–1
Department of the South 63, 72, 76–7, 97, 103, 105, 125, 127, 133
DeSaussure, C. A. 151–2

Index

Drayton, Thomas 58, 98
Dunovant, G.M. 57–8, 60
Du Pont, Samuel Francis 54–7, 98
Dustin's Brigade 140

Edisto Island 23
Edisto River 98, 120
8th Indiana Cavalry 139
11th South Carolina Regiment 67, 75, 78, 83, 85, 88, 97–9
Elliott, Henry DeSaussure 151–2
Elliott, Middleton Stuart 151
Elliott, Stephen, Jr. 7, 9, 47, 57–61, 63–70, 73, 75, 89, 136, 138, 147–8, 151–2, 154; attack on USS *George Washington* 68–70; attack on 3rd New Hampshire Regiment 66–8; Second Battle of the Pocotaligo 78–80, 82, 86
Elliott, the Rev. Stephen, Sr. 60–1
Elliott, William II 7
Emancipation Proclamation 2, 129

Fayetteville, NC 136–37
54th Massachusetts Infantry 126, 132
55th Massachusetts USCT 130
55th Pennsylvania Infantry 77, 80, 82
1st Battalion of South Carolina Sharpshooters 85
1st Massachusetts Cavalry 77
1st South Carolina Cavalry Battalion 74
1st South Carolina Regiment (Union) 15–55, 102–3; combat experience 110–5; competence in combat 116; Jacksonville expedition 118–9; military significance 121–2; recruitment 105–6
Force Bill of 1832 42
Fort Beauregard SC 56–61
Fort Sumter 47, 53, 124, 148, 150, 152, 154, 174–5
Fort Walker 56, 59–60, 98
47th Georgia Regiment 126, 131
47th Pennsylvania Infantry 77, 79–80
48th New York Regiment 77, 84, 99
14th U. S. Army Corps 136
4th New Hampshire Regiment 76, 80
4th South Carolina Cavalry 99
Free Soilers 103
Freedmen 30, 36–7
Fripp, Capt. John 28
Fugitive Slave Act 103
Fuller, Nathaniel Barnwell 149
Fuller, Robert Barnwell 51, 152
Furman Artillery 127

USS *George Washington* 69–70, 93, 150, 154
Gonzales, Ambrosio 133–4
Gullah 19, 30, 65–66, 156

Hall, Wilson 140
Halleck, Henry 125
Hammond, James 32, 38
Hampton, Wade 136, 138
Hardee, William 125, 127, 135, 137–8, 143–4
Hartwell, Alfred 126, 130
Hatch, John Porter 125, 126–8
Hayne, Robert 42
Higginson, Thomas Wentworth 102–3, 105–6, 108–20, 154, 156–58
Hilton Head Island, SC 56, 58, 61, 66–7, 72–3, 85–6, 90, 97–8, 101, 104, 124, 126, 147, 175
Honey Hill, Battle of 123–32
Howard, O.O. 133
Hunter, David 97, 104
Hunting Island 5, 16, 99

Jackson, George 129
Jackson, Nathaniel 139
Jenkins, John 126
Jenkins, Dr. William 16
USS *John Adams* 112–5, 117
Johnson, Thomas 84, 100
Johnston, Joseph E. 134, 143, 150
Jordan, Thomas 139

Kansas Territory 97, 103
Kilpatrick, Judson 138–9, 142
Knapp, Isaac 42

Lafayette, Marquis de 13–4
Lafayette Artillery 85–6, 127
Lee, Robert E. 63, 92, 133, 144
Le Gardeur's Battery 138
Leverett, Milton Maxcy 49, 57, 72–3, 87–92, 124
The Liberator 42–3
Lincoln, Abraham 20, 47, 53–4, 72, 77, 104–5, 116, 121
Long, Thomas 121, 155

McDowell, Mary 15
McLaws, Lafayette 137
McPhersonville, SC 13, 70, 76, 89, 126
Mickler, John 67, 67
Middleton, Henry A. 25
Middleton Plantation 25

Index

Mitchel, Ormsby McKnight 76–8, 103
Mitchell, Sam 19, 21–22, 25
Mosquito Fleet 57–8

Nelson Light Artillery 69, 76, 80
9th Pennsylvania Cavalry 139

127th New York Infantry 130

Pettigrew, General James 32
Pinckney Island 66–7, 98
Planter 84–5, 112
Pocotaligo, Battle of (first) 74–5
Pocotaligo, Battle of (second) 77–86
Pocotaligo River 82–3
Pocotaligo Station 74, 78
Polite, Sam 21
Pope, William 98
Port Royal, Battle of 53–62
Port Royal Ferry 7, 50, 65–6, 74–5
Potter, Edward 125
Praise House 24, 26
Preble, George Henry 126

Republican Party 46–7, 105, 171
Rhett, Alfred 138
Rhett, Robert Barnwell, Sr. 39–40, 43, 48, 98
Rhodes, Daniel Benjamin 144–5
Ripley, Roswell Sabine 56, 63
Rivers, Prince 108, 112, 155
Rogers, Seth 107, 113–4,
Rutledge Mounted Riflemen 74, 84

Sack of Lawrence 46
St. Helena Agricultural Society 17
St. Helena Island 3, 5, 7, 13–5, 21, 23, 25, 28, 30, 40, 43–5, 56, 61, 97, 126, 147, 152
St. Helena Parish 1, 2, 7, 9–10, 13, 20–2, 28, 32, 50, 64, 76, 97
Saxton, Rufus 103, 113, 147
2nd South Carolina Cavalry Battalion 78
2nd South Carolina Regiment (Union) 119
2nd U.S. Kentucky Cavalry 139
7th Connecticut Regiment 77, 82
7th South Carolina Infantry Battalion 83
76th Pennsylvania Infantry 77, 82
Sherman, Thomas W. 54, 72–3
Sherman, William Tecumseh 54, 56, 125, 127, 133–7, 142, 144

Simons, Thomas 47
6th Connecticut Infantry 80, 82, 119
slavery: religion 25–6; Sam Mitchel 19–20; slave health and medicine 23–4; task system 21; treatment by plantation owners 28–9
Slocum, Henry 133, 136–142
Smalls, Robert 84
Smith, Gustavus W. 127
South Carolina Bloodhounds 46
Southern Standard 45
Stanton, Edwin 77, 105, 110, 121
Stevens, Isaac 73–5
Stoney George 144, 150
Stono Slave Rebellion 33
Stuart, Henry Middleton 9, 48, 98, 124
Stuart, James Reeves 3–4, 150, 154
Sutton, Robert 112, 113–5, 156–7

Taliaferro, William 138, 145
Tariff of 1828 39
Tariff of 1842 43
Tattnall, Josiah 58
Taylor, Susie King 117, 156
10th Wisconsin Battery 138
3rd New Hampshire Infantry 66–8, 76
3rd Rhode Island Artillery 77, 84, 99
3rd South Carolina Cavalry 84, 99
3rd U.S. Cavalry 138
3rd U.S. Kentucky Cavalry 138, 139, 152
34th USCT 125
35th USCT 129, 130
36th USCT 125
Trescott, William Henry 48–50, 148, 171, 173
Trowbridge, Charles 105, 109–10, 154, 156
20th U. S. Army Corps 136, 139–40, 142

Unionists 40

Vesey, Denmark 36–8

USS *Wabash* 54–5, 58–59, 62
Walker, William 67
Waring, Cato 107
Wheeler, Joseph 136
Wiggins, Joseph 67
Wilmot Proviso 44
Woodward plantation 19

www.ingramcontent.com/pod-product-compliance
Ingram Content Group UK Ltd.
Pitfield, Milton Keynes, MK11 3LW, UK
UKHW042012140426
5217IPUK00015B/1130